The U.S. Man-Made Fiber Industry

The U.S. Man-Made Fiber Industry

Its Structure and Organization since 1948

David I. Goldenberg

PRAEGER

Westport, Connecticut
London

Library of Congress Cataloging-in-Publication Data

Goldenberg, David I.
   The U.S. man-made fiber industry : its structure and organization
since 1948 / David I. Goldenberg.
     p.   cm.
   Includes bibliographical references (p.) and index.
   ISBN 0-275-93360-1 (alk. paper)
   1. Man-made fibers industry—United States. I. Title.
II. Title: U.S. man-made fiber industry.
   HD9929.2.U52G65 1992
   338.4'76774'0973—dc20   90-14557

British Library Cataloguing in Publication Data is available.

Library of Congress Catalog Card Number: 90-14557
ISBN: 0-275-93360-1

First published in 1992

Praeger Publishers, 88 Post Road West, Westport, CT 06881
An imprint of Greenwood Publishing Group, Inc.

Printed in the United States of America

The paper used in this book complies with the
Permanent Paper Standard issued by the National
Information Standards Organization (Z39.48-1984).

10 9 8 7 6 5 4 3 2 1

To the memory of Arthur H. Yedwab, CPA. Art's zest for life, enthusiasm for work, courage, self-discipline, ready humor, consummate professionalism, and humanity will be sorely missed by all who knew him, and not just his family or this long-term friend and business partner.

Contents

List of Exhibits

FIGURES

TABLES

1

Introduction and General Summary

INTRODUCTION

The industrial organization branch of economics emphasizes identification and understanding of the factors critical to the survival and growth or decline of an industry and its constituent firms. Given that aim, an update and generalization of a near-classic study of an important industry with which I was familiar had considerable appeal. Jesse W. Markham's Competition in the Rayon Industry [1952] provided a fairly complete set of professionally accepted hypotheses to guide an effort focused on one key question. That question was: How well did Markham's major conclusions apply to the United States man-made fibers industry which evolved from, but eventually surpassed, the cellulosic fibers subindustry, which Markham called the rayon industry? A sound answer requires showing when Markham's specific conclusions about the pre-1949 U.S. cellulosic fiber industry's structure, conduct, and performance did and did not hold true for the larger and more complex post-1948 United States man-made fibers industry.

The structural issues are so numerous and complex that three consecutive chapters are devoted to them. Chapter 2 briefly introduces the U.S. man-made fibers industry to those unfamiliar with it. Chapter 3 treats the conditions of supply and demand. Chapter 4 examines the structures of the subindustries composing the U.S. man-made fibers industry. Chapter 5 discusses the structural determinants, including costs and economies of scale, existence, and integration. Two chapters are devoted to an examination of the industry's behavior. Chapter 6 focuses on the price aspects of behavior including price trends, cyclical and short-run price behavior, price structures, and selling terms. Chapter 7 concentrates on nonprice behavior, which is vital to one's understanding the industry and here essentially independent of price. Chapter 8 examines the industry's performance in terms of its overall social benefits, productivity, profits, and workability. This study's major conclusions are summarized below while the remaining chapters detail the hypotheses tested, the data gathered for such tests, and the conclusions derived from those efforts.

GENERAL SUMMARY

The U.S. rayon industry supposedly had essentially homogeneous products at least until the mid-1930s [Markham, 1]. As will be shown later, all major fibers, including natural as well as man-made, actually were and are heterogeneous in both sales and production in the United States. Two less familiar relationships between economic goods, displacement and complementarity, are vastly more important in this industry than the more usual relationship of substitution. Remarkably little substitution occurs in the United States man-made fibers industry.

Markham correctly identified the industry as natural oligopoly. He also made a remarkably accurate estimate, given the paucity of data available to him, of the minimum efficient size for a 150 denier rayon plant. Averages and trends of four firm concentration ratios were near but generally below the 80% level some regard as the threshold marking the existence of significant oligopoly power over price. Imports, especially of goods made from man-made fibers produced abroad, probably further reduce oligopoly power. Imports of products consuming man-made fibers made overseas gained so great a share of the U.S. markets by 1983 that those markets could no longer be deemed closed. Hence, future studies of this product family will have to deal with a global industry. Later and more complete data reveal that the U.S. man-made fibers industries are differentiated (rather than undifferentiated) natural oligopolies whose respective minimum efficient commercial plant sizes and costs at various scales also are quite distinct. Man-made fibers' short-run marginal costs (SRMCs) are a function of their respective costs of raw materials, direct labor, energy, and capacity utilization rates (CURs). SRMCs essentially are stable at a near-zero minimum in an optimal range of some 70% to 90% CUR, and climb rapidly as the CUR deviates in either direction from that optimal range.

Absent proof to the contrary, one must assume, as Markham did, that the industry consists of independent firms. However, at least one man-made fibers producers' cartel operated in the United States during the period Markham studied, although this was not publicly known until almost 30 years after Markham's book was published [Coleman, 401]. The continuation of that cartel is likely but not certain. Its efficacy is even less certain. Nevertheless, the actual or potential existence of a cartel influences one's views about an industry's structure, conduct, and performance.

Markham's study of 150 denier rayon's list prices discovered a declining secular price trend for an industry with administered, and hence relatively rigid, short-run prices. These become somewhat more flexible near the low points of severe business cycle contractions as rayon supposedly vied with cotton. Analyses of later data for more man-made fibers and forms lead one to a contrary conclusion. Representative man-made fibers' list and average spot trading price series confirm real secular price declines until, as Markham anticipated, a product enters the mature stage of its life-cycle. After that point, that is, in the mature stage, stagnant real price trends appeared. Our explanation of the cyclical behavior of prices diverges notably from

Markham's. A critical distinction between effective, spot trading, and list prices was found.

Markham hypothesized that rivalry with cotton in recessions explained the apparent cyclical price flexibility of pre-1949 rayon filaments' prices. Recent econometric tests found that view unsatisfactory for all major U.S. man-made fiber subindustries after 1948. Those tests simultaneously evaluated the influence of various man-made fibers' CURs on the cyclical prices of those goods, as this was an alternative hypothesis of Markham's. Again, no meaningful relationship was discerned. Allocation occurs near temporary cyclical peaks, that is, when CUR exceeds 90%, and relies on established business relationships rather than price. However, using cotton as a standard of short-run price flexibility confirmed the continued validity of Markham's hypothesis that man-made fibers' prices are rigid in the short run.

Interactive discounts apply to man-made fibers' list prices and influence effective prices in two important ways. First, the discount structure makes it impossible for either large buyers or sellers of man-made fibers to even approximately determine their individual or the industry's effective price for any particular product in any given period. Next, a conservative estimate of the 1975 average overall net effective price of man-made fibers found it to be at least 25% below the average 1975 list price, and probably more than 40% below it. Thus, most of the industry's output sells at large discounts in an environment in which rivalry plays the major, but a diminishing, role, as compared with price.

Aside from shunning price competition, each domestic man-made fiber producer sells allegedly competing versions of the same products at different prices. The bigger firms still retain a degree of control over man-made fibers' prices because technology imposes higher unit-output costs on smaller rivals. That would encourage asymmetrical behavior if the firms knew these realities. Specifically, a smaller producer would be far more likely to announce price rises in the hope that it would be confirmed by a larger firm (and thus "stick"), than would a larger rival. Similarly, fear would discourage knowledgeable smaller producers from precipitating an unwinnable price war with a unilateral price cut.

A realistic model of the U.S. man-made fiber industry's overall behavior was devised to take into account both the inherent uncertainties of price competition and nonprice rivalry typical of the industry. The model is decomposable to evaluate specific forms of rivalry and seems generalizable to other industries. It helps explain the industry's short-run and cyclical price stability, firms' parallel behavior, and sustained preference for nonprice rivalry.

Most of the U.S. man-made fibers industry's rivalrous activities affect perceived and actual uncertainty and extend the short-run horizon by years. Strategic alliances (that is, joint ventures, licensing, and mergers) aimed to reduce uncertainty through risk-sharing and accelerated market entry, but often were overwhelmed by unforeseen problems. A cartel probably continued to exist in this industry after 1945. Such an entity undoubtedly would further reduce uncertainty by deterring entry, stabilizing prices, and so on. However, neither the post-World War II presence of a U.S. man-made fibers cartel nor its efficacy could be established conclusively.

Another potent form of nonprice rivalry--strategic planning--was tried by most U.S. man-made fiber producers with mixed results. Those who carefully and patiently implemented a sound strategic planning system benefitted greatly. Those either dabbling with inappropriate systems or seeking an immediate miracle from any strategic planning effort were disappointed.

The U.S. man-made fibers industry enhanced the general welfare in ways that are hard to quantify. Lives have been extended and saved by products dependent on man-made fibers. The artificial kidney is one example. Man-made fibers also improved the quality of life and reduced costs, as evident in the price and performance trends of automobile and aircraft tires made of such fibers. These and other benefits from the U.S. man-made fibers industry were generated by a fairly small, well-paid, and highly and increasingly productive labor force.

Estimated pretax profits of the U.S. man-made fibers industry between 1958 and 1982 were clearly cyclical. Returns on gross values of fixed assets did not differ significantly for noncellulosic fibers from those for all U.S. manufacturing after the mid-1960s, but did differ significantly for cellulosic fibers.

Markham found the U.S. rayon industry workably competitive. However, the modern U.S. man-made fiber industry could not yet pass any of today's tests for workability. This conclusion partly results from the intrinsic difficulties of evaluating the merits and intensity of rivalry in an industry notable for differentiated goods and firms that vie primarily in a nonprice mode rather than, as traditionally premised, on the basis of price to sell homogeneous wares. The man-made fibers industry relies on product and marketing innovations for profit. Objectively measuring the kinds and intensities of rivalry in such an industry, and converting such ratings to price equivalents has so far exceeded human ingenuity. Perfect foresight would be needed to compare alternative marginal investments in research, product development, and advertising, and to trace the implications of appropriate but equally elusive elasticities on a firm-by-firm basis in a price-inelastic industry.

The U.S. man-made fiber industry experienced spasms of intense nonprice rivalry whenever a significant product or marketing innovation appeared. Then rivals had to quickly restore parity or risk permanent exile. What Markham termed "the rayon industry" eventually failed this brutal, on-going survival contest to become a sunset industry. Experience shows that the same fate awaits the rest of this industry in the (presumably) distant future, although the specifics are uncertain at the moment.

Price competition in the U.S. man-made fiber industry undoubtedly intensified in response to several factors, including decreased reliance on nonprice competitive practices and the weakening of earlier cartels. Always cost-sensitive, textile mill customers became more price conscious as they learned to efficiently process available man-made fibers, and the pace of man-made fiber product innovation slowed. Lack of recent major man-made fiber product innovations, coupled with growing consumer reliance on store and designer brands, instead of acceptance of domestic fiber producers' and needle trades' marketing efforts, opened the way to a veritable flood of imported final products. Almost half of all garments, a quarter of all home furnishings other than carpets and rugs, and some 10% of industrial textiles consumed domestically now are imported. Those imports of final goods, made from man-made fibers usually produced abroad, sharply eroded domestic demand for domestically produced man-made fibers.

Other factors also facilitated the rise of imports. Those additional import stimuli include: the lure of a large U.S. market; a strong U.S. dollar relative to most foreign currencies; ineffective U.S. import regulations and enforcement as compared with most other lands; the allure of foreign products for U.S. consumers; such imports' higher profit margins for U.S. retailers; the perceived superior quality of foreign products at the same retail price points; the willingness of U.S. consumers to shop at different outlet types rather than remaining loyal to a particular class of retailer; rising overseas sophistication in making and marketing substitute goods at fiber, fabric and final product levels; the willingness of U.S. man-made fiber producers to export fiber at prices near marginal costs despite an asymmetrical unwillingness to sell at such prices in the U.S.; and recognition by various domestic and foreign man-made fiber producers that efforts to, individually or jointly, control market participation, shares, prices, and so on were, although popular and persistent, generally futile.

2

The Industry's Background

This book tests two interconnected sets of hypotheses. The structuralist theory of oligopolistic industrial organization represents the more theoretical set of ideas for empirical reassessment. Jesse W. Markham's book [1952] provides the second group of hypotheses for reevaluation. Highlights of these points follow.

The structuralist theory propounds an objective, four-phase sequence to analyze the economic condition of an industry and its component firms in a market environment [Scherer, 4]. An industry's economic performance presumably results from its constituent firms' market conduct as conditioned by that industry's market structure, which, in turn, depends on the circumstances underlying the supply of and demand for that industry's output and its inputs. However, the structuralist theory quickly becomes complex and dynamic as market conduct provides feedback influencing both market structure and the basic circumstances of supply and demand. Changes in market structure may also impinge on the underpinnings of supply and demand. This effort aims to analyze the U.S. man-made fibers industry that evolved out of Markham's "rayon industry" in a way that permits testing some of Markham's more notable hypotheses and others.

Markham's four key hypotheses merit recapitulation now; others will be cited later.

1. The cross-elasticities of rayon, acetate, other new man-made fibers and even cotton are high over a long-period [Markham, 1].
2. Prices of rayon producers oscillate between the extremes of a monopoly price and a competitive one in a fairly regular manner during each economic fluctuation [Markham, 2].
3. Any monopoly powers derived from a pattern of strong price leadership and entry barriers in the rayon industry are highly constrained by that industry's operation in a larger market context wherein natural fibers experience a declining secular trend and a supply-induced, erratic variation in output and price [Markham, 2-3].

4. Large rayon producers are forced to bear an unduly high share of output reductions during recessions [Markham, 3].

The premise of high cross-elasticity of demand within and across fiber genera, and hence, commercial substitutability, would greatly simplify economic analysis of the U.S. man-made fiber industry. But it also would ignore some fascinating aspects of the industry's conditions, structure, behavior, and performance. Thus, positing low cross-elasticities is a reasonable alternative.

This industry's generic fiber families will be shown to be significantly differentiated. One indication of this is that the industry's terminology distinguishes competition across fiber genera (for example, between cotton and polyester staple) from that within a given generic fiber and form by suppliers of that supposedly homogeneous product. Competition across generic fiber families has been termed "interfiber competition" for over 30 years, while that among suppliers within any specific generic fiber and form is called "intrafiber competition."

A facilitating assumption of no meaningful product differentiation may have been valid in the pre-1948 rayon industry, or at least, without any apparent gross distortion then. Few, if any, knowledgeable industry observers would accept a premise of product homogeneity, even in an intrafiber competition context, as anything but ludicrous after World War II. Markham, however, adopted the idea that fiber data could, in principle, be adjusted to a standard denier [Markham, 1]. Markham's standard of 150 denier was a popular but not necessarily modal, let alone dominant, denier for either rayon and/or acetate in the pre-1948 rayon industry.

Furthermore, product proliferation and quality levels have increased so much since Markham studied the early U.S. man-made fiber industry that it seems wiser to initially assume differentiated oligopolistic competition than to blithely adhere to his facilitating premise of high cross-elasticity. A recent dissertation [Harrigan], done under Professor Markham's supervision, not only distinguished the rayon and acetate fiber genera but also characterized rayon as a differentiated commodity. Specifically,

1. Both rayon and acetate were deemed products of concentrated industries with relatively high exit barriers, and differentiated product traits [Harrigan, Ch. 3, 9].
2. There were differences between the filament and staple fiber made using the (a) viscose process; (b) acetate process; and (c) cuprammonium process for creating cellulosic fibers, which affected the characteristics of the fibers created and determined which man-made fibers markets a firm might serve [Harrigan, Ch. 10, 5].
3. The assets used in the intricate cellulosic fiber-extrusion processes were capital-intensive and highly specific to cellulosic fiber production. Some interchangeability between staple and filament equipment was possible. But very few assets used to produce rayon fibers were also used to produce acetate fibers [Ch. 10, 30].

4. The assets used to produce rayon or acetate (fine-denier filament) textile yarn were not necessarily the same as the assets that could be used to produce (high-denier filament rayon) tire cord yarn. The operating costs of a rayon filament plant, moreover, were higher than those of a staple plant because filament plants were more labor-intensive and workers in such yarn plants achieved only relatively low productivities. Also, more land would have been needed for a rayon filament plant than for a staple plant [Ch. 10, 37].

5. Because of the relative simplicity of producing filaments by the acetate process as compared with the viscose process, a lower capital investment was required for equipment used in the production of acetate yarn. This lower capital cost may be expressed in terms of plant cost of the annual pound, or the cost of yarn production measured by capital investment. In 1945, this cost was estimated at about $1.50 per pound of viscose yarn, but only $1.00 per pound for production of acetate yarn [Ch. 10, 43].

Much of this book's length resulted from the need to reassess the merits of a standard null hypothesis of industrial organization (that is, homogeneous products) across a larger and more complex U.S. man-made fibers industry in terms of the number of generic fibers. That in turn called for examining masses of disaggregated data instead of a few tables of highly aggregated figures.

Markham's finding of rayon prices oscillating between the extremes of a competitive price and a monopoly price in a discernible pattern over the course of business cycles before 1948 did not jibe with later experience in the broader man-made fibers industry. An obvious objection to Markham's finding is its simplicity as compared with post-1948 industry experience. Moreover, recent industry experience implies a less elegant, contrary view to the effect that prices are neither very flexible nor symmetrical but instead are quite rigid within a wide but commonly sustained critical band of capacity utilization rates (CURs). Prices, according to this hypothesis, only change in response to an unanticipated and prolonged period of operation outside that critical CUR band.

Markham's third conclusion is complex. After finding that the rayon industry has potentially significant monopoly powers, because of both strong price leadership and entry barriers, Markham identified competition with cotton as a highly effective constraint on any such monopoly powers. If correct, does this finding hold true after 1948? And is it also generalizable to all man-made fibers? It will be shown later that competition from cotton was not an effective restraint. Also, one could as readily attribute loss of monopoly power to the mere passage of time as to competition. Temporal erosion of price leadership and entry barriers reducing monopoly power to impotency are well-known economic phenomena. Occam's Razor favors this view over Markham's third finding. It also is reasonable to expect that even if this simpler explanation had not applied to rayon fibers by 1948, it well could have by the late 1980s, when rayon was still being produced.

Markham's fourth major finding ascribes an economic price (that is, the acceptance of a "disproportionately high share of output reductions in recessionary times") to dominant-firm price leadership in the rayon industry. This conclusion did not hold for long after 1948 as the basic character of price leadership in the industry changed. Sensitivity to antitrust cost and publicity encouraged the larger suppliers of each man-made fiber family and form to switch from the visible practice of dominant-firm price leadership to a less discernible price policy.

Markham also found that the rayon industry enjoyed "effective tariff protection" from imports [Markham, 36]. Whether, as according to Coleman [1969], this was more a result of cartel behavior is irrelevant. Today the U.S. market is effectively wide open to imports of foreign man-made fiber and goods made from such fibers. Hence, a key issue is the present and prospective viability of the more broadly defined industry in light of the vast increases in international trade.

Post-World War II evolution of the U.S. man-made fibers industry in terms of product families, structure, and overall economic significance, coupled with business cycle fluctuations of considerable variety in duration, intensity, and foreseeability, further enhance its appeal as a candidate for reappraisal.

The U.S. man-made fibers industry existed by 1910 [Markham, 16]. Some essentially pre-1948 corporate entities and generic fibers and forms still participate. However, new enterprises and products have entered with varying consequences. Therefore, a review of the earlier situation is necessary for a perspective about the U.S. man-made fibers industry since 1948.

Markham's study laid the groundwork. Markham focused on what he called the "rayon industry" primarily because that was the only part of the current, more broadly defined man-made fibers industry about which one then could get credible data.

BACKGROUND

At the outset one needs a coherent means to clearly distinguish and classify natural fibers from man-made and synthetic fibers. This is essential to prevent confusion arising from a complex situation. It also is necessary since Markham saw considerable competition between cotton and rayon.

Fibers either occur naturally, that is, without human intervention, or they need human effort to make. The former are designated natural fibers by the fiber and textile industries. The latter are called man-made fibers by the same groups. Natural fibers have animal, vegetable or mineral origins, as exemplified by wool, cotton, and asbestos, respectively.

Man-made fibers suppliers and their customers divide the industry's products into explicit and implicit categories. Synthetic fibers constitute an explicit subgroup of man-made fibers. Synthetic fibers are composed of selected polymers or long-chain molecules. Polymers are manufactured by chemically linking monomers made earlier by chemical synthesis of the elements carbon, hydrogen, oxygen, and nitrogen; hence, the designation "synthetic fibers." Synthetic fibers are identified readily whenever their chemically correct designations are used. Those names invariably have the prefix "poly," for example, polyacrylonitrile, to denote the presence of a polymer. However, fiber producers and their customers soon coined less technical names for the various synthetic fibers, which quickly became standard except among a few chemists (See Table 2-1). The technically correct terms are long, hard for some to pronounce, often even harder to spell, and thought to be unappealing to consumers and merchants.

The man-made fibers industry has no accepted term for the implicit set of man-made fibers that are neither derived from cellulose nor synthesized. Glass fibers are the most commercially important member of this class. The nonsynthetic man-made fibers group has two commercially important fiber families and several trivial ones. Regenerated protein fibers also fall into this latter group.

Markham's rayon industry will from now on be designated the "cellulosic fibers industry" in conformity with the Federal Trade Commission's (FTC) practice of defining generic fibers in terms of their dominant ingredient. From this point on, generic fibers are identified by the FTC's practice.

Cellulosic fibers derive from high purity cellulose, a naturally occurring sugar, as indicated by the suffix "-ulose." The FTC and the fiber and textile industries today apply the generic names "acetate" or "rayon" to cellulosic fibers according to the chemical process used and the resulting fiber's properties. Strictly speaking, the FTC recognizes at least two (rayon and acetate) distinct fiber families or genera within the cellulosic fiber industry. The industry and its customers acknowledge three rayon fiber families (viscose, cuprammonium, and nitrocellulose process versions), plus two acetate fiber genera (diacetate and triacetate), giving a total of five [Montcrieff, 157-262]. Within these and all the rest of the generic fiber categories are specific suppliers' offerings with detailed technical descriptions and, it is hoped, uniquely apt and favorably memorable brand names. Rayon, the progenitor man-made fiber, is neither the latest nor the most important in either commercial value or physical volume.

Producers of both viscose and cuprammonium process rayon filament fibers tried to emulate silk. An inexpensive silk substitute has been a goal of western cultures since the days of the Roman empire [Boulnois, 7-10]. Cuprammonium process rayon, often sold in the United States under the now-defunct Bemberg brand, generally was regarded as closer to the ideal of silk than viscose process rayons, acetates, and early synthetics until the advent of certain polyester filament variants in the late 1970s.

Acetate fibers, the second major branch of the cellulosic fibers family, also have disparate production processes yielding, at best, imperfectly substitutable products. Acetates were further attempts to imitate silk. While also cellulose-based, the two acetate variants have sufficiently different manufacturing processes and chemical ingredients as to yield fibers of such distinctive properties that the FTC and the textile and fiber industries acknowledged their existence as separate genera within the overall acetate fiber family.

Table 2-1 illustrates and clarifies the classification of man-made and natural fibers' generic names commonly used in the U.S. man-made fibers industry and this

Table 2-1

Fibers' Generic Names

Supergroups	Groups	Genera and Subgenera
Man-Made		
	Cellulosics	
		Acetates di - and triacetate
		Rayons (cuprammonium, nitrocellulose, and viscose)
	Noncellulosics Synthetics	
		Acrylics and modacrylics (polyacrylonitriles)
		Nylons (polyamides)
		Olefins (polyolefins and polypropylenes)
		Polyester (polyethylene terephthalate)
		Specialties (Aramids, Saran, Spandex, Teflon, and Vinyon)
	Others	carbon(ized), ceramic, fiberglass, metal (steel), and protein
Natural		
	Animal	Silk and Wool
	Mineral	Asbestos
	Vegetable	Coir, cotton, flax, hemp, jute, and sisal

Source: Author.

book. It is a considerable but, for these purposes, acceptable simplification to say that all fibers occur in either or both of two physical forms, filament or staple. Length is the critical determinant of a fiber's form. Staple fiber typically ranges from about an inch long in cotton to a foot or so for wool. By textile industry convention, natural fibers normally are considered to be staple rather than filament because they generally have rather short lengths. Silk is the exception. While theoretically unlimited in length, commercial filament fiber is made in continuous, multimile lengths. Form, in turn, determines many economically vital factors about a fiber, including but not limited to the detailed production path a given fiber must follow in textile processing.

Demand shifts to synthetic fibers at natural and cellulosic fibers' expense caused drastic restructurings of the U.S. man-made fibers and textiles industries in the almost 40 years following Markham's study. Progress in polymer chemistry led to synthetic fibers with price-performance properties often far superior to those of natural and cellulosic fibers.

By 1980 only four U.S. rayon firms had survived. Those were American Enka, Avtex Fibers, Courtaulds, and North American Rayon. All used the viscose process. Only Avtex also produced acetate fibers. Two others, Eastman Kodak and Celanese, were major producers of acetate fibers but not rayons. Celanese was the only acetate producer supplying both diacetate and triacetate fibers. Furthermore, only North American Rayon Corporation operated exclusively as a cellulosic fibers manufacturer. These six firms ran ten cellulosic fiber plants in eight locations in 1980. Then, 87 firms operated 168 U.S. noncellulosic fiber facilities [Textile Organon, 1951(6): 98-99, 142-43].

Sixteen firms operated 32 cellulosic fiber producing plants in the United States in 1948. Four supplied acetate fibers--one exclusively--from a total of seven plants. Two firms only produced cuprammonium process rayon in separate facilities [Textile Organon, 1948 (9): 137]. Also, three generic types of noncellulosic fibers, excluding fiberglass, were sold in the United States in 1948. One producer, American Viscose Corporation, made vinyl chloride fibers in a single plant [136]. The other domestic synthetic fiber producer, duPont, made nylon fibers at three locations and acrylic fibers in yet another plant [132].

The man-made fiber industry adopted the term "denier" from the silk trade, which defined it as the number representing the mass in grams of a 9,000-meter continuous length of a given yarn. Certain specific deniers are important but not necessarily dominant in even a bare majority of those markets, as measured by physical volume or revenue. Each end-use typically needs critically different combinations of values for over two dozen vital fiber properties, including denier, to meet the diverse requirements of its constituent fabrics or final products consuming those fabrics.

Detail available only in the Textile Organon's annual end-use issues is essential but insufficient to adequately understand the U.S. man-made fibers industry's markets. The information in those issues is subject to an important practical limit. Variations in individual man-made fiber producers' ability to decompose, and their willingness to report their real sales activity in confidence to the Textile Economics Bureau (TEB) in fully cross-tabulated detail by generic fiber and form, to comparably defined groups of markets limit the usefulness of those reports. At any given moment, some fiber producers act as if they believe it competitively advantageous **not** to report their activities to the TEB so that only they will know what really goes on in the markets. Rivals invariably detect such gambits quickly and have it corrected, as denoted by a "r" (for revised) or, in earlier issues, by a large black dot, in those tables. But anyone unfamiliar with the actual market segments pooled to form a particular end-use could readily be misled by relying solely on this published material.

The U.S. man-made fibers industry uses at least two distinct production means for each major generic fiber. Fiberglass typifies alternative technologies, with one process for batch operations on a modest scale and another for continuous production on a massive scale. Several factors influence the choice of a production process when the goal is making commercially acceptable fiber. Technical feasibility, costs, and market uncertainties become constraints.

Some uncertainties weigh heavily in any fiber technology selection decision. Each technology offers its own spectrum of attainable end-product properties and associated costs over a range of output volumes. One must carefully define the targeted end-use market(s) and learn their individual fiber property needs before determining which fiber genera's products can compete within a particular generic fiber family in that application. Sometimes an effective monopoly exists within parts of an end-use market but is disguised when pooling the data to form end-uses.

For example, consider the tire end-use. At first blush, six man-made fiber genera vie for tire business. Rayon, Kevlar Aramid, nylon, polyester, fiberglass and steel seemingly are rivals in this market. But things are not this simple. Not all rayons, Aramids or nylons are acceptable tire ingredients. Only the high-tenacity versions of viscose filament rayon, as compared with the other subvarieties of rayon, can make a commercially viable tire by today's standards. Other types of rayon and all acetate fibers lack the tenacity, heat resistance, and flex strength despite their low cost. It also explains the tire industry's rejection of all but one kind of nylon (Type 6, 6), although other types may be much lower priced.

Seemingly overly generalized nomenclature often confuses those first exploring the man-made fiber industry. That two fibers have a common generic name and form is no assurance of substitutability in intrafiber competition. Remembering a chemist's advice that water and alcohol are not always substitutes helps one avoid fallacious economic reasoning about substitutability when dealing with man-made fibers. Specifically, water and alcohol are adequate substitutes for bathing, but that does not make alcohol any less toxic, especially methyl alcohol, when ingested.

Fiber substitution needs at least suitable trade-offs on all the properties listed on Table 2-2 before money price becomes a relevant issue. Otherwise, an outsider is apt to think that experienced fiber and textile industry executives spout nonsense when asserting that a particular generic fiber, say, nylon filament, consumed in one end-use, say, sheer hosiery, is not substitutable for nylon filament in another end-use, such as tires. Fiber and textile industry convention assumes that one's colleagues will automatically and correctly know the unstated details of a specific fiber's description by the end-uses either cited or associated with whomever is speaking or writing. This convention makes outsiders to such discussions feel like Alice in Wonderland until they too learn the technical needs of the end-use market(s) under consideration.

Each of the six man-made fiber genera for the tire market serves isolated segments instead of competing head to head. Kevlar fiber's incredibly high resistance to being broken by force exerted on its long axis (that is, tenacity) and other technical properties well suit the needs of specialty tires for racing and other applications where price matters little when compared with performance. Fiberglass provides an inexpensive belt material but not a high performance one, as it lacks great flex strength and does not adhere well to rubber. Fiberglass is an inexpensive complement to tire cord in the declining belted tire segment of the market. Nylon fiber is displacing both high-tenacity rayon and polyester in original equipment and replacement segments of the tire market. Hence, one finds that the man-made fibers industry's terminology, end-product and end-use taxonomy, and publicly available statistics are complex enough to confuse even the most intelligent and diligent newcomers for a year or more and yet insufficiently detailed for practical planning and action within the industry's markets.

A second uncertainty in fiber technology selection concerns cost prospects, notably but not solely involving petrochemical ingredients as raw materials. The existence, if any, and persistence of a cost advantage between alternative petrochemical processes to make a given synthetic fiber is a matter of great importance to firms that must commit irreversibly to a production technology embodied in plant that can last for decades.

The above considerations highlight an important problem in studying this industry. The man-made fiber industry, its customers, leading retailers, and some consumers have learned that generic fibers usually are only partial substitutes at best. The man-made fibers industry's customers and final consumers paid dearly over the years in defective or unsalable products to discover that, suppliers of similarly described goods from the same generic fiber family may be, at best, partial substitutes and typically fail to come that close.

Sequential batches of similarly described products in the same generic fiber family made in the same plant may vary so widely on so many key properties that producers still take great care disclaiming liability for the consequences of ignoring differences in identifying merge and lot numbers, suppliers' names, fiber genera, and so on. Warnings to this effect appear on every fiber firm's package labels, technical bulletins, manuals, and invoices.

Production of man-made fibers involves many variables. Each crucially affect some key properties of the fiber and the ease of later processing. An unordered list of some of the more common fiber properties widely known to be critical in most end-use applications is presented on Table 2-2.

Table 2-2

Critical Man-Made Fiber Properties

1. Denier and denier uniformity
2. Number of filaments per fiber
3. Denier per filament (dpf)
4. Cross-sectional shape (for example, round, hollow, and so on)
5. Degree of crystallinity and crystal orientation
6. Tenacity and stress-strain hysteresis curves' values and shapes
7. Flex strength
8. Moisture absorption and transmission properties
   (hydrophobia versus hydrophilia)
9. Dye characteristics (for example, anionic versus cationic)
10. Number, type, location and uniformity of dye sites
11. Lusters (for example, bright, mid-dull, semi-dull, dull, and so on)
12. Thermal history
13. Glass transition temperature value
14. Twist (turns per inch and direction, clockwise or counterclockwise)
15. Optical properties (light reflection and refraction)
16. Density or specific gravity
17. Resistance to corrosive chemicals (for example, perspiration)
18. Shelf life and storage conditions
19. Colorfastness
20. Resistance to ultraviolet light degradation
21. Abrasion resistance
22. Finish on the fiber (lubricant, antistat, and so on)
23. Crimp frequency, amplitude, and symmetry
24. Compatibility with other merges and lots of the same genera
    and form from the same supplier
25. Compatibility with other suppliers' offerings of the same genera
26. Compatibility with other generic fibers
27. Physical form (monofilament, multifilament, ribbon or strip
    versus staple, tow, or fiberfill)

Source: Author.

Absolute control of all those factors within and between batches exceeds the present state of the art of man-made fiber production. However, control over these variables has improved markedly in recent years because of better understanding of the complex chemical structures and processes involved and improved process equipment and software. These improvements led to enhanced intermediate and end-product performance, quality standards, and intensified related aspects of nonprice rivalry.

Only in the last decade has the industry improved its process control enough to keep the variations of key variables within a $\pm 3\%$ tolerance within a given batch [Moncrieff, 7]. Variations of $\pm 50\%$ around standards over any given six-inch length of fiber were, of necessity, acceptable earlier. The variability of raw materials, ambient conditions resulting from changes in the weather, imprecise measurement equipment and controls, lagged equipment responses to adjustments in speed, temperature, and pressure, and other factors still make it impossible to produce synthetic fibers commercially, let alone economically, homogeneous from batch to batch. This is especially so as the standards for commercially acceptable man-made fibers have risen sharply in the almost 40 years since Markham's book appeared. During an April 1984 visit to Avtex's Meadville acetate plant the plant manager, William K. Mohney, told the author that even a 1600% improvement over the last decade in the fiber's resistance to breaking during knitting, according to a standard test, was not enough to ensure the plant's viability. Avtex permanently closed its Meadville plant a few years later. The man-made fiber industry and its clientele know these problems and try to compensate for them in several ways. Careful product identification, testing and adjustments to subsequent processing steps in converting man-made fibers into textile products, and price differentials are the more common steps currently used to offset the intrinsic variability of a given firm's output between batches of a particular generic fiber.

The TEB began tracking and reporting aggregated interfiber competition data across end-use markets in 1949. After duPont found it too burdensome to do so alone in 1957, the TEB became responsible for this effort. The costs were shared by all domestic man-made fiber producer sponsors of the TEB. The TEB reported its findings in tabular form in annual issues of or supplements to its monthly publication, the Textile Organon (TO), since 1951. Although an improvement to the prior lack of data, TO reports were limited to annual consumption data of cotton, wool, cellulosics and noncellulosic fibers in highly aggregated end-uses, with filament and staple volumes noted. Later, fiberglass detail was shown separately in a footnote to the appropriate end-use(s). Naturally, this was insufficient to monitor as many markets in as much depth or as often as many wanted. Quarterly data were sought on more than 100 vaguely and variably defined end-uses. Sometimes reliable data simply were not available even if the end-use market(s) could be operationally defined and measured. Moreover, correctly regarding knowledge as a source of power, the U.S. man-made fiber manufacturers sought better data on an exclusive basis.

The TEB satisfied its sponsors with exclusive quarterly reports on end-use consumption of man-made fibers by generic type and form. The latter reports were published as separate pages for insertion in a red three-ring binder called the Man-Made Fiber Producers' Handbook (MMFPH) with data on production and capacity. The MMFPH quickly became known as the "redbook." Its release was restricted to domestic fiber producers. It also was understood that details in the MMFPH were not to be given to non-TEB sponsors such as textile mills, needle trades firms, retailers, the financial community, the press, or the general public. These publications became available by subscription in the late 1970s, but until then, access to the MMFPH was reserved to fiber producers supporting the TEB with fees based on their total real fiber sales.

Specifying which generic fibers and forms are substitutes or complements generally or by end-use, and exactly how much of each falls into which category, exceeds the TEB's physical resources, technical expertise and authority, according to conversations the author has had over the last 30 years with the founder of the TEB, Stanley B. Hunt, and his immediate successors, Charles A. Whitehead and Robert P. Antoshak. That forced any interested man-made fiber producers to resort to other sources to get the information needed for such determinations. Consumer purchase diary panels are a particularly fruitful source of much of the data needed for such a purpose.

Celanese Corporation initiated the first and second multiclient consumer purchase diary panels, Market Research Corporation of America (MRCA) and National Family Opinion (NFO), respectively, to obtain longitudinal and cross-sectional data on a wide variety of products in a way that could be projected to each of the nine census regions and the nation. A client fiber producer, textile mill, or needle trades firm can buy three sets of data to help estimate elasticities. A set of demographic, but not psychographic, data is available for each household reporting each purchase. It includes family composition (numbers, genders, income, education, ages, relationships, and so on) and states who bought and who will use the product. A second set of data details the item bought by fiber genera, fabric structures, brand(s), source (domestic or import), units bought, price, and so on. A third set of data characterizes the transaction (that is, store type, on-sale or discounted item, whether the item was bought as a gift, the purchase date, and so on).

Table 2-3 presents average market share data by generic fiber and form within each of the TEB's 44 current end-uses. Certain features of this table require brief explanations.

The extreme left-hand column of Table 2-3 contains arbitrarily assigned end-use identifying numbers, in lieu of the TEB's longer ones showing how earlier end-uses were pooled to form this list. The TEB's taxonomy was otherwise adhered to, although, at first glance, it might seem desirable to further combine some end-uses into still fewer and larger ones. Domestic tires and export tire cord and cord fabric, numbers 29 and 43, respectively, are one case in point. Another is craft and handwork yarns, domestic sewing thread, and export yarn, thread, numbers 4, 34, and 42.

The format of Table 2-3 may create an illusion that most of the generic fibers are adequate substitutes in many end-uses. That illusion has two causes. Either the level of aggregation used by the TEB in compiling data for its end-use surveys, or an understandable but rarely stated convention of omitting industry-accepted qualifying terms describing the fiber products consumed within the various end-uses, may generate an illusion of generic fiber substitutability within and across end-uses in Table 2-3. While one can decompose the annual end-use data to generic fiber, and often firm, levels, that is insufficient to learn the existence, direction, and intensity of interfiber cross-elasticity within yarns, fabrics, and final products constituting that end-use. Interfiber and intrafiber competition, complementarity, displacement, or independence only occurs at these more detailed levels. The difficulties of sufficiently decomposing usage data and of correlating them with other essential data necessitates the publication of aggregated tables.

When different generic fibers appear to compete in an end-use, experience immediately suggests two things. It is wiser to reverse the usual premise of substitutability and assume at least independence, if not complementarity. The presence of different generic fibers and forms within an end-use most likely signals consumption either in isolated and noncompeting but overaggregated segments of that particular end-use market, or complementarity within a homogeneous end-use or a part of it.

Most complementarity arises from either of two causes. One is blending staple forms of fiber, which usually is done to produce permanent press fabric. The other is combining generically distinct filaments into a single yarn or fabric to achieve performance results impossible with either component alone. Extensive computerized analyses of both TEB and MRCA data conclusively prove these contentions but are affordable by only a few big firms. Such studies were economic and marketing research projects at some of the larger fiber firms after the mid-1960s. However, the reader now is on notice that any apparent substitutability of generic fibers in and across the various textile end-uses generally is more an illusion than a viable economic premise, let alone a fact.

The second column from the left of Table 2-3 displays either a "Y" or an "N" next to each end-use. A "Y" reflects the author's view, based on experience in analyzing and modeling these end-use data, that some significant degree of interfiber substitution conceivably happened during the 1960-69 period. An "N" denotes the contrary case of no significant degree of interfiber substitution having occurred. Lengthy rationales for the assignment of each "Y" or "N" are omitted. Ten-year market share averages within each end-use were used to minimize the potentially distortive effects of such phenomena as fads in fashions, business fluctuations, and so on. Even so, considerable innovation occurred during the period covered in terms of the large-scale commercialization of new man-made fiber genera and the development of new end-uses.

U.S. man-made fiber products typically "substitute" in a peculiar way for one another and other materials, including but not limited to natural fibers. High-tenacity rayon tire cord once reinforced rubber in tires, for example. It undoubtedly displaced

Table 2-3

Average 1960-69 Distribution of Generic Fibers by Form in U.S. End-Use Markets

(percent of pounds consumed annually)

Fiber Genus / Fiber Form — S = Subtotal; Ac = Acetate; Acr = Acrylic; Ny = Nylon; Ol = Olefin; Pol = Polyester; Ra = Rayon; Wo = Wool; Oth = Others; N = negligible; – = none.

End-Use Market	End-Use Substitutability	Filament S	Ac	Acr	Ny	Ol	Pol	Ra	Oth	Staple S	Ac	Acr	Ny	Ol	Pol	Ra	Wo	Oth	Total
Grand Total:		31	3	5	10	3	7	3	N	69	N	4	40	4	1	10	7	3	100%
Apparel		25	6	–	7	–	11	1	N	75	N	6	44	1	N	13	5	6	100%
1 Sheer Hosiery	N	100	–	–	95	–	–	5	–	–	–	–	–	–	–	–	–	–	100%
2 Anklets and Socks	Y	27	–	–	26	–	–	1	–	73	–	23	45	1	–	1	N	3	100%
3 Sweaters and Related Accessories	Y	13	2	–	11	–	–	–	–	87	–	53	5	1	1	2	N	26	100%
4 Craft and Handwork Yarns	Y	5	1	–	–	–	–	–	–	95	–	55	1	1	1	4	5	19	100%
5 Male Underwear and Nightwear	N	2	1	–	N	–	1	–	N	98	–	N	87	1	N	10	N	N	100%
6 Female and Infants' Underwear and Nightwear	N	55	19	–	32	–	1	2	1	45	–	2	38	N	–	3	1	1	100%
7 Robes and Loungewear	N	50	33	–	12	–	4	1	–	50	–	N	39	1	2	5	3	–	100%
8 Pile Fabrics	N	3	–	–	–	3	–	–	–	97	–	81	–	N	1	5	2	15	100%
9 Lining Type Fabrics	N	44	29	–	5	–	2	8	–	56	1	–	43	N	5	6	1	–	100%
10 Apparel Lace	N	77	17	–	55	–	–	5	–	23	–	1	18	5	–	1	–	–	100%
11 Retail Piece Goods	Y	32	–	–	1	28	3	–	–	68	2	–	40	N	15	8	3	–	100%
12 Narrow Woven Apparel	Y	25	4	–	4	2	12	3	–	75	–	–	70	1	–	1	3	–	100%
13 Other Apparel and Accessories	Y	10	–	–	4	1	5	–	–	90	–	5	72	4	1	4	4	1	100%

14	Y	Topweight Apparel Fabrics	18	4	-	6	-	8	N	-	82	N	4	48	-	-	23	6	1	-	100%
15	Y	Bottomweight Apparel Fabrics	23	5	-	2	-	16	N	N	77	1	3	42	N	-	15	6	10	N	100%
		Home Furnishings	23	2	1	13	5	1	1	-	77	N	5	38	13	2	9	8	2	-	100%
16	N	Carpet Face Yarn	35	-	-	31	4	N	N	-	65	-	10	2	30	3	10	5	5	-	100%
17	Y	Carpet Backing	56	-	-	6	50	-	N	-	44	-	1	25	6	10	1	1	-	-	100%
18	N	Bedspreads and Quilts	10	7	-	1	2	-	N	-	90	-	-	75	N	-	3	12	-	-	100%
19	Y	Blankets and Blanketing	4	1	-	2	-	1	-	-	96	1	29	18	4	-	20	17	7	-	100%
20	N	Sheets and Other Bedding	1	N	-	N	-	1	N	-	99	-	-	76	-	-	19	4	-	-	100%
21	N	Towels and Toweling	-	-	-	-	-	-	-	-	100	-	-	97	-	-	2	1	-	-	100%
22	Y	Curtains	38	5	2	-	-	27	4	-	62	-	-	34	-	-	10	18	-	-	100%
23	Y	Drapery and Upholstery	26	6	7	3	5	1	4	-	74	1	1	43	3	1	2	22	1	-	100%
24	Y	Miscellaneous Home Furnishings	17	3	4	2	2	4	2	-	83	-	4	62	5	-	6	6	-	-	100%
		Industrial and Other Consumer Type Products	52	N	18	15	4	7	8	-	48	1	N	31	1	1	7	7	N	-	100%
25	N	Narrow Fabrics	44	1	-	23	7	5	8	-	56	-	-	54	1	-	-	1	-	-	100%
26	N	Shoes and Slippers	2	-	-	-	-	-	2	-	98	-	-	91	4	-	-	3	-	-	100%
27	N	Medical, Surgical and Sanitary	3	-	-	1	2	-	N	-	97	-	-	44	-	-	4	49	-	-	100%
28	N	Transportation Fabrics	13	-	-	9	2	1	1	-	87	-	-	63	3	7	3	11	-	-	100%
29	N	Tires	99	-	4	47	-	24	24	-	1	-	-	1	-	-	-	-	-	-	100%
30	N	Hose	63	-	-	10	-	13	40	-	37	-	-	27	3	-	7	-	-	-	100%
31	N	Belting	41	-	-	20	-	12	9	-	59	-	-	47	2	-	8	2	-	-	100%
32	Y	Felts	8	-	-	4	-	4	-	-	92	-	-	27	11	-	4	17	33	-	100%
33	N	Filtration	19	-	10	2	5	2	-	-	81	-	2	24	-	15	13	27	-	-	100%
34	N	Sewing Thread	21	-	-	8	-	11	2	-	79	-	-	71	-	-	5	3	-	-	100%
35	N	Rope, Cordage, Fishline, Etc.	52	-	-	16	30	3	3	-	48	-	-	42	N	-	2	4	-	-	100%
36	N	Bags and Bagging	32	-	-	1	30	1	-	-	68	-	4	63	-	-	-	1	-	-	100%
37	Y	Coated and Protective Fabrics	23	-	3	11	7	2	-	-	77	-	N	59	-	1	10	7	-	-	100%
38	N	Electrical Applications	73	1	66	1	3	1	1	-	27	-	-	27	-	-	-	-	-	-	100%
39	N	Paper and Tape Reinforcing	78	1	65	3	-	-	9	-	22	-	-	14	1	-	2	5	-	-	100%
40	N	Reinforced Plastics	93	-	93	-	-	-	-	-	7	-	-	7	-	-	-	-	-	-	100%
41	N	Miscellaneous	16	1	1	6	2	2	4	-	84	4	2	32	3	2	31	10	N	-	100%

Table 2-3 Continued

	Filament								Staple										Total
	Subtotal	Acetate	Fiberglass	Nylon	Olefins	Polyester	Rayons	Others	Subtotal	Acetate	Acrylic	Cotton	Nylon	Olefins	Polyester	Rayons	Wool	Others	
Exports	22	4	-	6	1	9	2	-	78	-	2	57	2	-	8	7	2	-	100%
42 Y Yarn, Thread, Etc.	-	-	-	-	-	-	-	-	100	-	9	43	6	-	16	11	15	-	100%
43 Y Woven and Knit Fabrics	20	5	-	3	1	10	1	-	80	-	1	64	1	-	7	7	N	-	100%
44 N Tire Cord and Cord Fabrics	100	-	58	-	-	13	29	-	-	-	-	-	-	-	-	-	-	-	100%

Source: Systematic Forecasting, Inc., Hackensack, N.J.

Notes: N in the body of this table denotes negligible, that is, less than 0.05%.
N in the substitutability column denotes that no substitution occurred, while a Y denotes that some substitution
may have occurred.

the cotton yarns originally used for that purpose. Based on data at the bottom of page 30 in Markham's work, cotton accounted for 99.7% of U.S. tire cord in 1937 while rayon held the balance; by 1949, however, rayon accounted for 71.4%, of this market, with nylon and cotton fibers vying for the rest.

> *Since the early 1950's nylon has made significant gains in tire cord at the expense of rayon. The rayon industry in recent years has made product improvements with an objective of stalling off any further inroads by nylon in tire cord and possible gain back (of) a portion of its old market. . . . If rayon producers would have made improvements in the fiber, when nylon tire cord was first introduced or even earlier than that, rayon would still have had the total or a sizable segment of the nylon tire cord (Yale, vii).*

The rayon innovations Yale refers to include the development, refinement and marketing of high-tenacity, viscose tire cords. Moncrieff discusses these in depth. In sum, rayon tire cord was displaced by suitable products of vastly higher tenacity synthetic fibers starting with nylon [263-72].

There are four reasons the generic fiber displacement process is distinct from, rather than an extreme version of, conventional economic substitution. First, displacement is a prolonged process. Displacement occurs over a period of years because of imperfections in the relevant fiber and textile markets, as will be discussed in later chapters. Economic substitution, however, implicitly is a rapid phenomenon. Second, the displacement process better fits an "S" or logistics curve over time than the high frequency sine wave implicit in economic substitution.

Displacement occurs in at least two distinct steps. The initial displacement phase involves minute amounts and is very slow as the new fiber's producer develops product for a particular application, learns to market that good, and struggles to gain customer acceptance. However, the last-phase of displacement reallocates huge volumes of fiber and, to the outside observer, seemingly happens overnight.

Third, despite many instances of failure to complete phase one, displacement invariably is an irreversible process once phase two volumes are attained, as no case is known of a displaced fiber recovering to any significant degree, let alone recapturing, its original position in any market segment where such displacement happened. Finally, end-product physical performance requirements and the associated fiber properties are vastly more important determinants of the displacement process than the money price of either the fiber or its end product, while the latter is supreme in economic substitution.

Economic substitution implies several things simultaneously. First, a smooth and symmetrical trade-off relationship exists between prices and quantities of potentially competing goods, other things being equal. Second, substitution calls for a static period, that is, one characterized by little innovation, reasonably constant and known tastes, plus a well-understood manufacturing technology. In displacement, however, access to a dramatically higher final product performance with a new material matters enough to vitiate money price as an issue. Also, it is uncertain whether and how that desired higher performance can be achieved. Costly man-made fibers often displaced far cheaper natural fibers and other materials. Why? Because previously impossible but highly desirable things could be done only with this new material. For these reasons, generic fiber displacement is a process entirely distinct from that of economic substitution.

Generic fiber displacement by cellulosic fibers may have stimulated Professor Joseph A. Schumpeter's recognition of the process of creative destruction.

> *Professor Schumpeter had closely observed the bonanza days of the rayon industry in Europe and in the United States and frequently employed the industry as illustrative of his perennial gale of creative destruction [Markham, vii].*

Three more background points about the data in Table 2-3 are worth bearing in mind. As relative data were presented in a particular fashion, certain points may be obscured that would have been obvious in either an alternative format or absolute figures. First, unique combinations of three to six end-uses out of the 44 commonly account for over 70% of the usage of any particular form of each given generic fiber in the table. Next, within any given generic fiber and form, whether a man-made fiber or not, there are radical differences in the fibers, yarns or other textile structures made from these fibers and consumed in the various groups of end-uses. For this reason the TEB initially grouped its end-uses into five categories, later condensed to four. Table 2-3 explicitly presents only two of the main dimensions of those fiber differences, fiber genera and form. Third, while each end-use is homogeneous as compared with others, most are more internally heterogeneous and exhaustively segmented than an unfamiliar reader might expect. Cotton Counts Its Customers (CCIC), an annual publication of the Market Research Service of the National Cotton Council, illustrates the depth of final product disaggregation prerequisite to sensible discussion of generic fiber substitution better than do the TEB's end-uses. This periodical reports the quantities of cotton consumed in over 430 distinct items in 91 major end-uses. It also estimates the square yardage of fabric needed to produce given items, average weights per square yard, and other traits of relevant fabrics for most of the more important of those 430-plus items.

End-use numbers 11, 13, 24, and 41 report otherwise undecomposable poundages associated with products consuming only small amounts of fiber and traditionally included in the corresponding major end-use clusters. Any appearance of interfiber substitution in these miscellaneous end-uses is apt to result more from overaggregation than fact. However, some generic fiber substitution is assumed to have happened in all except end-use 41.

Two brief supplemental comments are needed to complete one's appreciation of Table 2-3. Spandex is the predominant component of the other filament column of Table 2-3. Spandex often is wrapped with nylon filament or cotton, depending on a given application's performance requirements. Wrapping compensates for this fiber's limited tensile strength and vulnerability to abrasion. Proper wrapping also confines the elongation and contractive force of this elastic fiber to values suitable to the particular final good. Hence, spandex fiber is consumed as a complementary fiber in sheer hosiery (end-use 1), anklets and socks (end-use 2), elastic parts of foundation garments (end-use 6), narrow woven (end-use 12), and stretch fabric for pants and bathing suits in bottom-weight apparel (end-use 15).

Nylon filaments' denier distribution in apparel (end-uses 1-15) range from 10 to 210 denier. However, only a few specific deniers or a very narrow denier range is feasible and acceptable for a given product in a particular end-use. The same principle also applies to all the other critical fiber traits given above on Table 2-2. Home furnishing end-uses (16-24 on Table 2-3) employ nylon filaments primarily in the 240 to 2,000 denier range. The two carpet end-uses (16 and 17) consume almost all the nylon filament of 1,000 denier and higher. The rest of the higher denier nylon used in this sector is consumed in upholstery fabrics. Those carpet end-uses have significantly different requirements for luster, filament cross-section (multi-lobal shapes are preferred to hide dirt and to get suitable light reflection properties), and such other traits as uniform and deep dyeing and ultraviolet and stain resistance. These explanatory remarks about nylon filament apply to all fibers and forms with suitable variations regarding the controlling properties and the distributions of those properties, although the net effect is the same--an industry of heterogeneous products.

CONCLUSIONS

Clearly, today's U.S. man-made fibers industry differs from Markham's rayon industry in many vital respects. Some of those differences were raised and discussed in this chapter. Their economic consequences and those of other differences yet to be identified will be treated in later chapters.

The current U.S. man-made fibers industry is far more complex than the one Markham examined. It has more generic fibers, producers, intermediate and final processes, and products today. Markham analyzed an industry of a single homogeneous man-made fiber, 150 denier filament viscose rayon. Many heterogeneous man-made fiber genera and products now exist. This latter point will be explored in later chapters.

Today's U.S. man-made fibers industry enjoys a long and detailed database. Nothing comparable was available at the time of Markham's research. End-use time series cross-sectioned by generic fiber and form, now taken for granted, were only being painstakingly developed when Markham wrote.

When viewed within end-uses and end-use items rather than in total, as Markham had to do, interfiber substitution is much rarer than either independence or complementarity in this industry. Inspection shows interfiber rivalry to be primarily a slow, irreversible, and money-price-insensitive process of displacement of an older material or fiber genus by a newer one, that is, a modern version of Schumpeter's process of creative destruction, rather than one characterized by rapid switching, as typified by an economic substitution process with its sensitivity to swings in the relative money prices of the rival items. Little substitution occurs either within or across fiber genera and forms. Conceptually substitutable fibers must balance their critical properties and satisfy a specific end product's needs before they can compete. Interfiber rivalry is confined to an individual item or a single end-use, as the fiber properties needed by other products or end-uses are so distinct as to bar any significant amount of substitution across most end-uses within a category (for example, industrial end-uses), let alone to or from an apparel end-use to or from either a household or industrial end-use.

Markham's rayon industry had glowing prospects. Although, as will be shown later, the current U.S. man-made fiber industry is still economically viable, its long-term prospects no longer are as indisputably roseate as they were to Markham.

3

Conditions of Supply and Demand

This chapter provides background information about the environment of the U.S. man-made fibers industry. Its two sections examine the conditions of the supply of man-made fibers since 1948, including economic features of the production technologies involved, and the demand determinants.

SUPPLY

Four issues were found to particularly affect the supply of U.S. man-made fibers. In order of discussion, those are production technology, raw materials, labor, and product durability.

Production Technology

Man-made fiber production has but a few basic steps according to recognized authorities [Corbman, 333-496; Inderfurth, 1-12; Moncrieff, 157-701; and Press, 50-91]. Those basic steps are mixing ingredients; reacting the mixture to form a monomer, the basic compound from which a polymer is formed; polymerization, or linking the monomer into a long chain molecule; extruding the polymer as a fiber or fiber spinning; and winding the fiber onto a package. These steps become complex in practice. Over ten variables have to be controlled and coordinated. There usually is at least one alternative to any selected fiber-spinning process, with often subtle, hard to evaluate but important economic and technical trade-offs. Essential secondary steps were omitted from this capsule description to emphasize the major features common to all man-made fiber production technology except for fiberglass, which is not a polymer. Because those secondary steps can crucially affect commercial acceptance of a man-made fiber product, they are introduced at suitable places in the more detailed technology discussion below.

A few distinct processes are used to make particular man-made fibers. Aside from significantly different technology, and inputs, it will be shown that each such process differs notably in minimum and maximum efficient scales too. Hence, one must continually bear in mind one caveat: Every guideline for man-made fibers' production has at least one exception. Even the well-accepted idea that man-made fiber production essentially is a chemical process breaks down with fiberglass.

Fiberglass manufacture fundamentally involves pulling molten glass, at temperatures of roughly 2,000 degrees centigrade, from an insulated furnace, letting it cool, applying a finish, and winding the product onto a package. Some fiberglass plants are backward integrated; others buy solid glass spheres, called marbles, about one inch in diameter and remelt them.

Four radically different man-made fiber-spinning processes exist. Melt spinning is appropriate to the manufacture of fiberglass or polyester fibers. It typically needs multifloor buildings to allow molten fiber to cool in the air without distortion as it descends under the force of gravity. Melt spinning also is energy intensive.

The viscose rayon process represents an early version of solution or regenerative spinning. It steadily squirts a viscose solution through a spinnerette into a congealing bath. A spinnerette is a metal disk with tiny, precisely shaped and positioned holes through which a spinning solution is extruded to form filaments. The spinnerette controls both the number and cross-sectional shape of the filaments. Solution-spun polymers react with the chemicals in a congealing bath to solidify into fibers. Obviously, a congealing bath chemically suitable to one generic fiber is inappropriate for any other.

A third fiber-spinning process extrudes polymer-bearing solvent through a spinnerette into an evaporation chamber. This process is called solvent or dry spinning. It too suits some generic fibers but not others. Diacetate fiber, for instance, is only made via dry spinning.

Many tiny but significant variations in man-made fiber-spinning technologies are possible and essential in practice. Ingredients' purity and uniformity of particle size and shape differs from batch to batch and sometimes exceeds practical spinning standards. Differences in ingredient mixtures as small as one part per million can significantly alter the properties of sequential batches of the same generic fiber. Differences in particle size affect the speed and completeness of chemical reactions.

The exact mixing process, its duration, and ambient conditions with respect to heat, light, moisture, and cleanliness, individually and collectively, can profoundly affect final product acceptability. Ambient conditions and the duration of exposure to them, plus the kind, form, and state of the catalyst used can affect the amount and purity of the monomer obtained. Some of these variables are more readily controlled than others. A noticeable difference in technology arises here.

Some man-made fiber producers are sufficiently backward integrated to make their own monomer or even the ingredients to produce monomer. Such ingredients are known as feedstocks or petrochemical feedstocks. A few large U.S. man-made fiber producers are partly integrated back into the oil business. Most larger firms prepare monomer for their own use to produce fiber and other products. Some have surplus monomer or polymer for resale from very large-scale plants that must be run steadily despite cyclical demand. Amoco, formerly Standard Oil of Indiana, may be the only U.S. man-made fiber producer essentially fully integrated back through feedstocks and even into petroleum gases and liquids.

Medium-sized synthetic fiber producers may either buy monomer and polymerize it or buy chips of a suitable polymer and liquefy them. Naturally, the less integrated the process, the more likely that ambient conditions will affect either or both the monomer and the polymer. Also, a less integrated process ties up more inventory and uses more energy per pound of output. Start and stop operation of a man-made fiber extruder prevents its temperature from stabilizing. That thermodynamic disequilibrium can erratically distort important fiber properties.

Energy is an often neglected but important aspect of man-made fiber production technology because the industry is characterized by Leontief-type production function in which all inputs are nonsubstitutable and must be used in exact and fixed proportions to get results. Man-made fiber manufacture is energy intensive [Ketterling, Sections VI and VII]. Synthetic and cellulosic fiber production depends heavily on electricity to heat and transport chemicals. Natural gas is burned to achieve the high temperature needed to make fiberglass.

Efficient commercial production of man-made fibers calls for more from electricity than just large quantities at low prices. An uninterrupted supply of electricity is essential. Many fiber polymers will quickly solidify in and then totally obstruct a fiber plant's piping unless kept at a proper temperature. Any power failure lasting long enough to let a polymer solidify necessitates a costly, prolonged, and technically difficult cleanup. A power outage lasting only minutes is a potential calamity in man-made fiber production. An uncontrolled man-made fiber plant shutdown is a rare but costly event. The machinery has to be completely taken apart and cleaned to get rid of all unevenly solidified polymer, then reassembled and precisely realigned. The system of polymer piping and containers has to be flushed to purge it of undesired and potentially reactive chemicals and minute particles, which can cause turbulence. Then the plant has to be restarted, one machine at a time, and restored to stable operating conditions before yielding commercial product. These steps can take experts months of intense effort.

Electricity for fiber production also must match the precision pumps' technical requirements regarding voltage, amperage, frequency, phase, and so on. Otherwise, an unacceptably uneven product results at the expense of decreased pump life. Electricity reliability problems are known to have made it impossible to produce polyester fiber and, later, the much more easily produced olefin fibers in Puerto Rico. Electrical concerns also influence siting decisions. It is not a matter of chance that almost all major, commercially successful man-made fibers plants erected since 1948 rely on the Tennessee Valley Authority or other equally trustworthy low-cost suppliers.

A man-made fiber needs further processing after extrusion to develop its strength and other properties. Drawing mechanically extends the fiber. A man-made fiber normally is extruded at a constant rate, say, at 1,000 meters per second. Actual extrusion speeds are confidential, but are widely believed to vary markedly by firm, fiber and form, product, and over time. A man-made fiber is extended or drawn at a faster rate per second than it was extruded to orient the fiber's crystalline structure. An insufficiently drawn fiber lacks strength; hence it is apt to break and interrupt later production.

An important but as yet unsettled issue in fiber production technology concerns the merits and disadvantages of various degrees of integration versus separation of the spinning, drawing, and winding stages. Rayon manufacture originally was a discontinuous process. A continuous process to make rayon was eventually developed by the Industrial Rayon Corporation (IRC) [Press, 60]. Typically, an integrated production process does not appear until the technology involved is well understood and developed; the risk of a superior technology arising is thought to be nominal; a superior product or a notably cheaper one results from the integrated process; demand exists to absorb the extra output; and adequate financing is available. Not all in the rayon industry were as confident about these matters as IRC's executives. The post-World War II noncellulosic fiber industry executives as a group have yet to become even that confident about the same issues.

A few supplementary but essential man-made fiber production steps now deserve attention. For instance, somewhere in the process a finish is applied to the fiber. A delusterant, such as titanium dioxide, also may be applied. Further fiber treatments may be necessary to produce a commercially viable product.

Fiber finishes are a chemical specialty unto themselves. Leading fiber producers develop finishes for their exclusive use. Smaller firms have to buy commercially available finishes. A finish is usually applied to a man-made fiber bundle shortly after it is extruded. That usually happens before the fiber is first wound onto a package but it may be done either before or after the fiber is drawn.

Fiber finishes typically serve several purposes simultaneously. A proper fiber finish keeps all the filaments together and lubricates the filament bundle to allow further processing without friction damage. A finish also should reduce or eliminate the effects of static electricity in later processing of the fiber. It also should protect the filaments from permanent staining because of momentary exposure to water, lubricants, perspiration and certain other chemicals. A finish may also enable or inhibit a reaction between the fiber and another substance. For example, some man-made fibers need special finishes to coat them or use them as a support material in end-use structures such as tires.

Fiberglass finishes are called binders because they bind the glass filaments together and protect them from friction. The major fiberglass producers feel that economies of scale in developing new and superior binders is a key reason for the decline of smaller fiberglass producers.

In the early 1960s duPont introduced a new version of its Type 6,6 nylon filament, called Rotoset, which did not call for twisting the filament bundle before weaving it into a fabric. A major part of the reason for Rotoset's success was its finish. Unfortunately, the Rotoset nylon finish did not work adequately when simply extended to polyester filament. It took almost two years to develop a new finish after a year's testing found that the finish was the cause of problems in the polyester fabric.

Some, once exclusively textile processes often are done by man-made fiber producers to ensure their fibers' market acceptance. Among those activities are plying, blending, yarn (as opposed to fiber) spinning, yarn (as opposed to fiber) dyeing, texturing, heat treatments, and warping. Before World War II, these functions were done by independent, specialized textile firms. Later, vertically integrated textile mills undertook these activities, first, for internal needs and subsequently as merchant suppliers. However, man-made fiber producers gradually felt compelled to undertake these textile functions since no one else had an incentive to learn to process large volumes of various man-made fibers on the textile equipment then available. Often extensive, expensive, and prolonged trial-and-error experiments are necessary to determine the changes to and the proper settings of commercial machines for volume operation.

Synthetic fibers and fiberglass are thermoplastic materials, that is, they exhibit a form of memory modifiable by a suitable heat treatment. Filament fiberglass' inherent brittleness is circumvented by processing it soon after heating it above the critical glass transition temperature. Man-made fiber genera have unique glass transition temperatures well under their (also unique) melting points. Some practical benefits result from exploiting this phenomenon; ignoring it can create intractable problems. Suppose, for instance, that an erratically elongated polyester thread were unwittingly woven into a fabric composed of thousands of otherwise homogeneous polyester filament yarns. That odd yarn would escape visual detection during weaving and other textile processes until heated to a high enough temperature in the finishing plant.

The stressed fiber responds differently when heated. It shrinks to ease the accumulated stress, which almost surely ruins the fabric. Enough such fiber in a fabric can destroy valuable textile equipment. Neither the imposed stress nor the overall temperature change need be very great to cause an impressive display of inanimate power. The author has seen 5,000 strands of inadequately heatset 70 denier nylon contract at the same time to crush a 5"-diameter hollow steel tube at the core of a loom warp beam in but a few hours.

The process of mechanically binding the filaments of one yarn into a helix is called twisting. When several yarns are so combined, the process is called plying. Textile mills specializing in twisting and plying are called throwsters. Some throwsters buy large volumes of man-made fiber to process for resale. They also wind their products onto special packages to facilitate weaving, knitting, or other textile processes. Man-made fiber producers generally want and wanted to avoid antagonizing these segments of the textile industry by forward integration.

The textile industry long ago developed machinery to process natural fibers and so prefers to deal with the more familiar staple form of fiber. The man-made fiber industry thus had to develop the technology to make a staple product, although man-made fibers originate as filaments. Making staple man-made fiber calls for additional production steps. Cutting filament into staple lengths is one such extra step. Commercial equipment from another industry was adapted to cut filament into staple, but there was a problem getting the staple to cohere so that it could be spun into a yarn. Crimping resolved this.

Crimping is essential to producing man-made fiber in staple form. Fortunately, the combination of a finish and twisting often suffices to form a yarn of filament fibers. Unfortunately, staple man-made fibers generally are too short and too smooth to be converted into a yarn merely with finishes or twisting. Man-made staples lack enough interfibril friction to cohere when subjected to textile yarn spinning. Crimping supplies the extra interfibril friction needed.

Crimping converts a smooth-surfaced man-made fiber into a microscopically wavy, three-dimensional spiraled material. The crimp pattern in any staple fiber only appears when it is examined longitudinally under magnification. Crimping can be done several ways. Filament often is mechanically crimped by running it between slightly separated gears before cutting it into staple. Self-crimping fiber can be made from a suitable combination of polymers.

A modern man-made fiber producer may provide a staple product or a special bundle of thousands of filaments, called tow, which a textile firm can later cut or tear into staple. A fiber producer may have to supply several incompatible and nonsubstitutable forms of staple from the same generic fiber family. Each version differs primarily, but not exclusively, in length so that it only can be converted efficiently into yarn via a particular yarn-spinning process. The machinery for each yarn-spinning process can only handle staple fiber within a range of lengths. For example, cotton spinning can convert fibers of some three-quarter inch to 2.5 inches long into yarn. The woolen process, however, can only convert fibers of roughly two to 16 inches long into yarn. The yarn from a given process also has distinctive features despite its fiber genus.

Further possible steps are not always mandatory in man-made fiber production. Delustering can change a fiber to suit an end-use's light-reflection requirements. Titanium dioxide is a popular delusterant. Delustering is easier and cheaper than altering a fiber's cross-section and/or polymer. The latter approaches are apt to invoke trade-offs with other important physical traits of the man-made fiber. Most man-made fibers come in bright, semi-dull and dull lusters. Some have added options such as mid-dull. Delustrants must be compatible with the fiber's finish and satisfactory in dealing with many of the same physical and chemical problems as finishes.

Man-made fiber firms had to show textile mills how to use man-made fibers. Mills could afford neither the time nor investment in equipment to learn by trial and error and lacked the expertise to independently try this with confidence. After all, if a new product's manufacturer cannot show a customer how best to use the innovation, then who can? Man-made fiber producers also found it advisable, if not imperative, to master textile technology to avoid being duped by hard-bargaining textile customers who sometimes blame their supplier's product for problems caused by the user's ineptitude, penury, or unwillingness to follow established procedures.

Some textile firms could not use man-made fibers in their original forms or on their original packages. When such textile firms formed a profitable market, fiber producers would forward integrate to supply the desired textile processing. Rewinding is a case in point.

Man-made fiber producers first supplied filament fiber on cone-shaped packages. The design of early man-made fiber production equipment dictated this package shape. However, parts of the textile industry needed other types and/or sizes of packages to fit their machines, balked at buying rewinding machinery, and disliked having to pay for such a service. Modern man-made fiber firms offer their fibers already put up on either single or multiend packages of various sizes, shapes, finishes, cost, and durability. Single end packages include both cones and a long narrow cylinder called a pirn. Different multifilament packages or warp beams are available for weaving and knitting. Man-made fiber producers forward integrated into rewinding to ensure both acceptable quality and product access at reasonable costs for filament weavers' warp beams, tricot knitters' warp beams, tire cord, and so on.

Commercializing each new man-made fiber typically involved difficulties in learning how to dye it, particularly in fabric or piece form. Sometimes the fabric's performance specifications seemed or were contradictory. How, for instance, to get different colors from the same generic fiber in the same length of fabric when the entire piece is to be subjected to the same dyeing and finishing process? The answer: Precolor either the darker or least needed threads in the design. If colorfastness specifications cannot be met by dyeing and finishing the fabric, then put the color into the body of the fiber instead of on the fiber's surface. Rayon producers soon learned to put a coloring agent into the congealing bath to do this. Solution-dyed fiber is colored during fiber production. Fiber colored after being produced is known as stock dyed. Coloring a yarn, rather than a fabric, is termed yarn dyeing. All these choices cost more than piece dyeing and raise the risk of amassing unsalable inventory. But solution-dyed yarn has superior color uniformity and resistance to chemical and ultraviolet degradation. Stock- and yarn-dyed fibers are mostly used in cost-sensitive situations calling for elaborate combinations of decorative colors.

So far, and despite vast expenditure of time, money and skilled effort, olefin fibers can only be solution dyed. An undyeable or unevenly dyeable man-made fiber or fiber that is expensive to dye is worthless to a market needing inexpensive coloration such as apparel outerwear. Some man-made fibers can only be dyed in a limited range of colors even under special conditions involving extreme pressure, temperature or costly chemicals. Satisfying those conditions may call for new capital equipment. The range of colors, uniformity and depth of shade, sunfastness and other related considerations may not be satisfactorily met or consistently reproduced between batches of the same generic fiber, let alone across man-made fiber families, despite the most attentive processing, at least until much experimentation has been done to establish new procedures, controls, and standards.

Synthetic fibers have two deficiencies as compared with the natural staple forms and, despite form, as compared with cellulosic fibers. Today's commercial synthetic fibers do not adsorb (that is, take moisture into their structure) and transmit moisture nearly as well as natural and cellulosic fibers. Most synthetic fibers adsorb little moisture from the air, as a percentage of their dry weight. As natural and cellulosic fibers can adsorb over 20% of their dry weight in atmospheric water, they are described as hydrophilic. Hydrophilic fibers tend to be more comfortable in garments and less subject to static electricity in processing. The adsorbed moisture may change their physical and chemical properties. None of the noncellulosic fibers really adsorbs moisture. They can, however, pick up some water on their surface by capillary action. The term "hydrophobic" describes synthetic fibers' insensitivity to moisture. Hydrophobic fibers are less comfortable in garments in humid weather and can build up large static electric charges. Hydrophobic fibers also are harder to color because of their impermeability to liquids. Furthermore, the smoothness of man-made filament yarns, as compared with a yarn, blocks air flow.

A staple yarn's microscopic bristle-like protrusions hold it away from one's skin. That allows air to circulate and makes such a fiber more comfortable. A filament yarn lacks "bristles" and so rests flat on the skin. Prolonged wearing of fabrics of such filaments next to large areas of skin feels uncomfortable. Those fabrics feel hot and dank in warm weather and chilly in cold weather.

Texturing is another important process to filament man-made fibers. Texturing has two mutually exclusive goals. It tries either to make filament fibers into functionally acceptable substitutes for staple fiber or to get 15% to 25% elongation and recovery from an otherwise inelastic material to improve various outerwear garments' comfort. The former aim is met via bulk texturing and the latter via stretch texturing.

In sum, the U.S. man-made fibers industry's technology has several important features. Chemical technologies are a major force in explaining the industry's origins and growth. Innovations in the man-made fibers industry often came in response to customers' needs or to gain new prospects' acceptance of these materials. The man-made fibers industry technologies are numerous, complex, sometimes interactive, as yet unperfected, and dynamic, at least in an evolutionary sense. Some scholars rate the results of duPont's commercialization of the developments in polymer chemistry (made by the team it recruited Professor Carothers to lead) as among the more significant innovations of this century [Jewkes, Sawers, and Stillerman, 71-72].

Complex technology technology implies an entry barrier resulting from imperfect or obsolete knowledge of the process, product, or market. Dynamic technology also implies a harsh reinvestment criterion. Those unwilling or unable to sustain a long-term commitment to the industry in the forms of on-going capital and intellectual investments are apt to be quickly left behind with expensive but obsolete plants and products. As will be quantified later, demonstrably significant cost differences exist across generic fiber families, and alternative processes within some of those fiber genera, notably nylon and polyester.

Raw Materials

The U.S. man-made fibers industry consumes a variety of raw materials. The cellulosic and synthetic sectors of the industry need huge amounts of water, while the fiberglass sector does not. Each sector of the industry uses large amounts of particular but distinct raw materials. Each also uses small amounts of many other ingredients. Man-made fiber recipes often have over 100 ingredients. Although important, those small-volume items must be ignored here. They often are proprietary in composition, source, purpose, costs, and so on. Also, the author knows little about them or their precise economic importance to the industry, and this book's focus is economics, not chemical engineering. Only a few aspects of their raw materials significantly affect man-made fibers' supply.

First, some man-made fiber ingredients are hazardous. Some are potentially explosive. Others, such as acrylonitrile, are carcinogens. Still others are highly reactive, such as, fluorine. Such ingredients need special handling or facilities, which invariably raises the investment in a fiber plant, and costs for labor, insurance, and regulatory compliance.

Second, man-made fiber producers differ in their backward integration into raw materials. Integrated firms can produce more uniform fiber in larger amounts, at lower costs with more stable operations. However, the economics of such integration dictate that a fiber producer be a large, multiproduct and multiplant firm with major activities beyond the scope of a strictly defined man-made fibers business. None of the U.S. man-made fiber firms is totally vertically integrated. But the more integrated producers typically are diversified into other uses of the key ingredient(s) to make fiber and/or non-fiber uses of the fiber-forming polymer itself. DuPont, for instance, mines the raw material for titanium dioxide and uses it not only as a fiber delustrant but also as a paint ingredient and for other purposes. DuPont also synthesizes polyester for molding powder, packaging film, computer diskettes, and other applications including fiber. Monsanto consumes the acrylonitrile it makes in one plant as a raw material in plants at various locations that produce two of its fibers, nylon and acrylic, plus sheet plastic, packaging films, and agricultural products. Backward integration in the chemical industry risks diseconomies as large plants are very sensitive to variations in utilization rates and are almost impossible to convert to other inputs or to make anything other than the originally intended output or output mix in fixed proportions.

The two key ingredients for cellulosic fibers, besides water, are wood pulp and a strong chemical. Viscose rayon requires caustic soda in its manufacture, while acetone is essential to produce acetate. Silica is the major raw material of fiberglass. Each man-made fiber has a characteristic large-volume ingredient or two. All acrylic fibers, for instance, derive from acrylonitrile. Type 6, 6 nylons consume adipic acid, while Type 6 nylons need lactic acid. Ethylene glycol is polyester's key raw material. But all the large-volume ingredients for synthetic fibers ultimately derive from carbon, hydrogen, nitrogen, and oxygen. The first three of these elements normally are extracted from oil or natural gas by refinery processes, with oxygen obtained from the atmosphere.

Most man-made fiber raw materials are obtained either by backward integration or purchase. Larger fiber producers tend to backward integrate into key chemical feedstocks. Such integration is limited by one's ability to market the output of a minimum-efficient-scale feedstock plant. Minimum-efficient-sized fiber feedstock plants commonly exceed 100 million pounds per year by significant multiples [Vietorisz], whereas, as shown later, the median size of merchant man-made fiber plants tends to be considerably smaller. However, some larger fiber producers found that a particular feedstock was essential to many product lines, not just fibers, which collectively warrant backward integration. DuPont, the largest U.S. producer of polyester fiber and film, is backward integrated into certain polyester feedstocks, although its fiber needs alone reportedly are insufficient to justify that investment. Monsanto made a similar commitment to acrylonitrile as a feedstock for its acrylic and modacrylic fibers, Type 6, 6 nylon fibers, spandex fiber, fertilizers, and other nonfiber products.

All larger U.S. man-made fiber producers have long been significantly backward integrated. Hence, one must conclude that the costs and risks of vertical integration are, at least for the U.S. man-made fibers industry, more than offset by the savings obtained. Conversely, the small, unintegrated firms neither lasted as long nor fared as well.

Labor

Running a viable merchant man-made fibers firm calls for a team of diversely skilled, educated, and trained employees. Man-made fiber technology also calls for continuous operation of large-scale facilities, which necessitates large staffs. Man-made fiber manufacture means coordinating a diversity of nonsubstitutable, specialized physical and mental skills into an effective team. That team has to function steadily at the firm's plant(s) and its sales and management offices as well as in the field at the customers' facilities. It also has to recreate and develop itself smoothly over time and across all functions to remain competitive.

Large production teams are needed to cope with refresher training programs, staggered vacations, illness, maintenance, multishift operations, and many kinds of equipment. A firm must also have adequately staffed technical support facilities.

Inescapable technical support involves such activities as process and product research and development at the fiber, yarn, fabric, and final product levels. Quality control laboratories are also needed to assess one's output and to assess the properties of products made from one's fibers or from competitors' fibers. Staffing these necessary quality control facilities further increases the number of specialized people required. These and other essential support activities require scientists in chemistry, physics, and statistics, plus engineers and technicians. Chemists with expertise in polymers, dyes, fiber finishes, and physical chemistry are essential. Engineers are needed with expertise in chemical, civil, textile, hydraulic, electricity and electronics, computer science, and mechanics. A modern fiber firm must also employ specialists in other disciplines who usually work in branch and headquarters offices. Such specialists include personnel managers; financial teams (accountants, credit and collections people, tax experts, analysts and forecasters); attorneys (corporate and tax law, contract, and patent and trademark); sales personnel; marketing and advertising people, including marketing researchers and planners; buyers; logistics personnel; technical field service personnel; color and style forecasters; maybe an economist or two; product and market specialists; secretaries and clerks; computer personnel (operators, systems analysts, and programmers); and a hierarchy of management from supervisors to senior executives. Major commercial U.S. man-made fiber producers thus commonly average hundreds of employees per plant or more.

While U.S. fiber manufacturers usually are multiproduct and multiplant operations, they typically are divisions of still larger, vertically integrated, corporations. The combination of a tendency to backward integration plus the need for large teams of diverse specialists creates an unusual entry barrier. Such teams are hard to assemble and maintain even if there were no difficulties in immediately financing a new organization big enough to warrant sufficient backward integration to compete with established man-made fibers suppliers. Historically, production and other personnel, as well as physical resources, are acquired over a period of years or decades. New entrants face a formidable barrier if they must speculatively fund a large and rapid investment in plant and personnel, despite an uncertain ability to sell and service a cost-conscious and skeptical mix of textile customers with product(s) of unproven properties, costs, and continuity of delivery.

Although not labor-intensive, man-made fibers manufacturing is highly dependent on human efforts. Experience gathered by the cellulosic fiber producers showed that most applicants lacked the physical endowments to perform satisfactorily as spinning machine operators. The requisite talents included ambidexterity, fast reflexes, sensitive touch, stamina, acute vision, and good depth perception. Few job seekers had all the necessary talents. Training might enhance the skills of those suitably endowed but it could not impart such talents. And, until quite recently, various types of man-made fiber production equipment needed special skills to operate.

Certain character traits also matter. Man-made fibers production workers have to be reliable, as high absenteeism is unaffordable. They also have to be able and willing to work with little opportunity for social contact with their peers since the jobs are paced by rather large-sized equipment that usually needs only one operator-inspector for every few machines. In Avtex's Meadville acetate filament plant, one person tended six extruders per shift in 1984. That machine load per worker had about doubled with modern equipment, which also yielded about twice the output per machine. Hence, at Meadville overall output per machine tender almost quadrupled in a decade in addition to a more than order of magnitude improvement in product quality.

Starting and bringing a man-made fibers plant to a stable operating state at rated capacity without damaging the equipment or risking injury to the employees calls for skilled and coordinated effort. Once in a normal operating mode, less human effort, but no less skill and coordination, can keep things on an even keel. In practice, the same labor force works overtime to bring a plant on-stream. Having done so, it has a strong incentive to avoid necessitating so strenuous an effort in the future. Some U.S. man-made fiber facilities have run continuously for so long that their employees lost the special skills and coordination necessary to restart the plant after an unexpected emergency shutdown. In one such instance, following weeks of unsuccessfully trying to restart MTC's Decatur, Alabama, acrylic plant after a fire caused a shutdown, the rather abashed inside joke was: "We've lost the recipe!"

In sum, man-made fiber firms are labor-sensitive but not labor-intensive. With backward integration also important, there is a significant entry barrier that is unlikely to dissipate until radical new technology appears.

Product Durability

Man-made fibers' durability is an uncertain but important matter. Man-made fibers typically are somewhat but not highly perishable and usually can be stored for months, if not years. U.S. textile and man-made fibers industries' technologies and practices on product liability and fees for package rental signal a practical shelf life for man-made fibers ranging from a few days to perhaps three years. In specific cases, such as producer-oriented feed yarn for texturing (POY), man-made fibers have to be shipped to and further processed by the customer within a few days after being extruded.

A man-made fiber's shelf life depends on several variables. Both the fiber's technical properties and storage conditions are critical determinants of its shelf life. All man-made fibers' surface finishes are composed of somewhat volatile substances. A man-made fiber becomes impossible to convert into a textile material once those volatile substance(s) evaporate. Sometimes the fiber finish can be restored or reapplied, but that is neither generally nor assuredly so.

Proper conditions can delay deterioration of the fiber finish. Drastic or frequent variations in transit and storage conditions can make a fiber unsuitable for its intended application. Excessive fluctuations in temperature and humidity are particularly troublesome. A leaky truck roof during a rain storm or a faulty air conditioning system for a storage room can make a shipment of fiber worthless. So can over or uneven heating in transit, storage, or processing. High or very erratic temperatures can damage the polymer and/or packages of man-made fibers. Temperature variations may unevenly distort man-made fibers' thermoplastic memory. Exposing fibers to sunlight or proximity to another heat source may cause uncorrectable problems later in fabric formation or finishing. If temperature variations of a few degrees last for a few hours, a man-made fiber may slough off its package and snarl or entangle on it. Such fiber is worth only a few cents a pound as waste unless it can be salvaged by rewinding, which costs extra in terms of both money and additional risk of further variations in stress and temperature.

Moisture can degrade a fiber's finish. It also can affect cellulosic fibers' physical traits and so raise the costs of converting a fiber to yarn or fabric. Too little humidity dries out cellulosic fibers. Too much moisture encourages hydrophilic fibers to stretch out of shape or to be pulled into abnormally low deniers of unacceptably weak and uneven dyeing properties.

Man-made fibers' limited durability and vulnerability to transportation and storage conditions complicates operations for their producers. These considerations restrict how long one can hold inventory for sale. As man-made fibers differ in durabilities and sensitivities to ambient conditions, a multifiber producer faces a more complex logistics and inventory control problem than a single-fiber manufacturer. Furthermore, knowing that man-made fibers have limited shelf lives, customers not only buy cautiously but try to return any purchases found lacking in demand.

DEMAND

Our examination of demand for U.S. man-made fibers has five sections. In order of discussion those are: substitutes and imports, the growth of demand, marketing methods, purchasing methods of buyers, and cyclical and seasonal demand. By definition, a discussion of marketing methods might better fit into a later chapter on nonprice behavior. However, that discussion was divided so that those aspects of the subject deserving immediate coverage appear below, while the rest were deferred until Chapter 7.

Substitutes and Imports

U.S. man-made fibers seldom are substitutable for one another in particular end-uses, as indicated in Chapter 2. They also are rarely even weakly or partly substitutable for natural fibers and vice versa, and then only under very specific circumstances. In both of the above cases the nature and degree of substitutability ultimately depend on requirements unique to the precise end-use market segment under consideration.

The U.S. Department of Agriculture researched this matter for cotton, wool, cellulosic and noncellulosic fibers in a little known series of econometric studies [Dudley 1973; Ward and King 1962; Donald, Lowenstein, and Simon 1962]. Parts of the latest report in that series merit quoting.

> *Cotton was price inelastic in all markets, ranging from an elasticity of 0.1 in men's apparel to 0.6 in industrial uses. . . . Noncellulosic fibers were also price inelastic except in the household furnishings market, where prices were slightly elastic. . . .*

Despite the price inelasticities, fiber consumption does respond to price changes. Although the changes are small, they are usually statistically significant [Dudley, vi].

This study initially tried an aggregate concept to measure elasticities which proved unsuccessful. Attempts to measure aggregate coefficients for total fiber demand and particularly its major components were generally unsatisfactory [3].

Cotton and manmade fibers compete for markets on the basis of both price and nonprice factors. Nonprice factors have probably dominated in the past. However, price competition and non-price competition are often hopelessly interrelated, due to extensive advertising and promotion campaigns by fiber producers, particularly manmade fiber manufacturers and marketers. These campaigns often are tied to fiber prices, and substantial discounts may be given purchasers at all levels between producer and retailer in consideration for joint advertising of a specified brand of fiber.

Price competition implies a drive for profit maximization, but the profit maximization motive itself provides drawbacks to direct interfiber price competition. For two products to compete directly on the basis of price, (1) they must be near or perfect substitutes for one another--that is, the marginal rates of substitution between the two products must approximately equal one, and (2) shifts back and forth between them must be easily made at all levels between producer and consumer. While cotton and manmade fibers may meet the first criterion (with certain very broad reservations), the second provides a much greater obstacle, particularly in the short run. While such substitution can be made without particular difficulty for many products and at many levels, at the mill level it is difficult and time-consuming to change from production of 100 percent manmade fiber to production of 100 percent cotton fiber, or vice versa. Major difficulties may even be encountered in shifting production of manmade fiber-cotton blends to production of 100 percent cotton fabrics. All of one fiber must be run out of the machines which are changing fiber and the machines must be thoroughly cleaned. This is a major undertaking and naturally quite time-consuming. During the change, neither labor nor machines operate at peak efficiency. So once a mill shifts from cotton to manmade fiber in response to an anticipated price or supply movement, it is unlikely that the change will be reversed unless planners at the individual mill level feel they must do so to avert a severe profit squeeze or in response to strong consumer demand. This explains in part the apparent difficulty cotton experiences when attempting to recover markets in a specific end use once it has been displaced. That is, the change is in response to anticipated long-run factors, and profit maximization drives would tend to counter the shutdown necessary to move back to cotton. This would also explain any lack of direct competitive short-run responses by cotton and man-made fibers to seasonal price fluctuations [21-22].

Research and development expenditures on fibers greatly affect consumption, particularly of manmade fibers. Such . . . have been sharply greater for manmade than for natural fibers. . . . Under the auspices of the Cotton Research and Promotion Act of 1966, upland cotton producers are assessed $1 on each bale of cotton they market. The money is earmarked for research and promotion. In addition, the Consumer Protection Act of 1973 authorizes the Secretary of Agriculture, at his discretion, to make available up to $10 million more. While cotton faces the handicap of late entry into research, development, and promotion fields, these sums are enhancing its competitive position. Although Government-sponsored money is fractional compared with the reported $250 million spent by the manmade fiber industry in 1968, no single manmade fiber has duplicated all of cotton's inherent desirable characteristics. . . .

Closely allied with research and development is promotion. In the past, producers of manmade fibers extensively promoted their special characteristics, spending perhaps 20 to 30 times as much as natural fiber producers. . . .

The availability and quality of supply is important in determining fiber demand, particularly at the mill level. Generally, this has been an advantage for manmade fibers in competition with natural fibers. Prior to the energy shortage, mills were generally assured of a predictable supply of manmade fiber of a constant quality and at relatively stable, predictable prices. However, production and quality of cotton is less dependable. Such factors as weather, insects, and Government programs, none of which can be predicted with certainty, affect quality, quantity, and prices of cotton.

Blending two or more fibers allows certain desirable properties of each to be retained. As a result, a fiber may lose part of an end-use category earlier considered its exclusive domain. An often-cited example of this is the bedsheeting end use.

Finally, as in any market operation, psychology plays a major role in determining cotton demand in relation to demand for man-made fibers. This psychology may operate at the mill, wholesale, and retail levels. Traditionally, mills have shifted to manmade fibers when they anticipated problems with cotton supplies, long-run higher prices, or shifts in consumer demand. . . . Once such a shift is made, the profit motive discussed above moderates a reversal, even if the anticipated structural change fails to materialize. At the wholesale level, anticipation of consumer preferences affects buying patterns. At the consumer level, certain promotional undertakings affect the substitutability of various fabrics or fibers. Of all nonprice variables, market psychology is the most difficult to measure. One can only note that cotton buying by the U.S. consumer has not increased proportionately to purchasing power.

Although the actual effect of consumption of one fiber on another or on the aggregate cannot be statistically measured, some comments are in order. Tastes and preferences at the consumer level, shaped largely by promotion at the producer or retailer level, are often important in determining demand for a particular product. Another facet of interfiber competition has received insufficient attention--the fact that markets may be expanded by the effect of technological advances. ...

Technological market expansion, for the purposes of this study refers to expansion of a particular market which is elicited solely by advances in the technology of production or distribution of a product. ... It can be characterized as an improved or substitute production which enlarges a traditional market with rather sharply delineated boundaries, rather than a product which is created and for which a market is achieved through promotion.

One of the best examples of technological market expansion is provided by recent textile demand. Traditionally, the fiber market was the exclusive domain of natural fibers. Cellulosic fibers were created. They competed somewhat with natural fibers, largely on the basis of price. Then noncellulosic fibers were developed, which were suitable for a great variety of end uses and for some uses were superior to natural or cellulosic fibers. As noncellulosics came into greater use, total fiber use began to increase very rapidly, exceeding any earlier responses elicited by the traditional demand factors. It seems logical that some of this increase resulted from the manmade fiber technology itself. Use of carpeting, as a general example, leaped as manmade fiber technological advances provided a fiber well suited for carpets in abundant supply at attractive prices. Income, availability, and price were somewhat important in increasing use of carpeting, but perhaps more important was the suitability of the noncellulosics for this end use [23-26].

Traditional analyses usually related cotton demand to a long-run demand shifter (income), own-price (deflated by some price index), and other variables peculiar to cotton. This implicitly assumes a demand for cotton per se rather than a demand for cotton as an increment of total fiber demand. A decade ago this was not patently unreasonable. But today, cotton no longer dominates the fiber market. Emphasis today must be placed on competition among or between fibers [33].

On the basis of price levels, cellulosic staple competed with cotton throughout most of the 1950's and 1960's. Due to discounting of rayon staple prices as cotton prices fluctuate, cotton prices may be a better proxy for staple price than producer list prices [37].

The Agriculture Department's study of fiber price elasticities is impressive for both its analytical comprehensiveness and its conclusion, contrary to cotton's interest, that is, that cotton, wool, cellulosic, and noncellulosic fibers generally were not substitutes for one another in the apparel, home furnishing and industrial end-uses during the period 1953 through 1970. While one might quibble over some minor technical aspects of this study, it remains an unsurpassed example of econometric research into a complex and dynamic industry. Since price elasticities tend to increase over time, the report's conclusions probably are valid for prior years, although the data needed to test this point were not available. Given the increased availability of data and computers to process such data since 1970, one might speculate about the lack of an update of this study. Maybe the findings are too well established and the underlying situation has not changed significantly.

Alternatively, the findings may have been ignored for any of several reasons. So sophisticated and little publicized a study may not have found much of an audience in a U.S. fiber industry with less than two dozen qualified economists. The study's conclusions surely were not what the cotton growers wanted to hear. They wanted to know exactly how to recoup business "lost" to man-made fibers. The report tells why that cannot be done just by their independent actions. Conversely, the man-made fibers industry would find little of value in the report, which tells them what they already believe: Continue with such nonprice competitive practices as marketing, promotion, planning, and product and process research and development as simply competing on price would neither be effective nor efficient.

This study offers two key results for our purposes. First, it greatly clarifies an important earlier finding of Markham, that long-run cellulosic fiber prices were heavily affected by competition with cotton and its more flexible prices [164-70]. As the above extracts shows, the Agriculture Department's most recent study still limits cotton's influence on man-made fiber to rayon staple. Second, based on the same study, it surely is inappropriate to hypothesize that any other man-made fibers are significantly influenced by competition with cotton. Man-made fibers' quantities demanded and prices generally should thus be regarded as independent of cotton activity.

Imports affected domestic demand for domestically produced man-made fiber both directly and indirectly. One must distinguish imports in various fiber forms from imports of intermediate and final products made from fiber. Intermediate and final products mostly composed of fiber and often imported include yarn, fabric, and apparel, home furnishings, and certain industrial products. Imports of generic fibers as fiber, regardless of form, are regarded as directly competitive imports, while fibers imported in intermediate and final goods are found to be indirectly competitive. Any comprehensive study of fiber imports must take both types into account since most fiber imports occur indirectly. Indirect imports, on average, accounted for some 52% of all man-made fiber imported between 1959 and 1982 [Textile Organon, March 1983, 38-39]. Disaggregating indirect imports into their specific generic fiber components is difficult but not impossible for major fiber producers. Such disaggregation needs a large computer plus access to consumer purchase diary panel data and Census Bureau import data tapes. Everyone else has to make do with highly aggregrated published data for indirect man-made fiber imports.

Direct imports of man-made fibers were treated as though they were another single domestic source of capacity named "imports" in appended market structure Tables A1-1 through A1-13. Direct imports' annual shares of domestic capacity for the period 1959-82 usually were well under the 10% figure generally thought to mark the threshold of potentially significant market disruption. Imports' total mean share was 3.0%, with a standard deviation of 1.4%. However, direct imports of five out of 12 generic fibers and forms occasionally exceeded 10% of total capacity, although this seldom lasted for more than a few years and often happened in years with a domestic capacity shortage.

Annual nylon staple direct imports exceeded 10% from 1961 through 1968 (except in 1965), with a 1966 peak share of 16.1%. The mean share of nylon staple's direct imports was 6.9% and the standard deviation was 3.9%. Olefin staple's direct import shares were exceptional. They exceeded 10% of total capacity in all but 1961, 1970, and 1979-82, and peaked at 31.6% in 1962. Olefin staple's direct imports' mean share of capacity was 13.0%, with a standard deviation of 8.4%. The nylon and olefin situations primarily appear to have resulted from the rapid acceptance of man-made fiber carpets.

Direct polyester filament imports captured capacity shares greater than 10% in 1970-72. The peak value of 15.0% came in 1970 during the early part of the double knit polyester apparel boom. But polyester filament's direct imports' mean share of capacity was 3.1%, with a standard deviation of 4.3%.

Direct imports of rayon filament exceeded 10% of capacity in 1976-79 and 1981, with the peak import share reaching 13.5% in 1978. Direct rayon staple imports accounted for more than 10% of capacity in 1959-60, 1963-66, and 1968, with such imports' share of capacity peaking at 19.0% in 1959.

The U.S. man-made fibers markets clearly were reasonably self-contained at least through 1982, although they clearly were never totally closed. The latter point will be examined in greater depth in the next chapter. However, the relevant finding is that at some time in the recent past, imports reached the point at which they effectively converted the domestic textile and, hence, man-made fiber industries from essentially closed to wide open systems. Our study focused on the period in which the U.S. man-made fibers industry essentially was a closed system. That was done to escape the difficulties of dealing with a massive global man-made fibers industry facing the unsettled complexities of international trade in fibers, textiles, and final products.

Several factors limited the significance of U.S. imports of all man-made fiber genera and forms before the mid-1980s. The simplest explanation of that constraint would be to credit the Multi-Fiber Agreement (MFA) and the General Agreement on Trade and Tariffs (GATT) as effective domestic market protectors. Such a claim is unjustified in light of the sustained gross inadequacy of funding for the U.S. Customs Service, which is responsible for enforcing the MFA and GATT [Freeston, 68-69].

Imports of final products became the bane of the U.S. textile industry and most domestic man-made fiber producers. Studies conducted by TEB and its parent institution, the Man-Made Fibers Producers Association, since 1983 show that final textile products imports captured more than all the growth in every market sector. As of 1984,

- about half of all the fiber used in apparel was imported as final products
- roughly 25% of all fiber used in noncarpet home furnishings was imported as final products
- only some 10% of all fiber used in industrial and other consumer products was imported in final product forms.

Even worse, the growth of such imports has been and, for some time to come, will continue rising faster than the growth of domestic demand for all textile end-products. Incentives to import final textile products are far more potent than any known combination of politically acceptable obstacles. Imports are more profitable to distribute and retail. Imports often carry a much higher profit margin than domestic goods. Imported goods frequently also are thought to be more fashionable and desirable to own. There are no effective tariff, quota or other barriers to direct or indirect fiber imports, given the U.S. government's penury. Such stinginess clearly arises from a naive commitment to a technically and historically invalid free-trade philosophy that few, if any, U.S. trading partners regard as worth more than lip service when negotiating treaties and especially when operating in the international business arena.

The Growth of Demand

The United States' population growth has always had a considerable long-term positive effect on demand for domestic man-made fibers. The growth of imports has had a negative influence, as explained in the preceding section. Shorter-term growth rates affecting U.S. man-made fibers' demand include that of the entire economy, plus specific industrial sectors and the development of new end-uses.

The U.S. population's growth rate slowed to almost a replacement rate by the late 1950s according to the U.S. Department of Commerce's Bureau of the Census. That change in historic growth rates resulted from a more restrictive immigration policy and a lower birthrate, as neither emigration nor death rates altered much since the end of World War II. However, the postwar baby boom and the lag effects of changes in population growth complicated demand forecasts in the U.S. man-made fibers industry. Population growth rate changes operate with a variable lag insofar as man-made fibers are concerned.

Changes in population growth rates almost immediately influence demand for diapers and infant apparel. Typically, 15 to 20 years pass before a change in population growth visibly affects demand for work attire, especially in occupations requiring graduate or post-graduate training. Longer spans are needed to see the effects of changes in population growth rates on the home furnishings and industrial sectors. While foreseeable, such effects generally were either not sought or, worse, were ignored until it was too late. U.S. man-made fiber firms' managements often acted as though such changes either would be intrinsically favorable or so distant in time as not to matter.

The U.S. economy's long-term growth potential decreased as population growth eased and services came to dominate the national income accounts. The long-term growth rate of the general economy edged down from the historic trend of just under 4%, annually compounded, to that of the population's new secular growth rate of approximately 1%.

Analyses of various U.S. man-made fibers' product life cycles were done at several economic and marketing research departments in response to an unpublished but publicized doctoral dissertation [Yale] by a then employee of Chemstrand, the joint venture fiber business of Monsanto and American Viscose Corporation, and the availability of macroeconometric modeling services. While proving the inherent impossibility of accurately predicting the exact shape of a given product's life-cycle curve, Yale pointed the way for others to devise reliable methods to at least do so after the fact. Ultimately based on TEB data on generic fibers' usage histories by end-use, these studies found that as man-made fibers saturated each of the 44 TEB defined end-use markets, they became increasingly vulnerable to the business cycle pressures unique to each such end-use. Eventually there would be no more big, new, fast-growing end-use opportunities to pursue individually or collectively.

That situation arose in the late 1970s and denoted completion of the U.S. man-made fiber industry's transition from a growth to a mature industry. A growth industry characteristically sustains real growth rates well above that of the national economy. Long runs of annually compounded, double-digit real gains in output, shipments, and capacity typify growth industries. However, internally generated real growth above a 15% annually compounded rate historically has never been sustainable for more than two consecutive decades, and often occurs for only much shorter intervals [Kornai 1972: 82, 121-22]. The U.S. man-made fiber industry was no exception to Kornai's limit, although it remained a growth industry for just over half a century by successively commercializing entirely new families of generic fibers.

Until 1974, the U.S. man-made fiber industry had high, often double-digit, growth rates, which were somewhat illusory. Part of the illusion resulted from calculations employing low base numbers. Another part of the illusion came from successive exploitation of new end-uses. Saturating some of those developing end-uses called for huge amounts of man-made fiber. Generally, however, those larger end-uses had low inherent growth rates owing to their products' durability. They also often turned out to have low replacement demand, coupled with considerable postponability. The U.S. tire cord and carpet and rug face fiber end-uses are notable cases in point.

By the mid-1980s, senior executives at the leading U.S. textile mills had reluctantly accepted the fact that theirs was a sunset industry. Slowing domestic demand for textile products plus marked and unstoppable increases in imports of such goods were the last straws. The U.S. textile industry has been unable to adequately restimulate demand, cut costs, or implement any other measures strong enough to restore its long-run profits to an acceptable level after decades of sporadic effort. The U.S. man-made fiber industry operated for only ten years or so as a mature industry before sliding inexorably into the transition phase on its way to becoming a declining industry, with characteristically low to negative growth rates.

Marketing Methods

It is an established general rule in U.S. man-made fiber marketing that the industrial end-uses are technically most difficult to serve, the apparel markets are the easiest, and the home furnishings applications form a middle ground. Industrial end-uses have lead times of four or more years. They also use rigorous and complex end product, fabric, yarn, and fiber specifications based on scientific tests. Sustained close personal relations also are essential to developing mutual trust, respect, credibility, and confidence.

Man-made fiber companies seek industrial business for several reasons. Industrial markets provide steadier sales volumes at stable prices. More importantly, industrial business proves a supplier's technical competence, reliability, and willingness to make and honor long-term commitments. These traits also are vital in both the apparel and home furnishing sectors. Although these latter market sectors need quite different marketing strategies and tactics, the same leading textile firms are involved; until recently, they developed and maintained strong and distinctive patterns of commitment to different end-use markets and man-made fiber suppliers.

The apparel markets usually have lead times of three years or fewer. They entail comparatively easy technical problems but impose challenging marketing and personality problems for new executives at man-made fiber firms. Apparel outerwear end-uses necessitate continuously coordinating five or more distinct seasonal programs, with 18- to 36-month lead times, through long and complex distribution channels by hard-nosed negotiations with many strong-willed individuals at every stage. Apparel fashion is a further complication. Fortunately, the economics of apparel fashion were so well established in Thorstein Veblen's classic The Theory of the Leisure Class that it can be neglected here.

Many law suits, court cases, trade press articles, and the establishment of formal arbitration processes show that ease of entry into the apparel textile, and especially the garment industries, has resulted in spasms of ruthlessly intense competition, sometimes for its own sake. Design piracy, counterfeit goods, breaches of contract, chiseling on quality standards, violation of man-made fiber firms' specifications for final products, and other "creative" dealings have been normal actions for many decades in that arena. Fiber company executives with strong technical backgrounds usually are conditioned to open dealings by experience in the oil and chemical industries, where one's word and one's employer's are a bond. Their first polite verbal reaction to the apparel branch of the textile industry often involves the adjective "Byzantine."

A U.S. man-made fiber producer opts for either a broad or narrow marketing strategy. A broad approach means dealing with almost all 44 end-uses simultaneously. That strategy calls for extensive product lines, specialized plants, and large and diverse support staffs. A narrow approach focuses on a few end-uses, usually within one sector or some of the customers in those markets. Most merchant, as distinct from captive, man-made fiber producers chose a narrow marketing approach, or were eventually forced to adopt such a strategy. DuPont, however, developed a broad approach with a remarkably wide and deep array of large volume acrylic, nylon, and polyester genera plus lines of specialty fibers, notably spandex, Aramids (Qiana, Nomex, and Kevlar), and Teflon. By the late 1960s, duPont had more distinct nylon fiber products than the huge 3,000-item Scotch Tape line of 3M (Minnesota Mining and Manufacturing, Inc.), and those were just in terms of polymers, deniers, forms, and lusters. Variations in finishes, dye properties, fiber cross-sections, and batches (merges and lots) would have vastly enlarged duPont's nylon product line.

Most large U.S. man-made fiber strategy failure producers failed with a broad marketing strategy before accepting a more focused effort. Those firms' leaders insisted on learning from personal experience about the complexities, difficulties, and costs of an across-the-board strategy rather than from observation, marketing research, or logic. Firms unable to sustain the necessary efforts include American Cyanamid, Avtex, Celanese, and Monsanto's Textiles Company (MTC). Others looked first and decided in advance that "the view isn't worth the climb."

Product Lines and Branding. No merchant U.S. man-made fiber producer has survived for long with only a product line for a single end-use market, let alone by selling only a single item. All major U.S. man-made fiber producers offer a wide range of products for several end-uses. Nylon and polyester filament and staple product lines are the most popular in terms of diverse end-use coverage. The acrylics, cellulosics, olefins, fiberglass, and so on have more restricted and often markedly seasonal opportunities.

All U.S. man-made fiber producers brand their product lines to some extent. At the bare threshold level, they settle for giving their product lines distinctive names. The ceiling could run into the tens of millions spent on advertising those brands, public relations campaigns, guaranties and warranties, contests, and so on. Few fiber brands achieved more than nominal consumer recognition and even less influence on end-product purchase decisions [Familiarity and Favorability with Synthetic Fibers and Brand Names and Their End Uses, iii]. However, a brand helps differentiate products in textile, fashion, and retail executives' minds. That at least partly justifies the multilayered price structure described in Chapter 6.

All merchant suppliers of man-made fibers brand their first-quality goods for several reasons. By more precisely identifying a fiber, brands reduce customer's risk of accidental mixing with fibers of the same genera. An unbranded fiber signals either quality concerns or price concessions. Fiber brands on end-product labels and hang-tags assure consumers of at least minimum levels of quality. Well-known brands may garner a price premium for an established consumer preference. There was some merit to this latter claim relative to the textile industry and natural fibers, at least until the early 1970s, when mills, the Cotton Institute and the Wool Bureau began promoting their own consumer-focused brands.

Textile clients and those further down the distribution channel(s) are only authorized to use a fiber brand by express permission on a case-by-case basis. In other words, a textile mill can buy exactly the same first-quality U.S. man-made fiber in any of three modes (that is, branded with promotional support, branded without promotional support, and unbranded) at quite different prices, as will be detailed in Chapter 6. No man-made fiber firm will allow off-grade or second-quality fiber to bear its brand(s). They may, however, permit a client to identify the fiber's producer and genera as, for example, X company's polyester, instead of by brand.

Promotional Efforts. All major U.S. man-made fiber producers use in-house, salaried sales forces to promote their products. They also use brokers selectively. No one has discovered how to sell man-made fibers without an in-house sales force, as distinct from an external sales agency or exclusive broker or via such impersonal methods as catalogs or mail.

Man-made fiber companies' sales forces are not organized or located according to any common pattern. The combination of product lines, end-use(s) served, geography, and specific clients' needs have to be balanced against a supplier's resources and attitudes.

U.S. man-made fiber producers' sales personnel have many duties. The most important of these involves communicating and, to some extent, negotiating deals within one of a few formats. Acting as a two-way communication channel, buffer, and field-intelligence gatherer are some typical additional functions of man-made fiber sales staff. Sales efforts alone do not differentiate man-made fibers or their producers. They can, however, either reinforce or vitiate such efforts.

Differentiation arises from a combination of individual firms' product lines and quality; customer and technical services; policies; and branding and marketing development efforts. The salesman has to communicate those points effectively to clients, on the one hand, and advise his firm of any changes needed to establish and maintain productive relations with his account(s), on the other hand.

Most man-made fiber producers realize that they cannot satisfy any and every mill with just one set of goods and policies. Prospective clients differ too much in terms of end-uses served, how they choose to serve those markets, the technology used, and their buying practices for one man-made fiber producer to satisfy them equally. So product lines, policy choices, and promotional practices further differentiate fiber producers. The salesman's biggest challenge is posed by a prospective account that has to be either very diplomatically spurned or used as a lever to revise his employer's policies in a way that will not alienate customers.

Valid sales contracts are rare in the U.S. man-made fiber industry. There are no enforceable short-term contracts in selling man-made fibers to major textile mills. The need to maintain long-term relationships between a man-made fiber producer and its customers reduces conventional sales contracts to a formality.

Textile mills breach short-term man-made fiber purchase contracts with almost total impunity whenever it is advantageous for them to do so. Conversely, mills insist that any such contract be honored to the letter whenever it favors their interests. Man-made fiber sales contracts often are waived by mutual consent to either preserve a desired long-term relationship or to save face by preventing it from being abrogated in routine exercise of a mill's momentarily superior bargaining power.

Most man-made fiber sales contracts call for compulsory and binding arbitration. Enforceable fiber sales contracts appear only when temporary monopoly power arises from significant product or marketing innovations. Thus certain aspects of U.S. man-made fiber sales are much closer to the free-market ideal than would be the case if sales contracts were binding and enforced.

U.S. man-made fiber producers offer four "contracts" in terms of time horizons and order size. Those are spot sales, bookings or orders for delivery in the next 90 days at going prices [Markham, 67-68], quantity orders at a modest discount, and "take-or-pay" contracts at far larger discounts. The last, adopted from the heavy chemical industry, is the only really binding and enforced sales contract, as spot sales essentially are for cash and the others are options. But all man-made fiber sales supposedly are final unless stated product property and performance specifications are not met.

A take-or-pay contract offers large discounts, often more than 20%, on a precisely defined fiber in exchange for:

- an irrevocable order for the year ahead
- an order of 10 million pounds or more
- exact delivery details as to amounts, locations, and dates when the order is placed
- assured acceptance of suitable product under all circumstances
- unusual handling of contractual breaches.

A take-or-pay contract simplifies fiber production scheduling and stabilizes capacity utilization.

Breaching such a contract invokes seven atypical rules against textile customers. First, disputes go to court instead of arbitration, which makes such behavior public knowledge. Publicizing these cases does several things. It warns other man-made fiber suppliers not to trust the defendant mill in similar circumstances, effectively barring the defaulting mill from purchase price parity for years to come. It announces an almost certainly favorable judicial outcome for the seller which reaffirms to all that such contracts are and will continue to be enforced. Naturally, the loser also bears the court costs and a degree of opprobrium for ineptitude.

Second, the price at once reverts to that in the spot market at the time of delivery of each part of the order. The price difference for past deliveries falls due on occurrence of the breach. Third, any resale of the fiber by the mill has to be made at the originally contracted price subject to approval from the producer, which is hard to obtain. Fourth, the fiber supplier can refuse any returns. Fifth, the mill cannot use the fiber brand on goods made from the fiber involved. Sixth, the seller no longer needs to offer the buyer such discounts in the future. Seventh, delivery may be accelerated, with payment called for on delivery, and technical and marketing services may be provided only at the supplier's convenience, perhaps for a fee.

U.S. man-made fiber producers assign national account managers to coordinate all activity between a large textile firm or a similar-sized, influential needle trade or retail organizations. Ten or more full-time national account managers usually are necessary. Smaller businesses are contacted by territorial sales people. Depending on an account's value to a fiber producer, the kinds and amounts of service needed, and the travel time involved, a territorial salesman may manage five to 30 accounts. That provides opportunities to develop sales personnel, given the regional concentrations of textile plants and the size distribution of their parent firms, without undue risk of losing a key order or account if a salesman errs or encounters an overly difficult client.

Advertising and public relations are less important promotional activities than sales efforts to domestic man-made fiber producers. Although usually second and third in importance and cost, after sales, advertising and public relations are non-trivial items in a fiber firm's budget. Each major fiber producer spent millions of dollars annually promoting its wares in trade and consumer media before the U.S. man-made fibers industry entered the declining stage.

DuPont, for instance, reduced traceable, consumer media spending on its Lycra spandex product line to $3.5 million in 1984, out of a total of $10.8 million on all fibers, from $5.1 in 1983. Those are impressive sums from two viewpoints. First, Globe, duPont's only U.S. spandex rival, does no consumer advertising and spends only token amounts on trade advertisements. Second, about 25 million pounds per year of Lycra is sold in the United States at an estimated average price of $10 per pound, while duPont sells some four billion pounds annually of all of its other fibers at a much lower average price, on the approximate order of $1.00 per pound.

Historically, MTC's fiber advertising emphasized its Wear-Dated program, which is discussed below under guaranties and warranties. In the late 1960s MTC's advertising budget was large enough to justify the effort to move everything in-house to save the 15% of media purchases normally paid to an advertising agency. MTC's 1984 traceable advertising spending on its fibers was down to only $5.5 million. By way of contrast, Celanese spent only $0.6 million advertising its fibers to consumers, while the rest of the U.S. man-made fiber producers spent only token amounts, if anything, in 1984.

Logistics, Technical and Marketing Support Services. Domestic man-made fiber producers sell free on board (FOB) their own loading docks and generally ship by truck. The major U.S. man-made fiber producers have their own truck fleets, as do their larger customers. However, some fiber shipments are sent by commercial truck or rail carrier.

Man-made fiber producers perform several technical services. A common one involves sending a technician or a team of experts to a specific textile plant for either of two reasons. Technical service personnel show a client exactly how to process a new product or prevent a recognized problem. They also help the clients to quickly define and resolve unexpected problems. Such services range from routine inspection visits to sophisticated, costly laboratory and field tests lasting years.

Textile executives have two reasons to call their fiber suppliers for help. When the problem may in part have been caused by a particular batch of fiber, the fiber producer is obligated to help. The mill generally can learn to handle, cure, prevent, or get recompense for the problem faster by cooperating with the fiber company. This is crucial in the cost-sensitive, efficiency-oriented textile industry. The mill must cooperate with the fiber supplier's expert(s) to prove that supplier's responsibility to qualify for compensation. Fiber producers provide technical aid to minimize their liability and to build distinctive reputations for competence in this vital area. The fiber firm with the best technical staff has a much easier time keeping mills happy with existing goods and cooperative in trying new ones. It also instills confidence in mill management that testing and commercializing new yarns, fabrics, and final products from existing or new fibers will not be as serious a problem as with other firms.

Technical staffs transfer knowledge too--a sensitive issue for mill managers. Each mill manager must balance the fear that an outsider will spot an innovation at the mill and spread it to rivals against the risk of delay in learning an important practical development long after his rivals. Fiber companies necessarily do considerable technical work with textile equipment besides man-made fibers. Early access to such insights can be crucial to a mill striving to adapt its peculiar machinery mix to another product or end-use or simply in evaluating new equipment.

U.S. man-made fiber firms traditionally provide many marketing services to textile, needle trades, and retail firms. These activities create opportunities to meet with and influence senior executives of customers and decision-makers of downstream firms.

Most large man-made fiber companies made elaborate quarterly or semiannual presentations to leading clients and prospects. These socalled "dog-and-pony" shows usually cover the outlook for the general economy and of relevant economic sectors and industries such as apparel, automobiles, and housing; demand by generic fiber within key end-uses and by major processes, such as knitting, weaving, nonwovens, carpet tufting, and so on; historic and projected spending by critical consumer groups; innovations of mutual interest; and progress reports on coordinated efforts. Detailed booklets recapitulating the meeting for attendees' later use as reference documents normally were issued too. This practice enabled the fiber producers to earn a reputation for marketing omniscience and generosity in supplying such information. Less astute audiences acted as if this service eliminated the need for their own marketing research and planning. Most large textile firms took decades to realize that they would have to match or surpass the research capabilities behind such presentations in order to recoup a balanced bargaining position.

Domestic man-made fiber producers' marketing services were not limited to presentations. An essential aspect of their services lay in devising and coordinating marketing programs along the entire length of the pipeline. Mills often knew some of the potential buyers for a new textile item. The top fiber companies made a point of being well acquainted with decision-makers at all major cutters, distributors, and retailers down to the last buyer and merchandise manager. That entree was potentially available to cooperating mills in two ways. U.S. fiber suppliers create and sell programs at the retail level and then carry the commitments back up the distribution channel(s) to cooperating firms at each stage. The fiber companies also supply such information to help those clients grow and diversify. In such cases, the client frequently needs to know whom to buy from or to sell to, how to buy and sell, and how to make an acceptable product.

Trouble shooting is a third marketing service of man-made fiber producers. A customer needing a bit of technical or marketing assistance, information, or help in finding either a qualified consultant or an employee often seeks his fiber suppliers' advice. Sometimes fiber producers know the answer and are willing to disclose it, or know of a suitable person available. At other times, they either do not know or, for some practical reason, prefer not to respond. Certain inquiries simply are too politically sensitive to respond to beyond expressing sympathy and saying something like, "Let me look into this and get back to you." However, the usual response saves the inquirer much time and money. Such services seem a great bargain, since a mill's out-of-pocket costs are negligible and the cumulative reputation for service, expertise, and being a good contact are of inestimable value. So is the potential for a reciprocal favor, as in a close bargaining situation.

Guaranties and Warranties. U.S. man-made fiber manufacturers found it necessary to guarantee more than the levels and continuity of their products' physical properties. They also had to accept responsibility for seeing that those goods could be efficiently converted into textile yarns and fabrics. Three added considerations compelled man-made fiber producers to extend the explicit guaranties on their first-quality wares. One such consideration was the difficulty of adequately testing a man-made fiber's performance before incorporating it into a final product. A second was that the fiber producer had greater knowledge of and control over its product than anyone else, although no one had absolute mastery or control. Perhaps the most convincing consideration, however, was a deep pocket theory of legal liability.

Textile mills could not afford to dabble with exotic new materials such as man-made fibers when suppliers supposedly knew how to avoid or minimize processing problems. Suppliers presumably could better afford those risks since they usually were part of far larger organizations and, ultimately, had to bear those risks to sell their first-quality goods. Hence, a U.S. man-made fiber producer might find itself liable for thousands of defective garments because of what a layman would misinterpret as a minor or undetectable flaw in a single pound of one of its fibers.

Man-made fiber is not made flawlessly, or even highly consistently. Some man-made fiber defects are serious enough to condemn an entire batch to be reprocessed (if possible), sold for a few cents per pound, or just scrapped. In such extreme cases there are no guaranties or warranties. However, a broad middle ground exists. When a batch of a man-made fiber has defects that could be ignored, hidden or offset, it might be sold at a discount or subject to a partial or limited guaranty. Specified defects and their derivative problems are no longer then the producer's responsibility.

What if, for example, a batch of polyester staple designed for dress shirts absorbs dye unevenly? If possible, it will be sold as a first-quality product with an unrestricted guaranty, but solely into an end-use or product not requiring dyed fabric. It may instead be discounted to sell into the original end-use with the explicit warning "for whites only," as such fibers are naturally white and so do not need dye.

A few U.S. man-made fiber manufacturers took the exceptional step of extending the brand concept into a related facet of their marketing. Chemstrand was the first to adapt a retail apparel warranty and give it a brand name, Wear-Dated [Forrestal, 132-33]. The Wear-Dated program initially warranted a year's "normal" wear or a free replacement or refund, at Chemstrand's option, for any apparel made of its fiber that met Chemstrand's specifications. This program was neither quickly nor widely imitated, as the liability exposure appeared enormous and uncertain. Rivals interested in developing a competitive program faced two further deterrents: the necessarily long-term technical development and seemingly large promotional commitments. Others preferred not to risk offending major retail chains, notably Sears, which had established but not heavily promoted, unconditional money-back guaranties on anything they sold. Only Allied, of the rivals that researched the Wear-Dated program, devised and implemented a similar approach, which included carpets. MTC, Chemstrand's successor and a wholly owned subsidiary of Monsanto Company, later extended its Wear-Dated program to upholstery and carpets. Such end-product, limited-warranty branded programs assure uncertain consumers of a minimum standard of durability. They still enjoy considerable success in non-industrial end-uses in which durability and value are hard for risk-averse consumers to evaluate merely by inspection. Notable among such end-uses are children's outerwear, upholstery, and carpet-face fiber.

Purchasing Methods of Buyers

Before World War II, U.S. textile mills bought natural fibers on either a hand-to-mouth basis or, preferably, speculatively in markets where hedging was possible. Textile profits often depended on luck or skill in buying raw fiber, since intense competition quickly neutralized other sources of advantage, that is, special equipment and new fabric and end product designs. Natural fibers' seasonal availability rarely synchronized with mills' demand timing. Man-made fibers' more regular supply let mills better match fiber buying with demand to cut raw materials' inventory risks and costs. That also gradually forced domestic textile mills to modify their management practices generally and in such critical functions as purchasing, raw materials inventory control, logistics, production, and marketing.

Man-made fibers' advent greatly weakened mills' ability to earn profits by hedging on raw materials. Man-made fiber was not readily resalable to offset a purchasing error, which increased downside risks. Worse, textile mills found it necessary to cultivate man-made fiber producers, in contrast to their established practice of exploiting natural fiber sellers.

Mills quickly found it essential to develop and maintain a friendly relationship with several man-made fiber suppliers, especially duPont. DuPont earned preferred supplier status with a long-standing record as the man-made fiber product and marketing innovator. Graceful demarketing of unsuccessful new products also enhanced duPont's reputation.

The first textile mills to master man-made fibers' strange new processing requirements could best exploit their seemingly miraculous properties to earn huge profits. Mills understandably equated late access to these new materials with reduced profits since they operated in a competitive industry. The same reasoning held for an inability to efficiently convert a new fiber into a salable good. Proliferation of man-made fiber genera and product variants forced each textile firm to recognize that future profits depended on friendly ongoing relationships as an established customer of a few man-made fiber producers. Established accounts get early access to innovations and protected supply positions during shortages, when man-made fiber producers normally allocate output proportionally to mills' recent purchases. New accounts take second priority in such times.

Allocation commonly occurs under three circumstances. First, it is traditional during the brief peaks of business cycles. Second, temporary shortages caused by insufficient expansion of various man-made fibers' capacities to meet developing end-use demand will trigger allocation. Finally, allocation is deemed an equitable response to external shocks.

U.S. textile mills buy from only a few, usually three, man-made fiber suppliers at any moment for two main reasons. First, it reduces risks, including loss of quantity discounts. Second, it reduces the strain on their limited information-processing capabilities. Problems at a sole supplier could cripple a textile firm's output indefinitely, especially during booms. A textile corporation risks sacrificing both production continuity and bargaining power unless it has multiple sources of supply.

The textile industry historically is very averse to supply-related risks. Regrettably, it has an equally strong record of blindly exposing itself to unnecessary demand-related risks, as shown by its nearly billion-dollar overinvestment in double knit machines in the late 1960s and early 1970s. However, multisourcing is a practical, albeit modest way to reduce a textile firm's supply problems associated with man-made fibers.

Severe quality and inventory control risks arise from dealing with too many man-made fiber suppliers. Most textile companies minimize these perils by having no more than three suppliers of the same generic fiber at one time. They also try to use similar generic fibers and forms from different suppliers in separate plants or, at least, in well-separated areas of the same plant. Larger textile firms implement an anticolonization policy, that is, making only one product at each plant, to prevent damage from the unintentional mixing of different suppliers' fibers--even of the same genera--while also attempting to capture economies of plant size and specialization. Furthermore, buying from too many man-made fiber suppliers sacrifices order size and cumulative volume discounts, as well as lowering manufacturing efficiency and increasing both the funds tied up in inventory and the risk of having to prematurely end a production run when a supplier changes merges.

A few significant changes occurred in man-made fibers purchasing by mills between 1948 and 1984. One was the introduction of take-or-pay contracts described above. At one time or other, every leading U.S. textile mill tried backward integration into one or more high-volume man-made fibers.

With few exceptions, all mill efforts to backward integrate soon failed. Some captive (that is, non-merchant) monofilament (that is, single filament fiber) plants extruded nylon, polyester, or olefin for parts of the rope, cordage, and fishline market. Many of these still survive.

Fiberglass also was an exception. Mills' attempts to backward integrate into fiberglass production usually died out slowly instead of quickly. That may be a result of a slower pace of innovation in fiberglass or less intense competitive pressures in its earlier stages. Save for fiberglass, monofilaments, and olefins, competitively-sized man-made fiber plants call for investments, that even the biggest U.S. textile companies apparently cannot afford. Moreover, the process technology and management philosophy are quite alien to textile firms.

The third major change in man-made fiber buying occurred when domestic mills began using foreign man-made fiber. Foreign man-made fiber quality is comparable with and often superior to or even technologically ahead of domestic products in certain respects, such as finer denier per filament (dpf) yarns. Imported man-made fiber prices can be quite favorable even after duties, freight, insurance, currency exchange rates, and extra paperwork costs. Imported man-made fibers lack brand recognition, promotional support, and technical and marketing services, but these are long-run, rather than immediately serious, concerns. Uncertainty about supply continuity and future prices, coupled with a need to make large, long-term, irrevocable commitments, deterred all but self-confident or desperate mills from importing man-made fiber.

American purchases of man-made fibers recently underwent two other major changes. J.P. Stevens and Company introduced sealed bids and single sourcing for a year at a time in buying polyester staple for sheeting fabrics [Chemical Week, July 24, 1985, 21] That put some 30 million pounds, an apparent record, out for bid at one time. Eastman reportedly got the order at $0.70 per pound, which broke the established $0.85 per pound price.

There also were nontrivial secondary effects. Rival sheeting mills quickly renegotiated polyester prices with their suppliers. Then, other parts of the same textile companies, using similar polyester staple, sought and won equivalent treatment. Depending on one's view, that either depressed polyester staple's price or enhanced the market's price competitiveness. It is worth mentioning that J.P. Stevens was the only U.S. textile company with more than one full-time, professionally trained and industry-experienced economist. Most domestic textile companies and man-made fiber producers could afford an able economist, but have none and never have had one.

Two U.S. textile mills simulated the entire fiber-textile-needle trades' pipeline in computers. These models predicted price changes more accurately than U.S. man-made fiber suppliers' more intuitive forecasts of fiber demand and supply overall and within end-uses. These materials balance models incorporate physical capacity constraints and inventory level adjustments at each stage of the distribution channels from fiber through final products, rather than relying on the highly aggregated and financially based systems of equations typical of Keynesian macroeconometric models. Various econometric consulting firms tried unsuccessfully to devise macro-oriented (that is, top-down) models to forecast cotton and man-made fibers' demand. Man-made fiber producers could have deployed such models by the early 1970s but chose not to do so. It will be interesting to see how long it takes them to identify and respond effectively to this latest major pricing challenge.

Cyclical and Seasonal Demand

The U.S. man-made fibers industry has become increasingly responsive to the cyclical and seasonal patterns of the domestic textile industry it serves. The industry's heightened exposure to its primary client industry's renowned seasonal and cyclical traits resulted from attaining significant positions in all textile end-use markets. As a generality, man-made fibers' sensitivity to end-use markets' cycles and seasonality rose much faster than fiber producer executives expected. A technically notable complication associated with the detection of the cyclical and seasonal patterns of man-made fibers is their variably lagged dependency on textile end-use markets with their own distinctive cyclical and seasonal patterns.

Certain outerwear apparel end-uses evolved a season pattern. Hosiery and underwear end-uses have but two major seasons each. Those are linked strongly to summer and winter weather. However, outerwear accounts for most apparel fiber usage and greatly influences the cyclical and seasonal demand of other apparel end-uses. Seasonal demand variations of apparel end-uses often dictate shifts in man-made fibers' quantity demanded by polymer, form, deniers, lusters, and so on in response to end-products' performance requirements. For instance, technical and social developments have moderated sheer hosiery's historically strong use-pattern in cold seasons. Air conditioning and women's rising labor force participation, with a concomitant need to "dress for work," have somewhat evened out seasonal demand for fine denier nylon filament in sheer hosiery and increased that demand as well.

Social changes, especially in the acceptability of fashions, have attenuated the once pronounced seasonality of many apparel items. More casual dress standards and better central heating and cooling effectively prolonged the length of seasons and widened the acceptability of casual and special purpose attire, such as sweatsuits. Conversely, the same factors slashed demand for business suits, topcoats, and other more traditional formal apparel. These shifts influenced the total and the seasonal demand for specific man-made fibers.

Home furnishings end-uses' seasonality results primarily from two factors. First, many home furnishings end-uses depend heavily on housing construction. Housing construction is both geographically and seasonally concentrated. Late spring, summer, and early fall are preferred for construction because more natural light is available and temperatures are warm enough for foundation cement to set without cracking or requiring costly ingredients.

Second, carpet face yarns account for almost two-thirds of home furnishings' demand. The carpet face yarns end-use overwhelmingly consumes man-made fibers as natural fibers such as wool, the traditional fiber, fell to a 1% carpet market share. Simple linear least-squares regressions of quarterly demand for carpet against new housing starts, with a six months lag, and a second independent variable for carpet demand from other sources (household carpet replacement, transportation, office, and temporary dwellings) typically showed, at a 95% confidence level or higher, that 85% of the variation in demand derived from housing starts and 12% from the second exogenous term.

Man-made fiber demand from industrial end-uses is the least seasonal, but some quite seasonal, large man-made fiber consuming industrial end-uses exist. One is the bags and bagging end-use, which includes sandbags and agricultural bale wrap. Sandbags are almost entirely used to build temporary, peacetime, flood control levees. Sandbags now are almost entirely made from olefin fiber, which displaced burlap. Demand for sandbags peaks in the spring as melting snow feeds into the Mississippi River drainage system. Agricultural bags and wrapping of man-made fiber experience their strongest demand during the late summer and fall harvest season.

Lockhart [43-44] and others reported that overall textile demand usually leads the general business cycle in downturns but coincides with the U.S. economy's upturns, while man-made fibers' cyclical pattern differs in two key ways. Man-made fibers' demand tends to turn down before the textile industry and so also drops well ahead of general economic contractions. Man-made fibers' demand also tends to recover after the general economy and so usually lags behind the textile industry during expansions. The increasingly high costs of unintentional inventory investments forced textile managers to learn to anticipate and react faster to business cycle phase changes and to function with markedly lower inventory to shipment ratios. This latter development heightened the man-made fibers industry's sensitivity to its customer industries' business cycles, as the practice was applied to all end-uses although each has a unique business cycle.

An ongoing analysis of the textile industry's cycle after World War I by Stanley B. Hunt of the TEB [Markham, 112] reported a remarkably regular two-year cycle, with peaks occurring in odd-numbered years and troughs in the even-numbered years. Hunt cited the textile industry's inventory policy of carrying a six-month supply of raw materials in normal times, a four-month supply in bad times, and an eight-month supply in good times as explaining this incredibly regular fiber consumption cycle.

Understanding of the textile industry's cycles has improved greatly since Hunt's day. Specifically, improvements have been made in the following areas. First, it is now understood that the textile cycle Hunt explored was chiefly an outerwear apparel cycle instead of a general textile industry cycle. That apparel cycle's roughly two-year duration results from a consumer level buying pattern; that is, those buying outerwear in year X tend to not re-enter the market for new outerwear until year (X + 2) because U.S. consumers habitually spend approximately 8% of their real disposable income on apparel on a two-year moving average basis. That insight, plus recognition of apparel's high rate of postponement, much enhanced understanding of the apparel cycle. Similar logic was later applied to the other textile end-use groups, or sectors, in which each was found to have distinct cycles based on individually unique initial and replacement buying patterns and ease of deferral.

Second, textile industry inventory policy targets were pared drastically; so were those at retail. By the late 1960s, Milliken and Company had slashed normal fiber inventory levels at its mills to less than a month's supply by skillful use of mathematical programming techniques. Other textile firms, needle trade companies, and retailers learned of this between the major recessions of the 1970s and early 1980s and some eventually adopted similar methods.

Third, analysis of the Federal Reserve Board's monthly Textile Mill Products Indices from 1957 through 1976 showed that the average general textile cycle lasts almost 40 months, not 24.

Man-made fiber suppliers have learned to do more than merely adjust their pricing over the course of a business cycle. The textile mills vary their buying strategies with the different business cycle stages. When fiber producers find capacity constraining production, as is typical near major cyclical peaks, they normally put customers on allocation instead of relying on price flexibility to balance supply and demand.

Opportunistic textile mills react in two ways to man-made fiber allocations. Multiple, enlarged orders are placed with established suppliers. New man-made fiber suppliers are cultivated in the simultaneous hopes of becoming a desirable new account and of impairing rivals' access to this resource. Trying to devise new fabrics from fibers not on allocation historically has not been a viable option. It takes years to do this, which is too long in a cyclical crisis. Scrabbling for position in times of allocation is soon replaced by reneging on orders as the cycle enters its contraction phase. In an especially severe recession, mills go beyond canceling orders before delivery. They next unilaterally void partially filled orders, return unused man-made fibers, and seek damages for work-in-process and finished goods inventory, claiming that the fibers' failure to meet specifications was not immediately detectable. Those unmet standards were drastically, arbitrarily, and unilaterally elevated retroactively by the mill. Such practices gave unwary U.S. man-made fiber producers the rare and dubious experience of negative shipments near the 1973-75 recession's trough.

CONCLUSIONS

Many complex and, when summarized, seemingly contradictory conditions affect the U.S. man-made fibers industry's supply and demand.

The notable point about labor in this industry is the necessity for large groups of diverse specialists to function as a closely knit team while operating from several locations. A man-made fiber producer must develop and maintain such a team to run efficiently. These teams represent an unusual technologically based entry barrier more normally seen in commonly managed traveling troupes of performers such as circuses or symphonies.

Man-made fibers vary widely in durability as to shelf life and when they are incorporated into final products. A man-made fiber's durability can range from days, with POY for texturing, to a few years. Fiber durability also varies so much across genera that no clear, simple general rule holds true.

Man-made fibers generally are about as dense as water; that is, their specific gravities are slightly above but close to 1.00. Teflon and olefins are notable exceptions. Some olefin fibers have a low enough specific gravity to float on water, which can be helpful in marine ropes. Teflon is roughly 13 times denser than water. In any event, man-made fibers' bulk versus value trade-offs seldom matter in a logistics sense. But these and other properties often interact with cost to determine users' choices of man-made fiber genera, details, and supplier to satisfy a given set of end-product performance requirements. An inexpensive, bulky, but low tensile strength fiber such as olefin might do well in some apparel end-uses if it only transmitted moisture adequately and was piece dyeable in a wide range of fashion colors at competitive rates. A dense Teflon fiber may be the only viable raw material for durable fabrics to filter hot and corrosive fluids despite its lack of dyeability, its brittleness, limpness, cost, and so on.

Man-made fibers' substitutability for natural fibers, materials other than fibers, or one another is a complex subject. Man-made fibers generally are independent from or complementary with, instead of substitutable for, either natural fibers or one another. Man-made fiber substitutability is both rare and limited to like forms (staple or filament) within, not across, specific end-uses and end-use groups, such as, apparel, home furnishings, and industrial.

Some prior analyses apparently neglected or misinterpreted the process of displacement of natural and early cellulosic fibers by later developed man-made fibers as that of substitution. Displacement and substitution differ profoundly as processes on several key points. Specifically, compared to substitution, displacement is a gradual, two-step, irreversible process, essentially independent of money price. As an added complication to interfiber competition, man-made fibers often generated wholly novel uses--for example, reinforced plastics and permanent press apparel and bed linens--that could not be made from earlier materials.

Imports of man-made fibers as either fiber or in intermediate and final products seldom had any major lasting influence on U.S. supply of or demand for such material between the end of World War II and the mid-1970s. By the late 1970s, imports of final products of man-made fibers manufactured abroad had noticeably but not significantly lowered demand for U.S. textile products, especially in apparel, and for the man-made fibers used in it. However, by the early 1980s, imports of final products containing man-made fiber had markedly reduced U.S. demand for all domestically produced man-made fibers except for specialty or exotic items. Repeated but sporadic efforts over the last 20 years to either defend or insulate the U.S. man-made fibers and textile industries from imports invariably failed. Until recently, the domestic man-made fiber producers saw no reason to respond to imports but now are engaged in a joint effort with the U.S. textile industry, which has been grievously affected by imports. Impeding imports' continued growth allegedly is crucial to these domestic industries' survival. The outlook for this effort is at best uncertain for many reasons. First, this initial cooperative approach may not have enough time to develop and implement an effective program, given the accelerating rush of imports. Second, persuading several federal bureaucracies to change their beliefs, policies, and practices is most improbable. Third, U.S. import protection history generally and specifically for the domestic textile industry suggests that any politically tolerable level of relief is unlikely to be either effective or adequate.

U.S. man-made fiber demand followed typical product life-cycle patterns. All major man-made fibers are now in or past the final transition into the declining life-cycle stage. Synthetic fibers enjoyed an almost 30-year growth stage. During their individual growth phases, man-made fibers often sustained double-digit real growth rates for capacity, production, and shipments. By the late 1970s, however, all large-volume U.S. man-made fibers had entered the mature phase of their product life cycles. At that time, man-made fiber growth rates for capacity, production, utilization, and shipments became less dramatic and far more erratic.

Recent structural changes and performance shifts in key sectors of the general economy and underlying population growth explain the lower and more cyclical growth of demand for man-made fibers once these goods had essentially saturated all prospective markets. Two outside developments accelerated the evolution of the U.S. man-made fibers industry from a mature to a declining industry. First, by the late 1970s, the U.S. population's growth had settled to a replacement rate of about 1%, annually compounded. Second, unrestrained imports converted a potentially low growth situation into one of modest but undoubtedly declining demand for the domestic textiles industry, and hence, for the U.S. man-made fibers industry.

Marketing methods of U.S. man-made fiber firms are notable for their diversity and aversion to price competition. The diversity of marketing methods results primarily from the distinctive requirements of the various textile sectors and their constituent end-uses. Man-made fibers' producers had to commit to one of two fundamentally different marketing strategies. A producer had to become either a broad spectrum supplier, serving essentially the entire domestic textile industry, or a specialist in a combination of end-uses with common features. Only duPont succeeded with the former approach. All others focused their marketing on a few end-uses, although not necessarily the same ones. Many man-made fiber firms adopted a tightly focused marketing strategy only after finding that they were unable or unwilling to sustain a viable broad marketing strategy.

Textile mills' man-made fibers purchasing has changed significantly over time. From the outset, established methods of buying natural fibers simply did not apply to buying man-made fibers. Mills also found it imperative to create and maintain an ongoing cooperative relationship with a few man-made fiber suppliers. This was essential to minimize costs and to ensure early access to important innovations in man-made fibers products and marketing.

The U.S. man-made fibers industry gradually acquired seasonal and cyclical traits similar to but slightly different from those of its markets. Seasonal demand for man-made fibers varies by major end-use groups. Apparel demand for man-made fibers is highly seasonal, with outerwear products having as many as five pronounced seasons. Home furnishings' end-uses typically show seasonal responses only to warm and cold weather. Certain industrial end-uses also have distinct seasonal patterns. Acrylic and fiberglass fibers' seasonal demand fluctuations are readily apparent, as their sales are concentrated in a few end-uses with common seasonal patterns. Other man-made fibers' seasonal demand patterns are obscure in aggregate since the end-uses consuming these materials typically have distinctive seasonal patterns that tend to cancel when combined. Polyester staple is a case in point, illustrating the need to evaluate seasonal demand at an end-use or, preferably, at a final product level.

Man-made fibers' demand also varies cyclically by end-use. Textiles are a notoriously cyclical industry. Hence, it is only reasonable to expect that critical textile inputs, including man-made fibers, would respond to cyclical changes in derived demand. Cycles in man-made fibers' demand are triggered by consumers' initial and replacement buying patterns, fashion, shifts in population demography, innovations, and the general economy. Modern studies of these fibers' cyclical behavior show sensitivity to but key differences from the cycles of both the general economy and the specific markets served. While man-made fibers' overall business cycle is too aggregated for decision-making purposes, that phenomenon's existence now is indisputable. So are some of its more important general features.

It once was popularly believed that a growth industry such as synthetic fibers is immune to business cycles. That myth was first challenged by the history of cellulosic fibers' exposure to the Great Depression and then unmistakably refuted by the recession of the mid-1960s. No one seriously doubted the industry's cyclicality after the severe 1973-75 recession. Thereafter, attempts were made to understand and then predict future cycles in time to act effectively. Those efforts were hampered by internal political problems and the task's difficulty. Contrary to earlier beliefs, the U.S. man-made fibers' aggregate business cycle is irregular in length, with an approximately 40-month average duration instead of exactly 24. Peaks and troughs occur erratically rather than consistently in, respectively, odd- and even-numbered years.

4

U.S. Man-Made Fibers
Industries' Structures

This chapter addresses one key question by examining the structure of the U.S. man-made fibers industry. That question is: How much price control, if any, do the firms composing this industry have? The causes of the various structures are primarily discussed in the next chapter and secondarily in the following ones.

Measures of industry structure indicate, somewhat imperfectly, how much control supplier firms have over price. Obviously, a potentially high degree of price control exists when the industry consists of a single firm and that firm makes a good without any close substitutes, the classic definition of monopoly. Conversely, price almost certainly falls outside the control of any given supplier when only small, undifferentiated firms constitute the industry and act independently while producing a homogeneous good. The U.S. man-made fibers subindustries fall between these extremes. If price control exists in these industries, it is apt to be a matter of degree instead of kind.

CONCENTRATION

Background

Concentration ratios (CRs) were used to study the structures of the industries. CRs are the decimal shares of the industry held by the four, eight, or 20 largest firms. CRs were chosen over more elaborate measures for two reasons. First, CRs are easier to figure. Second, using a more sophisticated device would not significantly improve our understanding of the industries' structures and price control as all measures of an industry's structure are highly correlated [Scherer, 56-58].

Background information in various MMFPH issues shows that E.I. duPont de Nemours & Co. dominated the domestic synthetic fibers industry until the late 1950s. Similarly, Owens Corning Fiberglas (OCF) dominated the fiberglass sector of the man-made industry until 1959. Cellulosic fibers' combined market share eroded from over 95% in the late 1940s to only 62% in 1959 and continued to fall after that. Every cellulosic fibers subindustry was quite concentrated before 1959 since their four-firm CRs consistently exceeded 0.800 by wide margins. However, this finding is not generalizable. The leading firms in certain man-made fiber subindustries, notably fiberglass and olefins, do not vie to any significant degree with other man-made fiber subindustries.

Semiannually, in May and November, the TEB publishes a census of all U.S. man-made fiber producers to determine industry capacities by generic fiber and form. The TEB does not report the details by firm or by plant. Subject to some qualifying remarks below, TEB's capacity data represent the potential maximum physical output of facilities in or ready for use if those plants made as much as possible of their respective outputs in the planned denier mixes. Hence these data erroneously imply static denier mixes at each firm and overall. Appended Tables A1-1 through A1-13 trace U.S. man-made fiber producers' estimated November year-end capacities from 1959 through 1982 by generic fiber and form.

The data in Tables A1-1 through A1-13 were estimated from such public sources as the trade press, company financial reports and press releases, Wall Street analysts' reports, consultants' reports shown or given to the author, trade interviews, the U.S. Department of Commerce, and, of course, the TEB's publications. Those estimates were rounded to the nearest one, five, or ten million pounds to reflect the inherent imprecision of the data and to highlight trends. Shortly before retiring, Stanley B. Hunt, TEB's founder and president, reviewed the estimates through the early 1970s and found them remarkably close to the TEB's census figures.

Our capacity tables bear a standard footnote: They are not adjusted for "waste" capacity, although the industry produces considerable waste fiber. Waste is recycled whenever possible and then reported as regular output. However, between 1975 and 1979, U.S. man-made fibers' average annual reported waste output ranged from a low of seven million pounds for olefin fibers to a high of 110 million pounds for nylons and Aramids. While waste production is reported apart from and less often than regular production, industry capacity data do not reflect such output.

Production lost to downtime can greatly change a firm's intended average denier. It might offset the first year's expected gain in capacity sought from such a change. Although they are common, minor denier mix variations (that is, less than 5%) have no practical effect for our purposes. However, some domestic man-made fiber producers defer reporting current waste production and actual denier mix to hide position in or plans for key end-uses, to delay rivals' detection of potential market opportunities, or to deter entry.

Capacity data initially were reported on a 50, rather than a 52-week production year because cellulosic fiber plants supposedly had to close two weeks a year for major maintenance. Production data eventually proved that this practice had been stopped, if it ever had been in effect. After that, capacity was based on operations 52 weeks a year. All of our capacity tables' data fit the latter premise.

As explained in Chapter 3, direct imports appear in these tables as annual totals, as though they were a single additional source of supply, instead of detailing them by country of origin. That was done for reasons of practicality.

Table A1-13 displays total capacities of the U.S. man-made fibers industry's 20 largest suppliers, including direct and indirect imports as appropriate. This enables examination of the effect of all man-made fibers' imports on this industry's structure. As explained in Chapter 3, only a few big firms could find out the effects of indirect imports on individual generic fibers and forms.

Four-firm CRs were calculated annually for each of Tables A1-1 through A1-13 and supplemented with eight and 20-firm CRs whenever feasible. Three-digit CR values were presented near the bottom of each table, with the minimum and maximum values noted. The results are summarized in Table 4-1.

Aggregate Concentration

Several aspects of the industry's structure are evident in Table 4-1. First, the overall industry appears much less concentrated than any of its component fibers at both its maximum and minimum values. This finding applies to the total four-firm CRs excluding imports of man-made products but including imports of man-made fibers, termed "unadjusted," and those designated "adjusted," which incorporate direct and indirect imports of man-made fibers. Those imports vie with the fibers of interest and so depress domestic demand for domestically produced man-made fibers. Aggregate four-firm CRs including imports of both man-made fibers and products thereof consistently are as much as 6% lower than estimates that take into account only direct imports; that is, when indirect imports are ignored. However, imports of man-made fiber goods attained over 20% of the total domestic market by the late 1980s, a period beyond this book's horizon.

Second, if Markham's view that all fibers are substitutes is taken to its logical conclusion, then one must include cotton and wool in the totals of Tables A1-13 and 4-1 Such an adjustment is only sensible if all fibers were substitutes. This hypothetical adjustment was not made because that premise was found to be false. But such an adjustment would approximately halve the overall U.S.fibers industry's concentration in any given year because spuriously including natural fibers would almost double the industry's size.

Although cotton represents roughly half of all fiber consumed in the United States, no single domestic cotton farmer grows enough to rate among the leading fiber suppliers. Wool usage is roughly a tenth as big as cotton; United States sheep herders are, individually and collectively, even smaller than cotton growers, and most wool is imported.

Third, there was a marked general trend of deconcentration between 1959 and at least the mid-1970s, if one interprets erosion of four-firm CRs in steps of 10% or more to below 0.870 as significant.

Table 4-1

Extreme Values of U.S. Man-Made Fibers' Annual

Four-Firm Concentration Ratios

(1959 through 1982)

Apparent Trend in Concentration	Man-Made Fiber Genera & Form	Maximumn			Minimum		
		Value	&	Year	Value	&	Year
	Acetate						
Stable	Filament	1.000		1973	0.071		1976
Stable	Staple	1.000		1959	1.000		1982
Down	Acrylic Staple	0.953		1960	0.861		1971
Stable	Fiberglass	1.000		1959	0.932		1978
	Nylon						
Down	Filament	0.985		1960	0.723		1972
Down	Staple	1.000		1959	0.674		1975
	Olefin						
Down	Filament	0.889		1959	0.446		1970
Down	Staple	1.000		1959	0.758		1964
	Polyester						
Down	Filament	1.000		1959	0.614		1974
Down	Staple	1.000		1959	0.781		1970
	Rayon						
Up	Filament	1.000		1972	0.858		1960
Up	Staple	0.994		1971	0.942		1967
	Total						
Down	Unadjusted	0.652		1959	0.520		1975
Down	Adjusted	0.643		1959	0.497		1972

Source: Appended Tables A1-1 through A1-13.

Fourth, the apparent trends in individual generic fibers and forms' concentration varied. Concentration ratios in acetates, fiberglass, and rayons fundamentally were high, over 85%, and stable.

Synthetic fibers' individual concentration trends essentially paralleled the general trend by declining from 1959 peaks to values well below 0.800, which usually is regarded as the threshold of significant monopoly power. By the early 1970s acrylic staple was the only large-volume synthetic fiber with a four-firm CR above 80%.

Four more aspects of the structure of the U.S. man-made fibers industry and its component fibers and forms deserve mention.

First, a large and persistent size disparity existed between leading firms and their nearest rivals. DuPont consistently was the largest firm in the total industry on a capacity basis, as Table A1-13 shows. It was almost 20% bigger than Avtex, its closest rival, in 1959. By 1982 duPont was over five times larger than in 1959; its total capacity exceeded that of the three next largest firms (Celanese, MTC, and OCF) by over 100 million pounds, or 4%. DuPont also dominated the acrylic, nylon filament, and both polyester fibers subindustries (see Tables A1-3, A1-5, A1-9, and A1-10). Similarly, Celanese dominated the acetate portions of the industry between 1959 and 1982 (see Tables A1-1 and A1-2).

Second, the relative positions of the two or three leading firms in each subindustry are notable for their stability over long time spans.

Third, most of the subindustries exhibit a persistent fringe of small producers. Captive or monofilament producers are those fringes' most notable and frequent constituents.

Last, some key points about fiber imports merit attention. As indicated in Chapter 3, until 1982 the industry was a closed system for practical purposes on both total and specific man-made fiber and form bases. That seldom was true after 1982. Industrial organization deals with effectively closed systems but not open ones, because the former are determinate while the latter are indeterminate. Imports also deserve close attention because Markham posited effective protection against them as a major reason for the success of the domestic "rayon industry" [Markham, 7]. However, neither Courtaulds, the American Viscose Company's (A.V.C.) founder and owner until 1941, nor others in the international rayon cartel effectively restricted U.S. imports before enactment of the 1930 tariff [Coleman, 280-82].

Table A1-13 shows that by 1959, the combination of direct and indirect imports of man-made fibers sufficed to clearly, albeit modestly, lower each year's four-firm CRs. By 1966, total imports effectively would have ranked as the fifth largest supply source if they had been produced by a single firm. Under the latter assumption, broadly defined imports would have ranked as the third or fourth biggest supply source in 1971-73, 1976-78, and 1981. Also, between 1971 and 1973, total imports held almost 10% of the market. It is well established that even a highly concentrated market's prices and profits are vulnerable when low-priced imports account for 10% or more of total supply. The U.S. man-made fibers industry and the markets it sells to seem to alternate randomly between closed and open states, with their trends to

CRs below 80% linked with stagnating domestic demand and rapid but erratic growth of imports. Such a system would become increasingly open as imports gained prominence. One can not consider the U.S. man-made fibers industry a closed system after 1986 because imports of man-made and man-made fiber products held so great a domestic role. Future studies of the man-made fibers industry, if not done on a global scale, will have to cover at least the northern hemisphere, since most man-made fibers are made, converted into intermediate and final goods, and consumed there.

Concentration within Subindustries

Acetate Filament. As mentioned earlier, Celanese dominated the acetate filament subindustry. It also was the only multimillion-pound acetate staple firm (see Tables A1-1 and A1-2). But Avtex and Eastman consistently jockeyed for the title of second and third largest suppliers in this arena, while duPont was fourth until 1976, when it exited this then mature subindustry.

Acetate Staple. The TEB's exclusion of acetate tow for cigarette filters from its acetate staple capacity data would, if corrected, enlarge that subindustry by roughly 250 million pounds. Such an act would only reinforce the finding of high concentration, since only Celanese and Eastman supply cigarette tow. Celanese is the only domestic producer of both diacetate and triacetate, a fiber genus distinct from the more commonly spun diacetate. Decomposing acetate filament and staple to the diacetate and triacetate levels would further elevate the high concentration levels found.

Acrylic Staple. The acrylic staple subindustry's structure was stable over the 1959-82 period at the four-firm level (see Table A1-3). DuPont dominated the industry with a proprietary dry-spinning process from the early years on. However, it also used and licensed or sold wet-process technology to some firms, notably Chemstrand. American Cyanamid and BASF, or its predecessors, usually were the third and fourth largest acrylic fiber producers. Before 1972, either Eastman or imports occasionally would capture third or fourth place for a few years.

The acrylic subindustry's structure is complicated by the presence of two suppliers that only spun modified acrylics, a separate fiber genus, according to the FTC, known as modacrylics, with unique properties and so tending to have limited end-use access, mostly as wig fibers or nonflammable specialties. The exclusively modacrylic producers were Eastman and Union Carbide. MTC also made small quantities of modacrylics. Applying a somewhat more rigorous subindustry definition to separate acrylic and modacrylic fibers would only replace an already highly concentrated subindustry with two even more concentrated ones. Both American Cyanamid and duPont tried but failed to commercialize acrylic filament. Thus this generic fiber's structure turns on a single form, staple, and so is restricted to certain end-uses and textile processes.

Fiberglass. Owens Corning Fiberglas (OCF), the inventor of glass fibers, captured and held over half of the fiberglass business from the outset (see Table A1-4). Together the merchant firms of OCF and PPG, Pittsburgh Plate Glass, routinely held first and second rank, respectively, in this subindustry. Both reportedly also had captive uses for some of their output, including insulation batting and reinforcement material for roofing shingles. Moreover, Manville, regularly among the top four fiberglass producers, was and remains primarily a captive supplier.

Nylon Filament. The identity and rank of the four largest nylon filament producers were stable over the 1959-82 period (see Table A1-5). As stated before, duPont was and is the pioneer and leading nylon producer. MTC was next, with Allied third and American Enka fourth. Surprisingly, most nylon filament producers are captive or monofilament operations. The latter usually are small, captive facilities. However, not all nylon monofilament spinners are small, as duPont and most of its merchant rivals also spin monofilament to complete their product lines with fishing line and similar goods. Redefining the nylon subindustries to exclude firms with some captive capacity would have an uncertain effect on concentration for both filament and staple but probably would not markedly change the conclusions already reached. Calculating nylon subindustries' CRs at finer levels by either or both polymer types (such as, Types 6; 6, 6; 6, 10; 6, 12; or 11) and subprocesses (such as, bulk-textured carpet yarn versus tire cord and so on) surely would yield higher values in every year. However, one often, but not always, finds at least partial substitutability within each generic fiber and form across polymer types or processes, but not across forms. So it is economically correct to examine concentration by fiber forms within generic fiber families rather than merely in aggregate.

Nylon Staple. DuPont started out larger in nylon staple than a hypothetical coalition of its rivals. But in the late 1970s, MTC "bought market share" with the goal of becoming this subindustry's leader (see Table A1-6). By 1982, MTC had about 50% more nylon staple capacity than duPont. Together these two firms regularly accounted for over half of this subindustry's capacity after 1960. Allied and American Enka consistently were the two next largest domestic nylon staple producers.

Olefin Filament. Until the mid-1970s there was no dominant olefin filament supplier (see Table A1-7). By the late 1970s, Amoco's olefin filament capacity exceeded its three nearest domestic rivals (duPont, Hercules, and Wayn-Tex). As with fiberglass, nylon, and polyester filament, the olefin filament subindustry has a fringe of captive and monofilament suppliers. Most captive olefin producers extrude monofilament to make rope and cordage, bags and bagging, or carpet backing. The olefin filament subindustry has the most populous and dynamic fringe as it is the easiest technically and least expensive segment of the man-made fiber industry to enter and exit. Olefin fringe firms about match the combined numbers and capacities of fringe suppliers in the other man-made fiber subindustries.

Amoco is an exceptional dominant man-made fiber producer in no less than four key regards. It is the only primarily oil company to "make it big" in the general U.S.

man-made fibers industry, and specifically in olefin filament. Exxon, Chevron, and Phillips are oil companies that also manufacture such fibers, but none was able or willing to expand as much or as fast by acquisition. Through the mid-1980s, Amoco was the only big U.S. man-made fiber extruder to rely almost totally on acquisition for growth. It also is primarily a captive, rather than a merchant, producer since it converts almost all of its output into various textile products, notably carpet backing. Finally, Amoco is the last huge firm to enter the industry.

Olefin Staple. The identity of the dominant firm in the olefin staple subindustry varied over time. No dominant firm was evident until 1966, when Chevron matched the joint capacity of its two closest rivals (see Table A1-8). By 1982, Hercules was the leader, as its capacity nearly exceeded that of the four next largest domestic firms (Amoco,Phillips, Chevron, and Avtex). However, imports usually were significant, as Table A1-8 shows. Direct imports of olefin staple imports were one of the four largest U.S. supply sources in 17 out of the 24 years covered.

Polyester. DuPont, again, was the dominant firm in both polyester subindustries, with Celanese next in each case. Usually these two firms held well over half of the capacity reported on Tables A1-9 and A1-10 to extrude polyester filament and staple. The top four producers regularly accounted for at least 77% of total domestic capacity to supply polyester staple. Although the identities of the third and fourth largest producers varied somewhat over time, only a few firms were in contention for these positions. The top candidates included Eastman, which usually was third, and Beaunit, which through 1967 usually kept fourth place. MTC moved up into fourth place in 1968 and 1969 before being temporarily dislodged by imports in 1970. MTC recovered fourth place in 1971, held it for a year, and then was displaced by Hoechst.

The polyester filament subindustry generally was both more dynamic and less concentrated than the polyester staple subindustry because, in part, of a fringe of small captive and monofilament firms. Imports of polyester filament were variously the third or fourth largest source of domestic supply from 1969 through 1973. Between 1969 and 1974, domestic firms apparently could not expand or enter the market fast enough to stay abreast of the jumps in demand from new uses, notably, double knit apparel and mechanical rubber goods such as tires, which attained commercial status and grew much faster than anticipated.

Most captive polyester firms spin only easy to make monofilaments. But Firestone and Goodyear extrude multifilament polyester for use in their mechanical rubber goods products, and a few others tried to become selfsufficient in apparel deniers. Multifilament captive firms are not as small as the exclusively monofilament suppliers. This implies a smaller minimum efficient size for a monofilament polyester plant than for a multifilament polyester apparel or tire cord yarn facility. More will be said on this point in the next chapter.

Rayon Filament. The rayon filament subindustry represents another distinctive situation (see Table A1-11). After World War II, Avtex and its predecessors dominated by default as other established producers first reduced their capacities and then exited the declining rayon filament subindustry. Four domestic producers (American Enka, Avtex, American Cyanamid, and Beaunit, or their predecessors and successors) regularly held over 85% of U.S. capacity to spin rayon filament from 1959 until 1972. Imports held fourth and then third place as a source of rayon filament after 1974.

Rayon Staple. The rayon staple subindustry was dominated by Avtex until 1980 (see Table A1-12). Then, financial pressures and pollution control regulations forced this successor to the once preeminent American Viscose Corporation (A.V.C.) to close its older capacity faster than Courtaulds, its parent and now nearest rival, which inched ahead into first place. The financial pressures on Avtex were intensified by the interaction of a waning demand trend, a cyclical downturn, and the terms of a leveraged buyout, which management sought to liberate Avtex from FMC. Three domestic manufacturers, plus imports of rayon staple, routinely held over 90% of U.S. rayon staple capacity. Those domestic producers were Avtex, Courtaulds, and American Enka. Over half of this subindustry's output was consumed in end-uses needing a stable supply of inexpensive hydrophilic fiber, such as the medical, surgical, and sanitary end-use, where more expensive acetate fibers and hydrophobic noncellulosics cannot compete.

Findings

The above discussion shows that the overall U.S. man-made fibers industry and its subindustries are imperfectly competitive in structure. More precisely, the U.S. man-made fibers subindustries comprise a set of oligopolies, not monopolies. First, the firms composing every U.S. man-made fiber subindustry are few in number, usually less than ten in any given year, especially after adjusting for captive facilities, pilot plants, and the early stages of startup situations, which individually seldom have over one million pounds of capacity. Second, suppliers' size distributions typically exhibited the unequal sizes characteristic of a particular version of imperfect competition. Third, over the years studied, freedom to enter and sustain operations within these subindustries was clearly imperfect, as many discovered too late. Fourth, the sustained presence of the same large fiber-producing firms as major suppliers in multiple subindustries signals the existence of economies of scale and existence that can start and perpetuate imperfect competition. Fifth, as already established, man-made fibers are heterogeneous and quite poor substitutes for both one another and for natural fibers. Product differentiation is another distinguishing trait of a particular form of imperfect competition.

The U.S. man-made fibers subindustries' structures examined above clearly are not those of pure monopolies since each had at least two, and usually more, very large producers throughout the 1959-82 period. This combination of facts precludes the possibility of monopolistic competition as a suitable common description of these subindustries' structures. The process of elimination leads to the conclusion that, save perhaps for acetate staple, U.S. man-made fibers subindustries typically were differentiated oligopolies between 1959 and 1982. The previously cited econometric study of fiber elasticities established the case for product heterogeneity. Anecdotal information and analyses in later chapters extend differentiation to the suppliers of those goods. However, understanding of an industry's structure requires some attention to the structure of its clientele, as monopoly power might be vitiated by a stronger, more aggressive or more astute monopsony or oligopsony.

Concentration within the U.S. Textile Industry

The U.S. textile industry buys almost all man-made fiber sold in the United States. At first glance, the U.S. textile industry seems fragmented since no firm has 5% of total sales. A different interpretation arises from a separate examination of major end-use markets. The 16 biggest of the TEB's 44 textile end-uses account for over 75% of the fiber consumed. Each also is an oligopsony. The textile leaders within any major end-use seldom hold such status in more than a few, if any, of the others. Hosiery manufacturers, for example, rarely if ever compete with tire makers or carpet tufters, but may dabble in apparel underwear or outerwear. As a further complication, the textile industry has been vertically integrating so that the small specialized firms still typical of the Orient and Europe are less viable here. U.S. man-made fiber producers thus face increasingly large and sophisticated textile mill customers. While all leading U.S. man-made fiber manufacturers are only divisions of much larger corporate entities, those fiber-spinning divisions usually have far greater sales revenues than their clients. Only six U.S. textile firms (Burlington Industries, J.P. Stevens, Fieldcrest Cannon, Milliken & Co., West Point Pepperell, and Dominion Textiles) usually have gross annual sales in excess of a billion dollars. Conversely, annual sales of most of the top 20 U.S. man-made fiber producers usually are well above that threshold; the others normally come very close to that target.

Another Facet of Concentration

One aspect of concentration in the U.S. man-made fibers industry is noteworthy. The topic held more than academic interest for the industry, based on papers circulated in it. The earliest known of these documents was a draft paper, "Generalized Distribution Rule" by John E. Reith in the early 1960s while working for duPont's Textile Fibers Department. Its claim to have found a "law . . . to account for the observed distribution of . . . market shares" reportedly generated considerable momentary interest within duPont. That socalled law asserted that the distribution of rivals' shares is basically a random [Sawyer, 69] and inverse function of the number of rivals. Obviously, this was quickly found not to be a valid or general rule. However, the flurry of interest aroused by that draft paper shows that the industry's leader sought to better understand this facet of its situation.

A second paper, "Structural Profile of the U.S. Man-made Fiber Industry," was published in 1971 and generated a record number of reprint requests. Its author, Leland S. Liang, is a renowned authority on and consultant to the industry. Liang revealed certain aspects of the industry's structure more clearly and concisely than anyone else and did so first.

> *This tendency toward domination of the manmade fiber industry by a number of firms has been advanced by the movement to multiproduct diversification. Of the sixteen companies, only Hercules produces one fiber--polypropylene--while all the others are involved in producing two or more fibers. In fact, it is almost impossible for any company to operate successfully unless it produces two of the three major non-cellulosic fibers. Indeed, even the longtime cellulosic fiber suppliers . . . have in recent years added the production of noncellulosics. . . .*

> *It is surmised that the oligopolistic nature of the manmade fiber industry stems from a combination of factors. Some of the most significant are:*

> 1. *The extremely high capital requirements;*
> 2. *The high level of technological knowledge and experience which obstruct entry of new firms even after the basic patents have expired;*
> 3. *The rapidly changing technologies which necessitate extensive and continuing expenditures for research and development; and*
> 4. *The enormous marketing effort required in the successful introduction of new fibers, the likes of which are not apparent even to the initiated.*

> *Large-scale operations are almost always necessary because of the economy of scale attendant to manmade fiber manufacturing. Integrated operations are deemed essential in most instances because the industry is a joint product industry, so that while producing one product, another is usually obtained as a by-product. To secure essential raw material supplies is another valid reason for backward integration on the part of the producers.*

> *Not only are high capital requirements necessary to operate a manmade fiber plant successfully, but fixed costs constitute a very high proportion of the value of the product. . . .*

> *Even if the capital requirements to enter the fiber operations could be met, it would be extremely difficult to hire qualified technical personnel and engineering talent, not to mention getting access to very closely guarded and highly secretive information relating to the intricacies of successful polymer and fiber extrusion.*

> *To be successful in fiber operations, it is always necessary to develop extensive product development programs, to improve fiber properties constantly so as to impart new attributes to the existing product, and above all, to work incessantly with the mills to engineer new fiber variants for specific end-use markets with eternal vigilance. It is, therefore, not surprising that interested producers might be deterred from entering the manmade fiber industry, especially in view of the erosion of industry profits during the last few years. [Liang]*

CONCLUSIONS

Concentration within the U.S. man-made fibers industry usually is only moderately high, about 80% for the top four firms, in each subindustry composed of a specific form of a particular generic fiber. Not only are the subindustries' four-firm CRs seldom high enough to denote the presence of significant price control (that is, monopoly power), but they also show significant erosion over time. The CR evidence as to price control clearly is ambiguous. Acetate filament and staple are glaring exceptions to this general conclusion. It is noteworthy too that many subindustries have pronounced fringes of captive or specialized producers. The U.S. man-made fibers industry seems far less concentrated in aggregate than its subindustries. This lower aggregate concentration results from the presence of some large producers specializing in but one or a few subindustries and end-uses. The two leading fiberglass firms, OCF and PPG, exemplify this phenomenon.

Another interesting aspect of aggregate concentration is the effect of imports. The concentration analyses by subindustry could only include imports of directly competing fibers. However, it was possible to examine the effects of indirect imports, that is, intermediate and final goods made abroad from foreign man-made fiber(s) on total concentration. This latter point is of great practical importance at the moment as low foreign labor costs, foreign government subsidies, an open U.S. market, and a relatively strong dollar combine to encourage increased indirect imports instead of directly competitive man-made fibers. The four, eight, and 20-firm CRs almost always were significantly but not greatly lowered by taking indirect imports into account instead of ignoring them.

A key conclusion of this analysis of concentration is that the U.S. man-made fibers industry has an oligopolistic structure instead of some more extreme form. More precisely, those man-made fiber subindustries typically are heterogeneous oligopolies, not undifferentiated ones. Heterogeneity implies that a degree of price control might exist that should not be arbitrarily ignored in either theory or practice.

The U.S. man-made fibers industry is in a transition between a mature and a terminal product life-cycle phase. Many of its subindustries indisputably are in their declining phase. Once well into or past its mature phase, an industry's structure is more apt to change as firms exit or merge instead of enter. Firms' exits or mergers heighten the industry's concentration. That inevitability of reconcentration is predictable. The pace of such reconcentration is, however, quite uncertain since, as yet, no valid theory exists to guide forecasts of it.

5

Structural Determinants

The various U.S. man-made fibers subindustry structures were established and discussed in the prior chapter. Here the aim is to identify and understand the determinants of those structures. Three of many possible structural determinants are particularly important. Technology probably is the most significant determinant of these industry structures. Technology dictates the exact method and the inputs needed. Decisions in these spheres commit a firm for considerable periods, as the earlier discussion of technology showed.

This chapter's focus narrows to two issues: differentiation of firms vying in a particular subindustry, and the cost structures involved in extruding that family of goods. Firm differentiation is examined in the first section below before devoting the bulk of the chapter to the more critical matter of cost structures.

FIRM DIFFERENTIATION

Product heterogeneity was treated extensively above. It should therefore suffice to restate a few key points about man-made fiber heterogeneity as a foundation for other sources of differentiation of U.S. man-made fiber manufacturers. Man-made fibers of a given form within a particular genus generally are not substitutes either for other man-made fibers or for natural fibers. Independence, complementarity, or displacement, as shown earlier, are more common among fibers than substitution. As the various fiber families have low cross-elasticities, interfiber substitution is improbable without relative prices undergoing larger swings for longer periods than have been experienced to date. The absence of such price fluctuations is shown in the next chapter.

One of the main reasons man-made fibers' cross-elasticities are so low is that fiber usually is a small part of the cost of most final products. Carpet is the only large-volume exception. Suits consuming some five pounds of fiber generally retail for well over $100 today, although their constituent fibers' prices normally are below

$2.00 per pound and often closer to $1.00. Even if a suit's man-made fibers were costless and those savings were fully passed to the ultimate consumers, it obviously would neither raise total fiber demand nor cause switching across fiber genera.

As mentioned earlier, man-made fiber producers within a subindustry engage in what the industry terms "intrafiber competition." A keystone of intrafiber competition is that even at this level of disaggregation firms do not always supply products sufficiently homogeneous to substitute for one another within a particular segment of a given end-use. Some times this is a result of policy decisions. At other times, it results from the choice of technology or skill differences in using that technology.

U.S. man-made fiber producers differentiate themselves from rivals in several ways besides operating within heterogeneous subindustries. Previously cited axes of supplier differentiation include the number, breadth, and depth of product lines; the kinds and amounts of technical and marketing services; skill and cooperation in dealing with firms located further along the diverse channels of distribution than textile mills; and innovativeness in both product and marketing. A survey of fiber buyers at textile mills indicated that they chose man-made fiber suppliers according to a combination of at least eight traits [Goldenberg, 244-45].

When choosing man-made fiber suppliers, textile mills rated the supplier's size, as measured by total capacity, as most important, followed by its pricing policies. The two essentially equally important tertiary considerations are the breadth and depth of the supplier's product lines and such product-related features as quality levels, consistency, and record of improvement. The two equally important fourth-level concerns were the intensity and expertise of fiber firms' sales efforts and similar aspects of their customer and technical service. Innovativeness in creating either new products or new uses for established goods was on a par with the supplier's market knowledge as fifth points of differentiation between man-made fiber suppliers.

U.S. man-made fiber producers subcontracted such studies for many years. Disclosing the sponsor might bias respondents. These studies were first done to establish benchmarks and obtain insights about their ratings compared with leading rivals among major clients and prospects. Periodic follow-up studies monitored the results of changes in one's practices and those of competitors.

Such surveys suffered from a common problem. Until recently there was no valid technique to pool results for individual traits to get a sound total rating by product(s) or customer(s). Various simple weighting procedures were favored in practice. This methodological problem is analogous to establishing a group's indifference curve. Although Saaty apparently solved this problem for strategic planning purposes in the early 1980s, no one in the U.S. man-made fibers industry seems to have realized that Saaty's analytic hierarchy process is equally valid for this purpose.

Certain fiber producers went out of their way to be accessible, flexible, and effective to all or, at the least, their main accounts. Others applied or were perceived as having adopted an opposite strategy. During the 1960s and 1970s mills surveyed usually would put MTC in the former class and duPont in the latter.

Several fiber producers devised a variety of marketing practices to differentiate themselves. Among the more successful of these devices were end-product guaranties or warranties and images of indispensability or product ties. MTC was the first to adapt a retail warranty with its Wear-Dated apparel program in the early 1960s. Final buyers of Wear-Dated apparel were assured that MTC would either replace any Wear-Dated garment failing to give a year's normal use, as demonstrated by returning the item with the sales receipt and the original Wear-Dated hang-tag, or give a pro-rata refund of the purchase price. This program appeals greatly to mothers of active and fast-growing children. Its less than a tenth of a percent return rate is a tribute to a massive effort to establish and enforce standards and labeling in an arena previously without norms, and the inertia of shoppers in seeking refunds with such tough evidentiary criteria. A similar five-year Wear-Dated guaranty was later introduced for carpet. Naturally, Wear-Dated products have to be made exclusively of MTC supplied or approved fiber(s) and to fully meet the end-product specifications developed by Monsanto so as to have the crucial Wear-Dated hang-tag. Allied is the only other fiber producer to develop a competing program.

DuPont has differentiated itself in many critical industrial end-uses by developing enduring product specifications that dictated use of particular duPont fibers even if potentially substitutable fibers existed. Setting standards only its products could meet enabled duPont to isolate markets and impose low cross-elasticities on other firms' products. DuPont also commercialized exclusive lines of specialty (fibers Nomex Aramid, Kevlar Aramid, Lycra spandex, and Teflon) and extended its more conventional product lines with such improvements as higher tenacities, heavy deniers, hollow filaments, and so on. Proprietary specialty fibers, plus broad and deep product lines, "lock in" duPont as the premier man-made fiber supplier. As a setter of end-product specifications and the leading developer of significant new fiber genera, duPont earned and enjoys a uniquely powerful position in the U.S. fiber industry, which it skillfully exploits in several ways.

One such approach calls for steering a course close to but distinct from the illegal practice of tying products usable as complements to the sale of a specialty item. That legal course strives to make customers too nervous to risk using other suppliers' offerings. Fear that duPont might cancel or delay delivery of a critical material or assign a lower priority of access to new developments deters some of its fiber customers from switching part of their purchases to other suppliers. Facets of the apparel, home furnishings, and industrial sectors are vulnerable to such a ploy. When nylon and spandex fibers must be used together, as in hosiery or swimwear, for example, there is opportunity for such a stratagem.

Formerly, the mix of duPont fibers, dyes, and dyebath additives provided another such opportunity to imply a risk of tying products. However, following an unfavorable antitrust case ruling against the U.S. dyestuff industry, duPont divested itself of this business.

Hence, there are many grounds for marked and significant but incomplete and imperfect differentiation of U.S. man-made fiber producers besides their physical products. DuPont is the premier supplier because of its size, price leadership, diverse product mix, innovativeness, large and sustained advertising effort, sustained and relatively thorough marketing research, sophisticated marketing and demarketing, long-term commitment to technical and other research, and effective use of market power. Several more tiers of U.S. man-made fibers suppliers exist on the basis of certain intangible characteristics.

A second tier of U.S. man-made fibers producers is composed of firms that, although less effectively differentiated from one another than from duPont, possess distinctive reputations or images among their immediate and prospective customers and among key decision-makers at major needle trade houses and retailers. The second tier of U.S. man-made fiber manufacturers, in alphabetical order and independent of their specific reputations, includes Allied, Celanese, MTC, and OCF. Whether American Cyanamid, American Enka, Avtex, BASF, Eastman, and Hoechst form a third tier of less well-differentiated domestic fiber producers or should be included in the second tier is uncertain. However, they clearly are much better known and regarded than the remaining large merchant producers: Amoco, CertainTeed, Chevron, Courtaulds, Phillips, Omega, PPG, Reichhold, Wayn-Tex, and Wellman. The latter, in turn, are clearly differentiated from the smaller, merchant, and captive producers by textile trade customers or rivals who are captive fiber producers.

In conclusion, the U.S. man-made fibers industry has a hierarchy of four and maybe five levels when differentiating firms on issues other than the properties of their products. Testing other dimensions via more advanced statistical techniques probably would enhance this simplistic identification of strategic groups within the U.S. man-made fibers industry for other purposes, for example, competitor assessment. It suffices here to show that firm heterogeneity exists in addition to product heterogeneity.

COST STRUCTURES

Introduction

U.S. man-made fibers' long-run average cost curves (LRAC) were estimated in order to address some specific issues. As demonstrated later, man-made fiber costs differ significantly, showing that these goods also are heterogeneous in production as well as in the market(s) they serve, as shown earlier. A second issue focuses on determination of the minimum and maximum efficient plant sizes, if both exist. It also is desirable to measure and compare these scales to one another, to Markham's earlier estimate for "rayon," and to see if efficient plant scales are static or dynamic. Differences in efficient plant sizes over time imply either the improved diffusion of an optimum technology or a transition from an early to some newer means of production. A third concern is the shape of the planning curves. This shows how costs vary with scale of operations beyond the minimum efficient size, if costs change with size. How much effect do economies of scale or other factors have, if they exist? Are those effects large enough to raise a high entry barrier? Are their sources enduring enough to perpetuate an entry barrier? Or are any obstacles to resource mobility into or out of this industry merely temporary? Capital to labor ratios (K/L) are another interesting aspect of man-made fiber costs. Are the K/L values constant across plant scales? Are they constant across fibers and forms? Last, two facets of marginal costs merit attention: How large are marginal costs, and what, if any, is their relationship to capacity utilization rates?

Background

A series of identically formatted cost tables were generated by major man-made fiber, form, and, where possible, alternative processes to answer the above questions. The results are appended as Tables A2-1 through A2-15. Each table presents key points along a planning curve based on all relevant merchant plant sizes over the long run, that is, between 1959 and 1982. Five more common facets of these tables need brief explanations before discussing their results. Those items are the headings, stubs, data sources, adjustments made to the basic cost data, and the modifications made to individual costs as plant size changed.

Tables A2-1 through A2-15 refer to domestic U.S. merchant commercial plants; purely captive or monofilament facilities were excluded. Plant sizes were derived from the author's capacity estimates and data TEB published about the firms. Those man-made fibers extruders with both merchant and captive or monofilament production were classified as entirely merchant providers of the proper fiber form.

The right-hand columns of each table detail costs at various plant sizes. The first of these scale columns, reading from the left, is entitled the "minimum efficient module." It shows the smallest component of a merchant plant thought economically efficient on a sustained basis in the United States as of 1975. Data about minimum efficient module sizes came from a 1975 Arthur D. Little study and a chapter in the Man-Made Textile Encyclopedia. Numbers in the minimum efficient module columns of the appended cost tables represent major revisions to the Little data, save for its premised crude oil cost of $12 per barrel, described below.

Actual plant capacities were estimated annually by firm, generic fiber, and form independently of the minimum efficient modules' sizes. The smallest and largest plant sizes were noted and used in the cost tables. Averages of actual plant sizes also were calculated, from the same data sets, as intermediate points along each planning curve.

The stubs or columns furthest to the left on each cost table are a modest extension, for clarity's sake, of that appearing in the Little study. That study was relied on as a starting point for the following reasons. Arthur D. Little has over 60 years experience in providing consulting services to the U.S. man-made fibers industry. The report is one of the few comprehensive studies quantifying man-made fibers' cost components by generic fibers and forms and stating the rationales behind those figures.

A slightly modified format was adopted for three reasons. First, it makes sense to those outside the industry without sacrificing any cost details. Second, the form, structure, and terms are acceptable to the industry. Finally, it enables examination of some effects of various sources of advantage over the gamut of actual plant sizes. The Little study did not address this latter point.

Little's 1975 U.S. man-made fibers' cost data were modified to even more realistic values whenever possible. The sources of those more realistic values are cited in association with each modification next to the initial data. Major adjustments were made to the Little data for: minimum efficient scales of operation; costs per pound of capacity at minimum efficient module scales; energy costs per pound; depreciation; and pretax target returns on fixed and working capital. The latter can be considered part of a normal profit from an economic perspective.

Little used only three minimum efficient module sizes. Reality is a bit more diverse and generally appears to call for notably larger minimum efficient module sizes. Actual plants would be integer multiples of their respective minimum efficient modules' scales if those data were accurate and well known. The Little study assumed that all man-made fiber filaments had a 15 million pound per year capacity minimum efficient-sized module, and that staple forms, except wet-process acrylics, have a 25 million pound per year minimum efficient-sized module, while wet-process acrylic staple requires a 35 million pound per year minimum efficient-sized module. These minimum efficient module sizes and their corresponding fixed capital costs per pound of capacity were revised whenever data from the Man-Made Textile Encyclopedia [Press, 54-55] warranted doing so. Data from the latter source were given greater credence because the author, C.O. Butler, of the chapter on the economics and engineering of man-made fibers' facilities was an executive of a firm, Von Kohorn International Corporation, responsible for designing and erecting commercial man-made fiber plants, while the Little study relied on data from interviews, publications, internal files, and past reports.

Little's energy costs per pound were reduced in accordance with data not available to that organization when its report was prepared. Energy costs per pound were lowered by 40% as per a report done for the U.S. government on energy savings attainable in response to the 1973 OPEC oil embargo. That report was prepared by the Foster D. Snell Division of Booz, Allen and Hamilton, with the cooperation of various industries including the U.S. man-made fibers industry [Ketterling, Sections VI and VII]. It reached two relevant conclusions. First, as much as a 40% average energy savings was theoretically obtainable in the long run, with a 25% short-run savings readily achievable. Second, energy savings varied markedly by firm; some U.S. man-made fiber producers had near optimal energy efficiency long before the 1973 oil crisis, but most had not.

The Little study assumed a ten-year useful plant life and employed linear depreciation. Actual man-made fibers plants usually last longer than 20 years, and often more than 30 years. However, with but 24 years of capacity data available, our man-made fiber cost estimates tables used 20-year linear depreciation.

The last sweeping revision to Little's data concerned 30% pretax target rates of return on both fixed and working capital. That facilitating premise, popular among outsiders assessing the industry, was lowered to a more realistic pretax return of 16% based on trade interviews and internal Monsanto documents shown to the author when he worked there.

Various computational guidelines were used to reasonably adjust specific costs at the minimum efficient scale to estimates at other plant sizes. Fixed capital per pound was revised according to the historic chemical engineering "sixth-tenths factor" formula of Williams [R. Williams, Jr., 1947a: 102-3; and 1947b: 124-25]. Williams worked for duPont and cited duPont fiber department data in his articles. According to the rule of thumb devised by Williams, the capital cost (C2) of a new, different-sized (S2) facility, with the same technology as an older one of known size (S1) and costs (C1), can be approximated within $\pm 18\%$ from the relationship:

$$\log(C2) - \log(C1) = 0.6[\log(S2) - \log(S1)]$$

Raw material costs were only pared selectively. If the largest actual plant size and largest average actual plant size differed, and both exceeded the minimum efficient scale, then those larger plants' raw material costs were reduced to reflect the potential effect of cost savings attainable from backward integration into key raw materials. The largest plant's raw material costs were lowered by 20% and the second largest by 10%. These figures were a judgment based on a wide range of vague literature references and discussions with executives at a number of major man-made fiber producers. The literature implied a range of direct benefits from backward integration from zero to 30%, and maybe as much as 50%. However, interviewees pointed out that the literature accepted the faulty premise of a 30% pretax return. There were other reasons for these actions whose benefits were much harder to quantify and to allocate to one group of products. Reliable sourcing of uniformly high quality raw materials may be a more important ground for backward integration. Interviewees regarded a 10% to 20% range as a more realistic estimate of the savings from backward integration captured at their firms' man-made fiber plants. Those fibers included acetate filament, acrylic staple, nylon filament and staple, and polyester filament and staple. A highly sophisticated study would be needed to establish more precise values for these benefits, but 10% to 20% undoubtedly is acceptable as a better, second approximation, given the earlier paucity of reliable data.

Labor costs were decreased by 20% as plant size doubled.

> *Higher equipment productivity and larger plant capacity are important factors in improving the cost-effectiveness of ... fibre production. ... according to the writers' calculation, capital expenditure decreases by 20% and labor productivity increases by that amount when the production capacity of the plant is doubled [Evsyukov et al., 290].*

Such labor cost savings should not be confused with any potential economies from learning or experience, as popularized by the Boston Consulting Group and its offshoots. The latter refer to changes in cumulative output independent of plant scale. The labor productivity gains from larger man-made fiber plants are, instead, intrinsic to the technology. Any economies of learning available to the man-made fiber industry, probably are captured by either suppliers of capital equipment and labor to the firms producing those fibers or customers, as happens elsewhere [Carroll, 154-59].

The energy, maintenance, taxes, insurance, physical inventories, and miscellaneous overhead components of the remaining conversion costs, plus sales and administrative expenses, were assumed to follow the well-known operations research economies-of-scale guideline. That rule of thumb has working capital costs, especially physical inventories, decline as a function of the square root of two as capacity doubles. So, the working capital needs of a plant twice as large would be roughly 41.4% greater--not 100%.

Table 5-1 presents cost highlights, from appended Tables A2-1 through A2-15, and is discussed next.

Long-Run Cost Results

Percentage cost differences from the cheapest to the most expensive items in Table 5-1 invariably exceed 87% regardless of the form or scales involved. But there is considerable difference in the identity of the least and most costly items across fiber forms and plant scales. PTA-process (polyethylene terephthalic acid) polyester is the least costly staple fiber, and Type 6, 6 nylon staple the dearest at their minimum efficient module scales. At the largest staple plant sizes, wet-process acrylic is the least expensive and Type 6 nylon is the costliest. At both extreme scales, 150 denier rayon is the least expensive generic filament fiber, while 70 denier Type 6, 6 nylon is the costliest.

Table 5-1 shows that cost differentials exist between producing filament and staple forms of the same generic fiber, and always favor staple with a slightly wider range, from 11% to 84%, at the minimum efficient module sizes. Similar but smaller differentials favor staple at maximum plant sizes over a narrower range, from 2.2% to 63.2%, than at the minimum efficient module sizes.

The cost differentials to produce the same forms of the same generic fiber via alternative processes range from 0.8% to 26.1% for staple and from 9.6% to 44.4% for filament. These differentials exceed 18% at the largest scales. However, the pattern of generic fibers' differential costs is obscure when form and plant scale are simultaneously taken into account.

Such large cost differences across generic fibers, forms, and scales clearly are nontrivial. This is especially apparent given the fact that customers usually are highly sensitive to fabric price variations of an eighth of a cent a linear yard. Fabrics having a third to a half of their costs directly determined by their fiber input(s) obviously

Table 5-1

U.S. Man-Made Fiber Cost Comparisons for 1975

(millions of pounds and dollars per pound)

		Economic Scale		
		Minimum		Maximum
		(M Lbs) ($/Lb)		(M Lbs) ($/Lb)

	Form:		Staple		
Genera and Process					
Acrylic--wet process		30	0.708	325	0.375
Fiberglass (*)		20	0.845	200	0.368
Nylon					
Type 6		25	1.091	110	0.768
Type 6, 6		35	1.101	185	0.760
Olefin--resin		25	0.586	131	0.366
Polyester					
DMT		25	0.700	450	0.382
PTA		40	0.555	218	0.355
Rayon--viscose		50	0.632	236	0.425

	Form:		Filament		
Acetate--diacetate 100 denier		20	0.765	93	0.502
Nylon 70 denier					
Type 6		15	1.240	110	0.867
Type 6, 6		20	1.421	143	0.874
Olefin 1,000 denier		15	0.847	113	0.466
Polyester					
DMT		15	1.058	140	0.544
PTA		25	0.914	125	0.452
Rayon--viscose 150 denier		20	0.702	70	0.485

Source: Tables A2-1 through A2-15.

---

* Fiberglass is deemed and undecomposable mix of staple and
    filament forms.

should be quite responsive to small changes in fiber prices, despite those fabrics' weight per linear yard. Given textile mills' sensitivity to fiber costs, one would expect considerable substitution across generic fibers and forms if such were feasible and desirable, provided the prices diverged enough for long enough. The rarity of such substitution proves that those necessary conditions are seldom met.

Perhaps the supposedly competing fibers simply are too heterogeneous. Perhaps relative price moves are too small. Maybe, as per the Agricultural Department study cited earlier, changes in generic fiber and form usage are essentially irreversible commitments over periods of several years, despite wide swings in relative prices within that interval. Maybe textile firms are still so heavily dedicated to particular generic fibers and forms that they cannot or will not recognize alternative raw materials. Perhaps textile manufacturers are deterred from substitution across generic fibers and forms by a dearth of accurate information on some critical issues. Important but hard to ascertain points of information needed by management for rational decision-making include: the prices and availability of potentially rivaling generic fibers and forms; the processing methods and costs of conversion of alternative materials into textile structures; marketing requirements, including access to and cost of operations in new channels of distribution; the comparative properties of final goods made from the new fibers and those items' acceptability over time. In other words, the demand determinant details of potentially rivaling final products made from alternative generic fibers are not well known.

The plant size estimates in Tables A2-1 through A2-15 are properly subject to some criticisms. Those plant size ranges almost always are overextended at both ends within each generic fiber and form. Small, pilot and start-up facilities may occasionally have been included, as consistently accurate identification was not always possible. Absent better information, two things might be done to compensate for this potential distortion. First, all merchant plants below the minimum efficient module scale could be ignored as aberrations. Otherwise, the minimum efficient module size is grossly in error, which is possible but unlikely. Second, each firm's plant sizes within generic fibers and forms could be traced until they stabilized near a peak value, save for minor denier mix fluctuations. Averages of such corrected peak plant capacities within a generic fiber, form, and process would better indicate optimum plant scales. Man-made fiber plants almost never extrude just the single denier shown on the filaments or a fixed combination of deniers, regardless of fiber form [Hollander, 31]. Some small and mid-sized facilities specialize in specific product deniers or mixes (for example, Type 6 nylon carpet filament or Type 6, 6 nylon tire cord and/or industrial yarn) but the identities and scales of those plants were not readily ascertainable. All plant size averages are potentially biased in unknown directions and to unknowable degrees by using those facilities' estimated total sizes. One can but hope that these under- and overestimates offset one another in practice.

The largest man-made fiber-producing facilities invariably are multiplant operations at a one site. By way of illustration, a single location could incorporate distinct plants of diverse optimal sizes. Specifically, a Type 6, 6 nylon facility could have under its roof:

- a plant spinning fine denier, filament, hosiery yarns;
- a second plant making 40 to 210 denier multifilament apparel yarns;
- a third plant spinning 240 to 500 denier multifilament home furnishings yarns;
- a fourth plant extruding high-denier multifilament carpet yarns;
- a fifth plant making monofilament, industrial and nontextile yarns of high deniers and tenacities;
- a sixth plant spinning high-denier and high tenacity multifilament industrial yarns;
- a seventh plant extruding ultra-high filament count yarns or tows to later be cut into short lengths to make staple fiber.

Using the actual size of the largest plant on each cost undoubtedly upwardly biases our minimum and maximum efficient plant size estimates to an unknown degree since the number of truly distinct fiber plants under each large facility's roof and the actual sizes of those component plants are not general knowledge. Again, one can but hope that any under- and overestimation biases offset one another so that the averages yield reasonably close estimates of the minimum efficient merchant plant sizes. Conversely, using the size of the largest actual facility as a cost basis ensures high estimates of the optimum maximum plant scales and low estimates of the associated minimum attainable costs if the base costs and scale corrections are complete and accurate.

Adjustments made for the above criticisms yielded more realistic estimates of optimal minimum and maximum plant sizes, rounded off to the nearest integer multiples of the minimum efficient scales. The associated cost implications were estimated via previously described methods and the results appear on Table 5-2.

Comparisons of the appended cost tables' minimum efficient module sizes with the smallest commercially viable plant scales on Table 5-2 show that real world plants usually are at least twice their minimum efficient module scales. Exceptions included both forms and types of nylon and olefin staple. The staple exceptions to the above smallest commercially viable plants were the same size as their respective minimum efficient size modules. The smallest efficient nylon filament plants are triple their minimum efficient module sizes. The largest efficient merchant plants' scales vary from three to seven times greater than their minimum efficient module scales, with three times being the modal value.

Some other important conclusions also derive from Table 5-2 or from comparisons of its contents with other data. Each generic fiber's staple form tends to be at least 10% cheaper than its filament form whenever both forms exist. The cost differentials between minimum and maximum efficient plant scales within generic fiber and form generally are much smaller in the cellulosic fibers than the noncellulosics. Only twice did noncellulosics fibers' cost differentials across efficient

Table 5-2

U.S. Merchant Man-Made Fiber 1975 Costs at the

Smallest and Largest Viable Commercial Plant Sizes

(millions of pounds and dollars per pound)

| | Economic Scale | | | |
| | Minimum | | Maximum | |
	(M Lbs)	($/Lb)	(M Lbs)	($/Lb)
Form: Staple				
Genera and Process				
Acrylic--wet process	70	0.580	140	0.495
Fiberglass (*)	40	0.650	100	0.479
Nylon				
Type 6	25	1.087	100	0.904
Type 6, 6	35	1.096	105	0.950
Olefin--resin	25	0.582	75	0.467
Polyester				
DMT	50	0.726	150	0.602
PTA	80	0.481	120	0.449
Rayon--viscose	100	0.555	150	0.522
Form: Filament				
Acetate--diacetate 100 denier	40	0.661	100	0.568
Nylon 70 denier				
Type 6	45	1.128	90	1.015
Type 6, 6	60	1.496	100	1.322
Olefin 1,000 denier	30	0.698	105	0.526
Polyester				
DMT	30	0.868	90	0.674
PTA	50	0.689	100	0.584
Rayon--viscose 150 denier	40	0.606	60	0.564

Source: Author.

---

* Fiberglass is deemed an undecomposable mix of staple and
  filament forms.

plant scales exceed $0.10 per pound; cellulosics' cost differentials are less. Acrylic staple and polyester staple via the PTA process are sole exceptions. The realistic ranges of efficient plant scales shown in Table 5-2 usually are much less than the corresponding ones on Tables A2-1 through A2-15 and thus have smaller absolute declines. Those more realistic ranges of plant scales somewhat moderate the various economies of scale incorporated into Tables A2-1 through A2-15 but do not eliminate them.

Some questions raised at the start of this section on the costs of producing various man-made fibers remain to be addressed. The details of the individual generic fiber and form cost tables make it clear that no substitution occurs in production across generic fibers or forms. The minimum efficient module or plant scales and the capital, raw materials, and conversion cost components differ significantly, as does the technology.

Man-made fibers' planning curves as established here do not conform to the classic V shape as found by Markham [Markham, 49] for rayon. But more recent information justifies reconsidering Markham's minimum efficient plant scale estimate for rayon. His 40 million pound estimate [50-51] held up remarkably well over the years for rayon filament. However, it does not fit the more recent rayon staple data. In fairness, one must stress that Markham was examining what is today the rayon filament industry. Rayon staple's minimum efficient 1975 module size was 50 million pounds, as per Table 5-1. A 100 million pounds is the best estimate of the smallest commercially viable rayon staple plant's size in 1975, as noted in Table 5-2.

The long-run average cost curves (LRACs) estimated for U.S.-produced man-made fibers in 1975 have documented economies of scale and integration built into the data underlying their shapes. Other sources of efficiency and inefficiency are known to affect the costs of manufacturing man-made fibers in the United States, although their consequences could not be precisely quantified.

Among the formerly neglected, potentially important sources of advantage in producing man-made fibers are economies from operating multiple plants, in and across generic fibers and forms. Prior discussion of quantified advantages focused on efficiencies between existing (presumably) single plant firms without allowing for multiplant firms. Entering firms presumably find that discussion's implications self-evident. However, besides the various economies of scale, integration and multiplant operations, potential entrants may face another obstacle. Sources of multiplant operating economies are both numerous and hard to quantify, according to the literature from Markham's industry specific discussion [42-57] through more general treatments of this phenomenon [Scherer, 81-118]. Earlier observations of the pervasiveness of multiplant operations [Markham, 43, and especially 154-55; and Liang] in this industry remain valid today. Each of the 20 largest domestic man-made fiber firms in 1975 ran at least two such plants in that year. Most--15--had plants producing two or more distinct generic fibers and forms. The example of the largest firm, duPont, is most informative.

DuPont operated 24 man-made fiber facilities at ten locations in six states as 35 plants in 1975 [Textile Organon, November 1975, 139]. One plant made acetate filament. Seven produced specialty fibers: one for spandex filament; three made various Aramid fibers (two for Nomex, one each for filament and staple, and one spun Kevlar filament); one made Qiana Aramid filament; and the last two produced Teflon, one each for filament and staple. The remaining facilities were divided into groups of two or more plants to make each of the four major generic fibers by forms and processes. That plant deployment was:

- Acrylic staple: one wet- and one dry-process plant at different sites;
- Nylons: six plants at six different sites on Type 6, 6 filament plus six more at the same sites making Type 6, 6 staple, and three at one location spinning monofilaments of Types 6; 6, 6; and 6, 12;
- Olefin: two (spunbonded) filament plants at different locations;
- Polyester: two plants on filament at different locations with complementary staple spinning units at the same sites plus a monofilament plant at a third location.

DuPont's complex multiplant pattern presumably made greater economic sense than any alternative. At least in concept, duPont instead might have geographically centralized its fiber production; specialized in one generic fiber and form at a single plant; erected uniform-sized plants across locations; or, conversely, made the same fixed proportionate mix of its generic fibers and forms at each site. The merits of these options surely are theoretical instead of real since duPont shunned them for decades. DuPont fiber department executives undoubtedly knew their realistic options through experience, if not exposure to years of technical literature, consulting advice, and internal analyses. Hence, the distribution of duPont's man-made fiber plant sites and sizes probably reflects the best technology known at the times of the decision to erect or to expand those facilities. Others clearly could have deferred such decisions in the face of great uncertainty about the state of technology. However, as the industry's indisputable technological leader for the period covered, duPont's decisions about plant size, site, process, and product mix are most revealing. Those choices must have made more sense to duPont than any of the conceptual options cited above but rejected in practice. Presumably, duPont sized and sited its man-made fiber plants not solely according to the optimal scale of the best technology for the particular product to be made at the moment, but instead balanced or traded off these and other issues over time. Those balancing considerations surely included forward and backward integration and similar matters outside our purview. They are known to have included the capability to "retrofit" plants as superior technology was discovered and embodied in new equipment.

For many years duPont would build a new plant to field test the latest technology as incorporated into the equipment it also constructed. Once everything checked out at full scale duPont would then modernize all its facilities making that form of that fiber. This latter process is termed "retrofitting." For several reasons, duPont was one of the few, if not the only, domestic man-made fiber producer to retrofit as a matter of standard practice.

DuPont was the most technologically innovative U.S. man-made fiber firm. Until recently, duPont designed, built, and installed its own production equipment in its own plants. It occasionally did the same for rivals, for example, Eastman Kodak and Chemstrand. DuPont favored multiplant operations for each of its generic fibers and forms. Last, its strategic, marketing, and operational planning processes far surpassed those of most of its rivals.

The historic pattern of multiplant operations in the U.S. man-made fibers industry yields a clue about the size of its benefits. This practice's benefits must more than offset any savings from changing a hypothetical plant's sizes from the lowest average total cost on the appropriate appended cost table to the corresponding largest plant size on those same tables. Those estimated values of multiplant operations within the same generic man-made fiber and form range from $0.035 per pound for polyester staple made from PTA to $0.358 per pound for Type 6, 6 nylon filament. Note that duPont has six plants extruding subspecialties within this latter product group and another six committed to spinning Type 6, 6 nylon staple, which apparently enjoys the second largest advantage, $0.280 per pound, from multiplant operations. These estimates of the benefits of multiplant operations are significant and conservative as they omit multiplant economies known to exist across generic fibers and forms and from vertical integration, except in raw materials.

Among the potentially important sources of disadvantage in producing man-made fibers were rapid changes in technology and product properties demanded, Leibenstein's X-Inefficiency and decision rules imposed by higher authorities at parent firms. The latter presumably aim to optimize corporate performance despite their effect on the man-made fibers division's efficiency.

U.S. man-made fibers industry average costs do not hold well across the firms composing the industry. These firms did not build identical plants over time or simultaneously. They also vary in aggressiveness and cost-consciousness in exploiting opportunities to increase efficiency. DuPont, for instance, refused for decades to license its dry process to make acrylic staple, while producing some of its Orlon brand acrylic by that process for decades. Presumably, duPont's view was that the internal savings from this decision outweigh the social benefits from a greater diffusion of technical know-how, even if the company could extract maximum licensing fees.

Our cost tables show important differences not only between the costs of producing the major man-made fiber genera and forms in the U.S. but also between the alternative processes and the firms in each of those categories. Hence, process selection is as important to a man-made fiber producer as its choices of product and scale, since every generic fiber can be made by two alternative routes and usually in a diverse mix of deniers, forms (filament versus staple) and other critical traits.

All the appended cost tables have two extra rows just below their totals. The first extra row displays the capital-to-labor ratios (K/L) at the various plant scales. That information was sought because the man-made fibers industry reputedly is capital intensive. Total capital costs, that is, fixed capital costs per pound plus working capital costs per pound, formed the numerator of the K/L ratios. Direct labor plus half of the sales, administration and research expense (SARE) formed the denominators. The second extra row shows the percentage reduction in total costs from quantifiable economies of scale between various plant sizes and the maximum plant size.

A merchant man-made fiber firm needs a senior management team, some sales, technical, and customer service, and support personnel such as secretaries. Obviously, SARE does not vary directly with output. Experience suggests that 50% would be a reasonable estimate of the fixed proportion of SARE. Many man-made fiber producers cut nonproduction personnel by a combination of layoffs, early retirements, and even purges in reaction to sharp and prolonged but often unforeseen demand reductions. Many targeted 25% to 30% reductions in SARE. The few successful such retrenchments took thorough planning and usually substituted capital for labor, with computerization replacing much of middle management. None is known to have survived a one-time cutback of 50% or more in SARE. Presumably, therefore, about half of the U.S. man-made fibers merchant producers' SARE essentially are inescapable fixed costs. These costs are also highly labor-intensive.

Conversion costs were considered fixed because they do not vary significantly with plant output unless an entire plant is either started or permanently closed. Man-made fiber plants tend to have Leontief production functions because their inputs are not substitutable for one another and have to be used in fixed proportions, set by technology, to produce any output.

Temporary plant closings risk breaking up production teams that are hard to establish. That is avoided as it is very difficult to restart the facility as planned if key workers are unavailable when needed. Two alternative strategies are preferred: first, changing the product mix to the most durable and salable items and investing in nonperishable inventory while affordable. If or when that becomes too burdensome, lower the capacity utilization rate to work off inventory and spread the cutback across the labor force. Option two does not significantly affect operating or conversion costs until very drastic cutbacks are made, as discussed in the next section on marginal costs.

Man-made fibers clearly enjoy large economies of scale as their planning curves decline steeply over a considerable range. The precise total of all accessible economies of scale, establishment, multiplant operations, and so on is unknown. But the net effects of the various economies evaluated are not trivial and the benefits of the rest simply would enlarge those quantified gains.

It is possible to partly substitute capital for labor in the production of man-made fibers by choosing the proper new technology for a new plant. But incurring higher fixed costs only makes sense if management is confident about its demand and cost forecasts. This industry's marginal productivities of labor and capital differ notably over the 1959-82 period, with capital productivity probably improving faster than that of production labor.

A capital-intensive industry poses an inherent entry barrier if firms are unequal in their ability to raise or use finance capital. A capital-intensive industry with net positive economies of scale, establishment, and so on would generate a potentially formidable entry barrier since only a large-scale entrant might have a reasonable chance of success. Successful late entry would be quite problematic as the economies of scale call for an oligopolistic industry structure. The domestic man-made fibers industry's products differ significantly in cost, and not all producers supply all products to all end-use markets. In such a differentiated oligopoly, some established suppliers are sure to notice that they have been directly and substantially affected by a large-scale new entrant. The Sylos Postulate should alert prospective entrants to expect retaliation in such circumstances.

> *The following well-defined assumption: that potential entrants behave as though they expected existing firms to adopt the policy most unfavorable to them, namely, the policy of maintaining output while reducing the price (or accepting reductions) to the extent required to enforce such an output policy. I shall refer to this assumption as "Sylos' Postulate" because it underlies, more or less explicitly, most of his analysis [Modigliani, 217].*

Established firms have pronounced advantages, which were cited earlier, to deter or squash entry.

Table 5-2 is based on the premise that merchant commercial plants would be integer multiples of the appropriate minimum efficient scales. That is reasonable only if those modules' sizes and our plant size data are both correct. One also would expect firms to expand capacity as integer multiples of the appropriate modules. But as neither of these expectations is always met, an explanation is needed. Inaccurate estimation of module or plant sizes aside, several possibilities deserve consideration. First, many firms may have entered or expanded without knowing the minimum efficient module size. The 1975 Arthur D. Little study apparently was a rare, too late, and not well known or widely accepted document. Many entering firms were small. They may have failed because the largest plant they could afford was too small to be competitively viable over the long run.

Starting with too small a plant may result from excessive caution, insufficient financial resources, or many other reasons, including ignorance. However, all rationales for entering an industry with too small a plant bear a trace of either willfulness or arrogance, which surely does not impart a rosy cast to the firm's prospects.

Second, given the visible economies of scale, realistic minimum plant sizes generally are significantly larger than the minimum efficient modules sizes in the Little study. Third, minimum efficient scales may have increased over time. If so, then smaller expansion increments were more advisable before than after 1975. However, entrants and smaller firms in the business probably put greater reliance on readily available information about minimum efficient capacity scales and increments--that is, past behavior of rivals--than forecasts. Fourth, some producers may opt to erect the largest man-made fibers plant affordable instead of the largest affordable multiple of the smallest efficient module. Fifth, plants may be designed and built with debottlenecking in mind, which does not preclude the other options from also influencing management's decisions.

Plant expansions by debottlenecking imply higher starting capital costs to simplify rapid expansion later if future demand warrants. That form of hedging accepts imbalances in input relationships and suboptimal costs until peak plant capacity is reached. A debottlenecking strategy exchanges higher beginning capital costs per unit of output for minimization of the total amount of capital at risk. That only makes sense when demand is uncertain, management is risk-averse, and incremental investment is feasible.

A debottlenecking strategy also can deter entry by raising industry uncertainty about a plant's, and thus the industry's, capacity and when that capacity will come on-stream, that is, creating uncertainty about the long-run equilibrium of supply and demand. A leading firm could easily compound rivals' uncertainty by including in its announcement of a new plant a deliberately vague statement to the effect that the new facility's starting capacity can be expanded, via debottlenecking, by unspecified but large increments or to an enormous size to allow rapid capture of any faster or unexpected great demand growth over its projected useful life. Such an announcement gains credibility when the firm previously made and successfully executed similar threats.

Marginal Costs

The U.S. man-made fibers industry's short-run marginal costs (SRMCs) respond to changes in capacity utilization rate (CUR). Markham reported that average marginal unit costs fell to a low point at a gradually slowing rate as a rayon plant's CUR rose from below designed levels and then soared almost vertically in response to any attempt to exceed designed or optimum values [Markham, 151].

The modern view agrees that SRMC initially falls rapidly as CUR rises; it further agrees that SRMC soars whenever CUR exceeds a critical value. But the current view holds that SRMC stays constant at a low value within an optimal CUR range. Hence, Markham's V-shaped SRMC curve has been modified into a U-shaped curve by technology and CURs. Three lines of argument support the hypothesis of a U-shaped SRMC. Those rationales are industry belief, technical conditions, and regression analysis. These are discussed below.

Middle to senior executives currently at or recently retired from U.S. man-made fiber producers with thorough knowledge of the industry's technology and their firms' costs were interviewed. All were helpful when given a pledge to respect the confidentiality of their employer's potentially proprietary information or reputation and their job or pension security. Although far more intensely concerned with average total and average variable costs than with marginal costs, these interviewees supplied guidelines to the shape of a generalized man-made fiber's average variable cost (AVC) curve. The consensus was that AVC about doubles for each 20%

decrease in CUR below the 70% threshold of the optimal CUR range, and about triples for each 5% rise in CUR beyond the 90% upper end of the optimal CUR range. If so, then the SRMC curve's shape should be similar, with the flanks to its horizontal region even more steeply sloped than the corresponding legs of the related AVC curve. This view is supported by Bremer's experience with polyester staple pricing and CUR, as described in the next chapter; the public information discussed earlier and used to develop the appended fiber cost tables; and the industry's technical character, which is discussed next. Further, it is consistent with the regression results discussed later.

The technical rationale for a U-shaped man-made fibers' SRMC curve has to be stated in steps, one each for attempts to produce at suboptimal, optimal, and superoptimal CURs. Short-run attempts to produce man-made fiber beyond the optimal 70% to 90% CUR range conflict with the process's inherent technology. Man-made fiber is extruded at a fixed rate, according to the state of the art of chemical engineering as embodied in a given plant's machinery, notably its process controls, pumps, and take-up winders. That technologically determined production speed is unique to a particular combination of generic fiber, form, and certain other physical properties, notably denier. Both production speed variations and steady operations at an inappropriate speed yield inferior quality fiber at high cost. Technology also determines peak capacity per extruder quite precisely, although the semiannually reported capacity statistics may be slightly inaccurate.

A man-made producer's exact capacity to make a given fiber simply represents a temporarily absolute ceiling to its ability to supply a specific product or product mix within a particular generic fiber family and form. The rare and brief breaches of reported capacity ceilings have several possible causes. The 1967 105.0% CUR on appended Table A3-1 illustrates this case. When demand is unexpectedly strong, the industry tries to defer scheduled maintenance to a slow period to maximize sales. Chance also intervenes in at least three ways. Unscheduled repairs, exogenously induced shutdowns, and innovations essentially are random events from this industry's viewpoint, as they happen unpredictably even within any given six-month reporting period. But every producer soon learns from experience to allow some production downtime for the first two of these eventualities to protect its reputation for honoring commitments to customers. More downtime is needed to implement innovations in product or process at a plant. True peak CUR values potentially could be overstated by roughly 5% because of lags between reaching a given capacity target and the TEB's semiannual capacity surveys.

Hence, only three basic ways exist to produce more of a given man-made fiber:

1. Run the existing extruder at normal speed for enough extra time to get the added output desired.

2. Reset the synchronized pumps and take-up winders on some extruder to operate above designed speed while hoping that product quality does not

degrade too much and that the machine does not break or wearout too fast from the increased stress.

3. Buy and install another extruder.

The last of these options is inconsistent with the SRMC concept. The last two options also may expose the firm to high-risk trade-offs. The second option gambles the possibility of a momentary small gain in output against the risk of damaging or destroying an extruder worth millions of dollars.

The 70% CUR value marking the lower end of the efficient region of a man-made fiber plant's SRMC curve results from the technology, as discussed above. The pressing issue is to explain the industry's belief that a 90% CUR marks the upper end of its optimum operating range. The rationale has two intertwined parts. First, U.S. man-made fiber producers' inescapable maintenance requirements, both pre-ventive and repair, make sustained operations above a true 90% CUR infeasible for any given fiber and form. Experience-based industry practice is to schedule two or three days yearly per extruder for routine preventive maintenance but to report annual capacity on a 52-week basis. Second, despite having many spinnerettes, a commercial extruder can only make one very precisely defined product at a time as it has only one polymer source and, until recently, only a single valued control system. However, demand for its output varies seasonally and cyclically. Fortu-nately, a man-made fiber extruder need not be permanently dedicated to one precisely defined product, although that is very efficient and done whenever possi-ble. An extruder can be stopped and reset in just a few days to make another well-defined item of given polymer, package size and type, fiber finish, and so on within a fiber family. Necessary preventive maintenance can be, and usually is, performed during such change-overs. Industry experience shows that, on average, about five weeks of an extruder's potential yearly output is lost to emergency repairs, routine maintenance, and change-overs to satisfy the variations in demand just described when these tasks are done independently.

Two sets of estimates of marginal costs were developed. The primary set of estimates of SRMCs covered two broadly defined man-made fiber industries, cellulosic and noncellulosic fibers, from 1959 through 1982. Those estimates are appended as Tables A3-1 and A3-2. The primary estimates relied on the common formula equating marginal costs to a fraction, with the year-to-year change in deflated total variable costs as its numerator and the change in total production between the same periods as its denominator. For this purpose variable costs were defined as material and fuel costs plus total direct labor payroll from the U.S. Department of Commerce's Annual Censuses of Manufactures for each subindustry. The two estimated total variable cost series were deflated, as usual, with annual GNP implicit price deflators from the Statistical Abstracts of the United States, and reported in constant 1975 dollars. Corresponding yearly output and capacity data came from the TEB's Man-Made Fiber Producers' Handbook (MMFPH). The latter series made it possible to calculate annual CURs for the two subindustries for which SRMCs could be estimated.

Both estimated SRMC series were regressed in quadratic form with CUR as the independent variable. The occasional "negative" SRMC values were not excluded because their minus sign merely denotes out-of-phase directions of change between the numerators and denominators of the fractions used, instead of the conventional interpretation, that is, a SRMC value of less than zero. The regression equation was:

$$SRMC = a + bCUR + cCUR^2$$

where a refers to the intercept value of SRMC, b is the coefficient of the linear CUR variable, and c is the coefficient of the CUR squared term. Four regressions were run, two each for cellulosic and noncellulosic man-made fibers. These two man-made fibers subindustries' deflated SRMCs were regressed over both the entire gamut of actual CURs and a narrower CUR range of 70% to 95% for the following reasons. That 70% to 95% CUR range brackets the 80% to 90% CUR the industry thinks optimal, but allows for overestimation of both CURs and the low end of the optimal range. Furthermore, as explained before in describing cost tables, U.S. man-made fiber producers' costing practices include a targeted 16% return at their presumed breakeven 80% CUR, although production would continue until CUR was expected to permanently fall below a true breakeven CUR. A simple ratio shows that a 69% CUR approximates the real breakeven level. These regressions' results are presented as Table 5-3.

The common and key result is that none of the regression coefficients or overall coefficients of determination was significant, although the signs were correct. Several explanations seem plausible. First, there may not have been enough data available to reliably discern the SRMC curve shapes. Second, the 1973-74 OPEC oil embargo clearly induced pronounced and atypically large jumps in current dollar costs of materials and fuels, which were not fully compensated for by the GNP's implicit price deflator. That oil shock equally clearly depressed man-made fiber production. Third, the SRMC data are highly aggregated for both fiber groups. Cellulosic fibers include filament and staple forms of rayon and at least filament acetate and probably some acetate staple. Noncellulosic data include both forms of fiber and a far wider variety of generic fibers. In both cases the proportions of filament to staple across generic fibers and subprocesses changed markedly, but the cost data could not be disaggregated to reflect such changes. Fourth, production is highly cyclical and the secular trends for cellulosic and noncellulosic fiber production differ. The cellulosic fiber production trend has changed significantly; its growth trend ended in 1967, as can be seen on appended Table A3-1, and become a sustained falling trend. The noncellulosic fiber production trend continued despite occasional cyclical disruptions, as is evident on appended Table A3-2. Last, each fiber, form, and process apparently has a unique minimum cost and efficient CUR operating range. Aggregating in so dynamic and uncertain a situation, although

Table 5-3

Regression Analysis of Short-Run Marginal Cost

Capacity Utilization Rate Range	Intercept	CUR	CUR^2	Overall $\bar{R}^2$	N
Cellulosics					
65.2% to 105.0%	5.5834 [0.1774]	-0.0778 [-0.1008]	0.0002 [0.0417]	0.0212	24
69.9% to 95.01%	135.3279 [1.2058]	-3.1940 [-1.1634]	0.0188 [1.1257]	0.1099	21
Noncellulosics					
54.2% to 94.5%	44.5388 [0.7714]	-1.0638 [-0.7571]	0.0063 [0.7412]	0.0298	24
69.6% to 95.01%	92.3102 [1.0173]	-2.1857 [-1.0593]	0.0129 [1.0078]	0.0501	22

Source: Author.

Notes: 1. t ratios in brackets.
      2. CUR = capacity utilization rate.

unavoidable, may have obscured the actual SRMC data so much that ordinary statistical techniques cannot discern the facts.

Although weak, these regression results are consistent with both industry belief about SRMC curve shape and the technical conditions detailed earlier. As the regression coefficients do not differ significantly from zero, SRMCs apparently fall to a low value and then hold constant over a fairly wide CUR range before rising again when CUR climbs to a maximum. Hence, this industry very probably has flat-bottomed or U-shaped SRMC curves instead of the traditional V-shape.

Do the suboptimal (that is, under 80% CUR) and superoptimal (over 90% CUR) ranges' SRMCs differ significantly from those of the optimal range of 70% to 90% CUR? Tables A3-1 and A3-2 have separate columns of absolute values of SRMCs for each such CUR range. Averages and standard deviations were computed twice for SRMCs over the suboptimal, optimal, and superoptimal CUR ranges, once for all SRMC values and again for SRMCs under $3.00 per pound as higher SRMC values were suspect. SRMCs over $3.00 per pound were considered suspect because none of the large-volume man-made fibers sold for so high a price in the period covered, but some low-volume specialty man-made fibers sold at prices far above $3.00 per pound. Cost data on the latter were included in the reports relied on as a source. These average SRMCs and standard deviations are summarized in Table 5-4.

Only one average SRMC was more than 1.96 standard deviations away from zero. None of the others differed significantly from either zero or the adjacent ranges' SRMC before or after excluding potential outlier values of SRMC. The exception was cellulosic fibers' average SRMC below $3.00 per pound for superoptimal CURs. Hence, the answer to the question in the prior paragraph is: With one exception, no significant differences were found in the average SRMCs across the suboptimal, optimal, superoptimal, overall CUR ranges across cellulosic and noncellulosic fibers with available data. However, while the data analyzed are the best available, they are subject to potential flaws owing to overaggregation, as discussed earlier.

The second set of man-made fiber SRMC estimates was derived from the data on the appended cost tables. These estimates were made as a precautionary cross-check on the aggregate SRMCs developed above. Since the cost tables' 1975 data estimates assumed an 80% CUR, they are fully comparable with the primary SRMC estimates save that these SRMCs were approximated by the minimum average variable cost (MAVC) from each cost table. For this purpose, MAVC was defined as the costs of raw materials plus energy and direct labor. Those MAVC values would be lowest at the largest merchant plant size in each cost table because of the various scale economies incorporated into the tables, as described earlier in this chapter. This alternative method yields consistently smaller SRMC estimates than those of the primary approach. However, comparisons between the primary and secondary sets of SRMC estimates have two minor flaws. First, the primary noncellulosic SRMC estimates exclude inexpensive fiberglass, but a fiberglass cost table is appended. Second, the primary SRMC estimates include expensive spe-

Table 5-4

U.S. Man-Made Fibers'

Average Short-Run Marginal Costs 1958-82

(1975 U.S. dollars per pound)

CUR Range	Cellulosics	Noncellulosics
	[1]	[2]

All SRMCs

CUR Range	Cellulosics	Noncellulosics
Under 80%	$1.388 [0.5458]	$0.906 [1.0055]
80% - 90% [b]	$0.807 [1.9123]	$1.557 [0.5149]
Over 90%	$3.198 [0.6336]	$0.375 [1.1981]
Overall [c]	$1.629 [0.5623]	$1.094 [0.5177]

All SRMCs Below $3.00 per Pound

CUR Range	Cellulosics	Noncellulosics
Under 80%	$0.548 [1.4383]	$0.906 [1.0055]
80% - 90% [b]	$0.807 [1.9123]	$0.653 [1.5221]
Over 90%	$0.678 [a] [2.3542]	$0.375 [1.1981]
Overall [c]	$0.654 [1.7487]	$0.681 [1.0879]

Sources: 1. Table A3-1.
_____ 2. Table A3-2.

Notes: a. = Significantly greater than zero
         but not from optimal range SRMC
         Value in this group of cellulosic
         fibers.
      b. Optimal CUR Range.
      c. 59.6% to 105.0% CUR for cellulosics
         and 94.2% to 94.5% CUR for noncellulo-
         sics.
      d. t ratios in brackets.

cialty man-made fibers, such as spandex, Aramids, Teflon, carbon fibers, and so on, for which it was not possible to develop cost tables. Such specialty fibers' capital and raw materials costs are much higher than those of ordinary man-made fibers. Hence, inclusion of these newer fibers' costs undoubtedly raises the primary SRMC estimates. But the size of the distortion is unknowable, just as is the effect of the excluded and included fibers on the CURs used in conjunction with the primary SRMC estimates for noncellulosic fibers.

The information developed above confirms Markham's finding that man-made fibers' short-run marginal costs (SRMCs) fall to a minimum as CURs rise out of the suboptimal range but differ at CUR values above the lower limit of the optimal CUR range. That lower limit to the optimal operating range is at least 69% CUR and may be, as the industry sometimes claims, 80% CUR. Our information shows that SRMC remains at a minimum value until CUR exceeds the upper end of the optimal CUR range. That upper limit is at least 90% CUR and may be as much as 95% CUR. Then, SRMC rises at an accelerating rate as production moves up through the superoptimal range to a theoretical maximum of 100% CUR.

Minimum SRMC values for fiberglass and Type 6, 6 nylon filament were combined with the generalized AVC curve's slopes in order to estimate lower envelopes to the nonhorizontal parts of their SRMC curves to develop illustrative low- and high-value SRMC curves for the complete family of major man-made fibers. Those SRMC curves appear as Figure 5-1.

Figure 5-1
U.S. Man-Made Fibers SRMCs

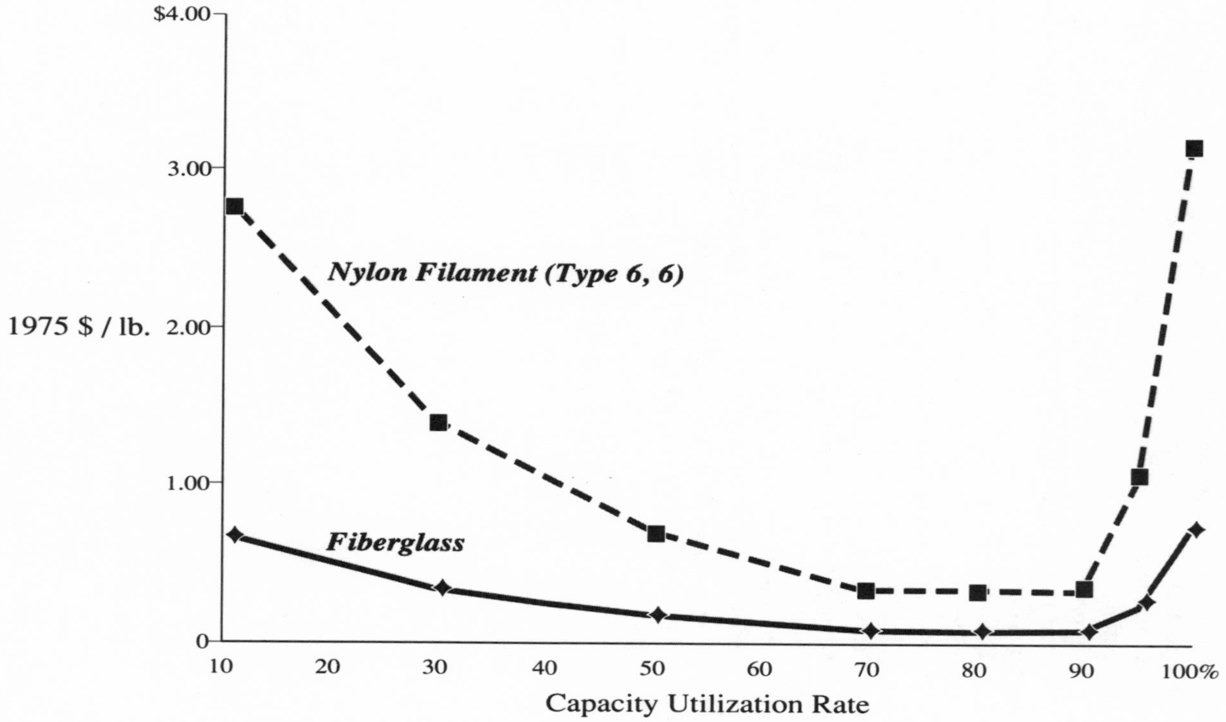

CONCLUSIONS

Logic and anecdotal evidence prove that the U.S. man-made fibers industry's firms are differentiated into a multilevel hierarchy. DuPont alone occupies the top of the hierarchy. Some less distinguished rivals compose a distant second tier. A third tier of differentiated firms also exists and contains newer, smaller, specialty or limited product line firms. Captive producers form yet another tier.

Demonstrable differentiation across both firms and products' physical, market, and cost traits leads to the conclusion that the U.S. man-made fibers industry and its subindustries exemplify differentiated oligopolies. Whether this structure is workably competitive becomes a key issue once the industry clearly is not perfectly competitive. However, resolution of that issue depends on evidence about pricing and performance, which are discussed in later chapters.

Cost structures were derived from public data for all major U.S. man-made fibers and forms. Those realistic 1975 costs per pound were recalculated at various actual minimum, average, and maximum plant sizes to find the effect of those economies of scale and integration that could be quantified. That information was used to generate planning curves for the various fibers and forms, make realistic estimates of their minimum efficient plant scales, and trace the patterns of capital intensity as capital/labor ratios.

At the largest actual plant sizes attained over the 1959-82 period, U.S. man-made fiber costs ranged from a low of $0.274 per pound for polyester staple via the dimethyl terephthalate (DMT) process to a high of $1.274 per pound for diacetate process staple. However, the maximum scale for such acetate plants is so small that a less biased comparison results from a contrast between DMT process polyester and the $0.773 cost per pound of the second most expensive fiber, which was Type 6, 6 nylon 70 denier filament. When fiber costs at maximum actual plant scales are arrayed in ascending order, the differences between adjacent costs ranged from a low of $0.005 per pound between the rayon and olefin filaments, or a 1.1% increase, to a high of $0.501 between Type 6,6 nylon 70 denier filament and diacetate process staple, a 64.8% increase. The average cost differential was $0.067 per pound in absolute terms and 11.6% in relative terms. The U.S. man-made fiber cost differentials are another indication of this industry's heterogeneous character.

The net effect of measurable economies of scale and integration is to lower total costs per pound of man-made fiber by at least 46% and perhaps as much as 89% when the decline in total costs is measured from the smallest to the largest actual plant sizes of each generic fiber, process, and form. The effect of all the other potential sources of economies was not assessed. Economies of scale and other entry barriers undoubtedly go far in explaining the persistent natural oligopoly in each of this industry's key fiber families and forms.

> *The rayon industry is an oligopoly. ... Perhaps the chief limitation to the number of firms is an economic one: the shape of the long-run cost curve for the firm, at least to the extent that it is indicated by*

> *available plant cost curves and other data, places the rayon industry*
> *among the natural oligopolies [Markham, 193].*

U.S. man-made fibers' SRMC are quite low relative to average total costs per pound for both cellulosics and noncellulosics. Minimum average variable costs (MAVC) derived from cost tables for each major generic fiber and form were used to check the primary SRMC estimates. Raw material costs account for the major part of each MAVC, followed by direct labor costs and energy costs. Industry belief, technological considerations, and quadratic regression analyses suggest that cellulosic and noncellulosic man-made fibers' SRMC curves fall to and then remain at a minimum in their optimal CUR operating region. The industry places that optimal CUR region between 80% and 90% CUR. Our analysis widened that range to 70% to 90% and suggests that it may be as wide as 69% to 95% CUR. Outside of that technologically determined optimal CUR region, SRMC reportedly rises with increasing rapidity as CUR diverges toward either 0% or 100% values, as Markham reported earlier. Industry descriptions of a representative average variable cost curve for man-made fibers about double average variable costs for each 20% decrement in CUR from the minimum optimal CUR, and about triple such costs for each 5% increment in CUR above the maximum optimal CUR.

6

Price Competition

This chapter discusses four main points about price competition in the U.S. man-made fibers industry. The first two of those concern prices' secular trends and shorter-term rigidity. Price types and structure constitute a third important issue. Pricing strategies and practices represent the last aspect of price competition to be discussed.

SECULAR TRENDS

Rayon list prices underwent a significant secular decline, according to Markham [Markham, 7]. Did this secular decline in real price continue after 1948, or is it merely a phenomenon associated with the embryonic and growth stages of such product's life cycle? Either a horizontal or rising price trend is possible, too. Which of these three trends best fits the newer man-made fibers' prices?

Three groups of 21 price series were collected, deflated, and regressed against time to test their slopes for significant departures from zero, that is, a horizontal trend. The 21 regressions' results are presented in Table 6-1. The regression price data were classified into one of three groups according to source and character on Table 6-1.

Eight list price series, complied from monthly issues of the now defunct Modern Textiles magazine, formed one group. These series were chosen both to represent the largest-volume fiber genera and forms and to be large-volume items in those categories for the longest possible spans between 1948 and 1972. A 150 denier rayon series also was included to directly reassess the product Markham used in his secular trend test. Modern Textiles stopped publishing list prices in early 1973. As its tables of prices increased from roughly four in the early years to over 20 this public service became too onerous to sustain without support from the man-made fiber producers. Those firms were loath to subsidize such an effort as they already gave complete

Table 6-1

Deflated (1) Prices' Regression (2) Statistics

Product Description	Intercept	t Ratio	Trend Coefficient	$\bar{R}^2$	Period Covered
List Prices (a)					
Acrylic/modacrylic: 3 denier per filament (dpf) staple	2.8617	73.3761	-0.0841	0.9210	1950 - 1972
Fiberglass: DE 150/11/1Z, multifilament on beams	1.1763	15.7330	-0.0240	0.9183	1962 - 1966
Nylon: 70/0.5Z/SD regular tenacity, round cross-section	3.6895	70.0950	-0.0779	0.9593	1948 - 1972
Nylon: 15 dpf bright, regular tenacity, not crimpset, 3 to 4.5 inch long staple	2.9077	24.1999	-0.0893	0.9120	1954 - 1972
Olefin: 840/0.5Z	1.9050	72.0926	-0.0404	0.9915	1962 - 1972
Polyester: 150/ low twist/ regular tenacity, round cross-section	4.3614	26.7630	-0.1117	0.8981	1954 - 1972
Polyester: 1.5 dpf/SD/ 1 to 5 inch long staple	3.7705	31.8899	-0.1320	0.9590	1954 - 1972
Rayon: 150/ regular tenacity, multifilament twisted on weaving cones	1.4569	77.4087	-0.0171	0.8990	1948 - 1972
Price Indices					
BLS' Man-Made Fiber Yarns and Fiber Price Index (1957-59=100) (b)	213.4977	111.4779	-5.3240	0.9819	1947 - 1963
BLS' Rayon Yarn (Viscose and Cuprammonium Process) (1972=100) (b)	146.4806	18.5744	-0.6438	0.1540	1958 - 1982
BLS' Non-Cellulosic Organic Fiber Price Index (1967=100) (b)	189.5715	17.1984	-3.4667	0.8548	1967 - 1982
duPont's Domestic Fiber Price Index (1967=100) (c)	340.4923	47.6878	-9.1962	0.9565	1947 - 1982

Average Spot Prices for Branded Man-Made Fibers (d)

Acetate: 55 denier multifilament, for tricot knitting	0.5400	4.6086	0.0040	0.0846	1971 - 1985
Acetate: 150 denier multifilament for weaving	0.6842	15.2609	-0.0017	0.1034	1971 - 1985
Rayon: 1.5 dpf regular tenacity staple	0.3080	3.3226	0.0021	0.0401	1971 - 1985
Polyester: 150 denier multifilament feed yarn for texturing	2.7028	5.9212	-0.0654	0.6222	1971 - 1985
Polyester staple:	0.4123	6.0413	-0.0015	0.0396	1971 - 1985
Nylon: 40/SD/ round multifilament on tricot beams	1.2863	5.7436	-0.0088	0.1099	1971 - 1985
Nylon: 2,000 to 3,000/ Type 6 multifilament for carpet	0.9505	5.4268	-0.0082	0.1523	1971 - 1985
Nylon: 18 dpf/ Type 6 staple for carpet	0.5052	2.4839	0.0006	0.0007	1971 - 1985
Acrylic: duPont's 2.5 dpf/ Type 75 Orlon for cotton system processing	0.8846	7.6730	-0.0122	0.4726	1971 - 1985
Acrylic: duPont's 15-20 dpf/ Type 42 Orlon for worsted system processing	0.4606	3.2119	0.0018	0.0118	1971 - 1985

Sources: a. List prices refer to data published in various monthly issues of Modern Textiles magazine between January 1948 and December 1972 for first-quality, branded fibers bought in truckload amounts for spot delivery and unadjusted for discounts, allowances, and so on.
b. U.S. Department of Labor, Bureau of Labor Statistics.
c. Courtesy of the Textile Fibers Department of E. I. duPont De Nemours & Company, Incorporated.
d. Courtesy of the Johnson Redbook Service of Prescott, Ball & Turben, Inc. of New York City.

Notes: 1. Prices were deflated with the GNP implicit price deflator (1972 = 100). Monthly price data were annualized with simple unweighted averages in the absence of poundata for those specific goods.
2. Ordinary single-stage, least-squares, linear regressions were calculated with time in years as the independent variable and either deflated to 1972 U.S. dollars per pound or used as index numbers.

and current tables of their individual list prices to customers. U.S. man-made fiber manufacturers' refusal to subsidize publication of list prices implicitly acknowledged buyers' long-standing objections to highly condensed list price tables, which greatly differed from trading prices. Moreover, abbreviated list price tables fostered the illusion of homogeneous products, as all suppliers of each specific item normally strove to maintain identical list prices while their selling prices differed.

Price indices from two sources were compiled to form the second group. The three longest and most typical Bureau of Labor Statistics (BLS) price series were chosen from the many such brief series in various U.S. Department of Labor publications. One such index provides an overview of the U.S. man-made fibers industry's prices; another deals exclusively with rayon prices; the third concentrates on noncellulosic fibers' prices. BLS man-made fiber price series have long been subject to intense, and regrettably, often justified criticism. The fourth index in the group is duPont's domestic fiber price index. E. I. duPont DeNemours and Company's Textile Fibers Department responded favorably to a request from the author for data from their Selling Price Index.

The duPont letter transmitting that data to the author described that series as follows:

> *The Textile Fibers Department Domestic Sales Price Index is a statistical measure of the change in prices of products sold by the Department. The Index related prices prevailing in a given period to those prevailing a base period through the use of annually revised fixed weights to reflect changes in the mix of products sold and a December chaining formula, and also permits the comparison of any two periods through their separate relationships to the base. Data used to develop the Index are generated from the accounting records of the Department [that is, invoices and related documents].*

The duPont domestic price index is a very long, consistently prepared series from the only producer to develop and publicly release such data.

The Johnson Redbook Service (a Division of Prescott, Ball & Turben of Manhattan) allowed the author to compile monthly averages of its commercially published spot trading price series. That firm collects its price data by telephone surveys of major U.S. textile mills. It has published on-going man-made fiber price series since January 1971. These spot trading price series were a matter of Hobson's choice; all those available were used.

All price series were deflated with the gross national product implicit price deflator series based on 1972 = 100. Monthly price data were annualized with simple unweighted averages because of the absence of product specific poundage data. DuPont's domestic price series already was in annual form.

Several distinct rationales support the claim that the few series used adequately represent the price trends of their generic fiber families. First, Markham (1952) set the precedent for applying this technique to this industry by using 150 denier rayon prices to assess the industry'sprice trend. Second, it would be an intolerable burden to collect and analyze all the prices. Last, the BLS, the organization most experienced in collecting and analyzing price data, "lets the well defined product represent the class of the product" [Stigler and Kindahl, 5].

Ordinary single-stage, least-squares linear regressions were calculated with time in years as the only independent variable and deflated annual prices in either U.S. dollars per pound or index numbers as the dependent variable. Standard "t" tests of the regressions' slope coefficients were done. If the result had both an appropriate negative sign and an absolute value above 1.96, then and only then was the slope interpreted as a significant secularly declining trend for the particular product series.

All 12 price series in the first two groups of Table 6-1 show statistically significant secular declines. This result extends the validity of Markham's finding into the early 1970s.

But evaluation of a third group of nine more recent series shows that by the early 1980s, the established falling price trend was no longer a general rule but a characteristic of newer fibers. Regressions of the nine spot trading price series against time yielded mixed results, as shown in the lower part of Table 6-1. Six of these nine series had negative slopes (150 denier but only two polyester and feed yarn duPont's Type 75, 2.5 denier per filament Orlon staple for cotton system processing) were significant. The other seven series in this group effectively had slopes of zero.

Several conclusions follow from the U.S. man-made fibers' secular trends. First, until at least the early 1970s, the hypothesis of a declining secular price trend remained valid. Second, the older fibers' real prices apparently began to level off after the early 1970s. A declining secular pricetrend cannot last eventually it must either level off or climb. Thus man-made fibers' price trends have passed a notable turning point.

CYCLICAL BEHAVIOR

Introduction

Markham found man-made fibers' list prices to be rigid in the shorter run and less flexible over the cycle than cotton prices but not totally inflexible [Markham, 126-27, 143, 164]. Man-made fibers' price flexibility is discussed below in terms of the short run first and then over the cycle.

Short-Run Price Rigidity

A neutral standard was needed to find out whether man-made fibers' prices are flexible or rigid in the short run. Markham found rayon's short-run prices rigid because they met an accepted definition of administered prices [Markham, 108].

A cotton price series was adopted as the standard of competitive price flexibility for the following reasons. First, cotton prices are competitive since only one widely traded, fairly homogeneous quality grade of cotton is involved, and prices of the many other grades of cotton tend to parallel it. Average spot trading prices of cotton were taken from the Commodity Year Book of the Commodity Research Bureau of New York City. The cotton prices quoted refer to strict low midding 1 1/16 inch-long cotton staple of grade 41 after August 1975. Through July 1951 the prices refer to cotton of midding 15/16 inch. Between August 1951 and July 1975, the cotton prices refer to midding 1 inch. The cotton grading criteria and terms changed over the years, but these three staple lengths and quality grades are apparently accepted by both the trade and the publisher as comparable. The latest grade reportedly accounts for by far the largest volume of some 80 presently recognized, distinct grades of U.S. grown cotton and is the only one for which so long a price series exists. The prices used are averages across all local U.S. cotton markets in each month.

Second, cotton is supplied by many small and more geographically dispersed farmers than there are man-made fiber producers. Third, cotton historically had little, if any, nonprice product or supplier differentiation activity. Fourth, essentially continuous auction markets throughout the country set cotton prices in a multitude of small transactions. Last, cotton is consumed in almost all 44 major end-uses tracked by the TEB and those end-uses consume all domestically sold man-made fibers.

Between 1948 and 1985, reported cotton prices varied from the prior month at every opportunity but two. Man-made fibers' list prices seldom were a tenth as dynamic. Between 1971 and 1985, man-made fibers' average spot trading prices were about five times more volatile than list prices, with changes from the prior months occasionally happening as often as three times per year. Percentage changes in cotton prices tended to be much larger than man-made fibers' even when the latter prices were about the same level as cotton's. Percentage changes in man-made fibers' prices from the prior month rarely exceed 10% and typically occur in 5% increments. Hence, man-made fibers' short-run prices clearly remain administered because they still are not as responsive to fluctuations in short-run supply and demand conditions as they could be.

Cyclical Price Rigidity

Markham observed that 150 denier rayon's list price series tended to fall in recessions and to partly, but not fully, recover in later expansions. The reality of heterogeneous, nonsubstituting natural and man-made fibers, with producers of the latter favoring rationing near temporary cyclical peaks instead of letting price serve as an allocator, does not fit the picture established by Markham. Two alternative hypotheses are offered and discussed in turn.

Hypothesis I: Prices Respond to CUR Fluctuations. This hypothesis was advanced by Charles Bremer while at Chemstrand in the 1960s. He graphed polyester staple prices against that industry's monthly capacity utilization rates (CURs) and found the apparent cyclical correlation worth exploring. Bremer learned that polyester staple's invoiced prices always fell once that product's CUR remained below an 80% threshold for three consecutive months. He also noted that those polyester staple prices usually, but not always, were raised after its CUR had exceeded 90% for a similar interval. Bremer found that polyester staple price hikes were only sought when the industry expected to operate for an unforeseeably long time, that is, "permanently," at more than a 90% CUR. As an employee of a leading U.S. man-made fiber producer with a vested interest in pricing advantageously, Bremer could monitor the industry's CUR expectations by a combination of personal contacts among other Chemstrand employees and by tracking TEB data on industry capacity expansion plans, inventory, and shipments. TEB restricted that information to the man-made fiber producers until the late 1970s. Bremer believed that U.S. polyester plants earn above-normal profits at CURs over 80% and cannot sustain CURs above 90%. Hence, the industry has little incentive to vary prices when its CUR lies within a narrow 80% to 90% CUR range and even less inclination to do so when it expects to only briefly operate at CURs above 90%.

Bremer also noted that temporary shortages (that is, when CUR was expected to only briefly exceed 90%) were handled by allocating output according to textile mills' established shares of their polyester staple suppliers' output. Bremer informally but repeatedly successfully tested his polyester staple price hypothesis empirically over 20 years for his employers, first Chemstrand and then West Point Pepperell, but did not generalize it to other man-made fibers.

Some practical considerations limit any test of a generalization of Bremer's theory. Today one could not match Bremer's access to invoiced, instead of list or spot trading prices, and industry CUR expectations, unless employed at a comparable or superior level in either a U.S. man-made fiber producer or a leading textile mill. The industry's capacity and expansion plans, inventories, and shipment data, which only became generally available for a fee from the TEB in the late 1970s, continue to have restricted circulation even within those organizations. Moreover, access to those data is necessary but not sufficient. Experience and detailed, intimate knowledge of industry conditions also are essential to convert those data to reliable signals of the industry's CUR expectations. Questions about the expansion timing and inventory issues, such as commercial quality level and the proportion of voluntary versus involuntary inventory accumulation, still are beyond the ken of most monitors of and executives in the industry. Hence, no outside observer has had or can get as consistently reliable an indicator of fiber producers' CUR expectations as Bremer devised. That restricts our test of Bremer's hypothesis to price cuts. Even then one must rely on less accurate, publicly available spot trading prices. Bremer, however, had access to invoiced prices covering purchases for spot delivery and orders subject to various discounts, discussed later in this chapter, and scheduled for later delivery. His prices were therefore much closer to effective prices for a much greater volume of fiber than is sold for spot delivery. As will be shown later, both list and spot trading prices are considerably higher than effective prices.

Six price series were generated and examined to see if Bremer's experience held true for all major man-made fibers and forms with publicly available list or spot trading prices when using actual instead of expected CUR data. Average spot price data for acetate filament, acrylic staple, nylon filament, nylon staple, polyester filament, and polyester staple did not show the relationship evident in Bremer's original graph. Two factors limited the man-made fiber genera and forms that could be examined in this way. One was the availability of average spot price series as proxies for invoiced prices and the period covered by those series. A second constraint was imposed by the varying availability of CUR data by fiber and form.

Examination of the six series did, however, clarify certain points.

1. The man-made fibers and forms' CURs examined are unambiguously cyclical.
2. Those CUR cycles were visibly distinct. They differed sharply in timing (onset, end, and duration) and amplitude.
3. Four pronounced recessions, that is, sustained operations below 80% CUR, were common to at least four of the six products. Those major recessions' dates were: 1966-67; 1970; 1974-75; and 1981-83. All six fibers' CURs fell drastically in 1974-75 and 1981-83. Acetate filament escaped the other two general man-made fiber industry recessions, while nylon filament escaped the 1966-67 contraction.
4. CURs of 95% or more are rare and of brief duration. Acetate filament set the record (seven months) for the longest run of operations at 95% CUR or better, followed by nylon staple with a maximum run of six months. Nylon filament's longest such run lasted five months. Acrylic staple's greatest such run was but four months long. Those for staple and filament polyester were even shorter--three and two months.
5. These six fibers' CURs usually remained in the 80% to 90% range.
6. Price rises did not visually correlate well with sustained CURs of 90% or more.
7. Price decreases are somewhat visually correlated to prior sustained CURs under 80% but neither very consistently nor strongly.
8. When it persists for at least three months, CUR direction of movement seems a better predictor of price changes' timing and direction than CUR levels.
9. Current spot trading prices later usually more than recouped any recessionary cuts but did so only gradually. The exception was polyester filament.
10. Current dollar declines in spot price tended to be rarer but larger and faster than current dollar price rises.

Thus neither list nor spot prices for U.S. man-made fibers move with CUR. Those prices remain stable within an 70% to 90% CUR range, and possibly over a 70% to 95% range, and do not necessarily go up or down outside that range.

Hypothesis II: Man-Made Fiber Prices Move with Cotton Prices. Two independent variables, cotton prices and rayon filament's CUR, were cited by Markham as explaining the cyclical variability of 150 denier rayon filament near cyclical troughs to 1948. Stepwise multiple linear regression was used to see if those two independent variables explained any significant amount of more recent cyclical changes in rayon filament or any other large-volume man-made fibers' deflated prices. The analytical procedure and a few particularly notable results are briefly described next.

Fourteen man-made fiber and form price series were subjected to the same stepwise, multiple linear regression procedure involving all 32 plausible independent variables derivable from changes in deflated cotton prices and the CURs of the man-made fiber and form whose deflated price change was the dependent variable. It was not possible to calculate CURs for rayon. The TEB no longer publishes the necessary monthly data since too few manufacturers remain and releasing such data equates to either signalling business data between supposedly competing firms, with attendant antitrust risks for all involved, or revealing company confidential data, which risks ruining TEB's reputation. Hence, CURs of other man-made fibers of appropriate form were used as proxies for rayon's CURs in this analysis. For reasons of availability, list price data of various duration over the period of June 1948 through December 1972 were used for seven man-made fibers, while average monthly spot trading prices from June 1971 through December 1985 were used for another seven fibers. Three sets of independent variables were created for cotton prices; three similar sets were generated for CURs, plus dummy variables for CURs below 80% or over 90%. These potential independent variables are listed and defined in appended Table A4-1.

The independent variables accounting for the greatest percentage change in a given dependent price series were automatically chosen by the computer program subject to entry and retention conditions of a 0.25 level of significance to establish the most potent explanatory equation from the available independent variables for each case. These regressions' total and partial coefficients of determination were consistently unimpressive. Those results are detailed in appended Table A4-2. The overall results are summarized in Table 6-2 and briefly discussed in the next few paragraphs.

The highest overall coefficient of determination, 0.4512, was found for 1.5 denier per filament (dpf) polyester staple's list prices (equation IX in Table 6-2), but its more important independent variables did not support Bremer's hypothesis. The three next best overall R squares were: 0.2903 for 150 denier rayon list prices, equation XI; 0.2063 for 150 denier acetate average spot trading prices, equation III; and 0.2030 for 70 denier nylon filament list prices, equation IV. The remaining overall R squares were even poorer, with the lowest value, 0.0429, in equation VI for 2,000 denier Type 6 nylon filament for carpet.

Table 6-2

Summary of Regression Results of Man-Made Fibers' Cyclical Price Behavior

Equation [1]	Generic Fiber (Dependent Variable) Family	Form [2]	Price [3]	Number of Data Points Used	Number of Independent Variables Selected	$\bar{R}^2$	F	Probability of Getting a Greater F Value	Significance Level
I	Acetate	F	T	163	7	0.1742	4.67	0.0001	**
II	Acetate	F	T	163	7	0.2063	5.75	0.0001	**
III	Acrylic	S	L	115	6	0.1130	2.29	0.0402	I
IV	Nylon	F	L	115	6	0.2030	4.58	0.0003	**
V	Nylon	F	T	175	4	0.0847	3.93	0.0044	*
VI	Nylon	F	T	175	3	0.0429	2.43	0.0657	I
VII	Nylon	S	T	115	7	0.1889	3.56	0.0018	*
VIII	Nylon	S	T	175	5	0.1084	4.11	0.0016	*
IX	Polyester	S	L	79	8	0.4514	7.20	0.0001	**
X	Polyester	S	T	175	5	0.1780	7.32	0.0001	**
XI-A	Rayon	F	L	295	5	0.2903	23.64	0.0001	**
XI-B	Rayon	F	L	115	8	0.1503	2.34	0.0232	I
XI-C	Rayon	F	L	115	8	0.2088	3.50	0.0013	*
XII-A	Rayon	S	T	175	7	0.1334	3.67	0.0010	*
XII-B	Rayon	S	T	175	12	0.1920	3.21	0.0004	**
XII-C	Rayon	S	T	175	6	0.1190	3.78	0.0015	*

Source: Table A4-2

Notes: * = significant at 0.01; ** = significant at 0.001; I = not significant at 0.01.
1. For details see the correspondingly numbered equation on Table A4-2.
2. F = filament; S = Staple
3. L = list; T = average spot trading.

Thirteen of the 16 overall F values were significant at the 0.01 level or better. However, the generally low overall and partial coefficients of determination did not support the logical extension of Markham's hypothesis to the effect that cotton prices influence other man-made fibers.

Although in principle the computer program might have selected any or all independent variables, it chose from three to 12 independent variables to build each of the equations.

The most frequently picked independent variable was used only six times and seldom was the most potent. After excluding five, never selected, potential variables, the average usage of any potential independent variable was three times. The chosen independent variables' relative impotence is evident from their low partial R squares. Only twice did a partial R square exceed 0.0883. Equation XI (150 denier rayon) was a notable exception, as DELTACP (changes in deflated current month's cotton prices from the prior month) had a partial R square of 0.2692, the highest such value obtained from these equations. Equation IX (1.5 dpf polyester staple) was the other exception; there, XDIF3 (the change in the change of deflated cotton prices lagged three months from the current month) had a partial R square of 0.2493. In sum, this analysis shows that no independent variable based on either cotton prices or a given man-made fiber's CUR, or any combination of them, adequately explains the behavior of any man-made fiber's list or spot trading prices at any peak, trough, expansion, or contraction phase of their CUR cycles between 1948 and 1985.

While list prices between 1948 and 1972 generally did not show it, U.S. man-made fiber's average spot trading prices were at least somewhat responsive to CUR cycle conditions after 1976, although they were neither completely nor symmetrically flexible. A theoretically sound examination of the cyclical behavior of man-made fibers' effective prices or their available crude proxy, average spot trading prices, depends on surmounting two sets of obstacles. The first such set involves data problems including:

- a paucity of reliable price data on a sufficiently large number of transactions, products, and subproducts;
- lagged responses to demand changes;
- gathering enough data on each of the variables identified.

The second set of obstacles derives from the current state of economic theory. As yet there is no sound theory to cope with problems of the following kinds, which routinely occur in this industry:

- persistent price inelasticities deterring reliance on price as an allocator;
- the presence of annual purchase contracts plus enduring business relationships and incidents of pronounced government intervention;
- the important role played by management expectations or forecasting skills;
- a continuing reliance on some form of price leadership.

Hence, current economic theory implies a relationship between a man-made cyclical price and the prices of suspected substitutes and complements (such as, cotton) and other putative demand determinants that may not be detected in available data because they either do not exist or appear in unanticipated ways.

In sum, two different analyses of man-made fibers' shorter-run pricing flexibility were considered. Short-run man-made fiber prices remained inflexible after 1948, as Markham proved for rayon before 1948. However, neither the cyclical relationships at the troughs with either cotton or CUR previously reported by Markham for 150 denier rayon nor those Bremer detected for polyester staple were supported at a significant level by publicly available data.

PRICE STRUCTURES

Introduction

The U.S. man-made fibers industry normally sells each of its products over a remarkably wide range of prices to fit subtle but important distinctions in product quality, associated services, and the specific producer's character. A complex structure of adjustments further widens those price ranges. These points are discussed below.

Prices for the "Same" Product

Every producer of a first-quality, branded man-made fiber publishes a list price for spot delivery in truckload amounts; these prices tend to be identical across producers. List prices are called "wish prices" by the trade. The latter term arose once it became known that, save for specialty and very new items, producers aspire to these prices but do not seriously expect to get them.

A second set of prices, the real asking prices for spot delivery in truckload amounts, would be more useful. However, such prices have not been published by man-made fiber producers. Published list prices presumably sufficed in the past. As explained earlier, the Johnson Redbook Service estimates and publishes spot trading prices monthly for a few representative fibers within key man-made fiber genera and forms.

Invoiced prices represent a third set of prices. These obviously are not published. They vary temporally and by item. Invoiced prices are negotiated order by order and, more important, are subject to myriad interactive terms. Thus, invoiced prices are well below list and spot trading prices but generally quite a bit above net or effective prices. The more important of those interactive terms include but are not limited to:

- discounts for both order size and cumulative volumes bought in a given year;
- quality allowances;
- promotional and other subsidies;
- adjustments of package types;
- various premiums for specific options;
- liability for defective products.

Details on these points seldom are written, let alone publicized, but, as will be shown, they profoundly influence the net prices received by U.S. man-made fiber producers.

The above variables' most important practical and theoretical consequence is that they totally obscure net or effective prices at both the time of sale and, with certain added complications, afterward. One such major complication arises from textile mills' practice of paying many invoices with a single check. The time span needed to first convert fibers into salable final products and then to sell those goods is long--often more than a year and sometimes as much as three years. That exposes all man-made producers' receipts to potentially huge contingent liabilities, as described in Chapter 3, for years after the textile mill has paid for its fiber purchases. The most potent obscuring force arises from each producer offering cumulative volume discounts across its fiber forms and genera. Merchant U.S. man-made fiber producers thus function with no more than extremely crude estimates of their actual net asking and effective net prices for every specific fiber product. Whether this ignorance continues as a matter of choice or results from external forces and the reasons for it are as yet unresolved questions. It does, however, make the business of buying and selling U.S. man-made fibers one of the most bizarre bazaars known.

Man-made fiber prices normally involve a simple set of terms of trade but a complex and interactive structure of adjustments. Most of the information in the next six paragraphs was excerpted from notes to the monthly list price tables in various issues of Modern Textiles magazine.

Terms of Trade

U.S. man-made fibers are sold on net 30-day terms, without discounts for cash. Poor credit risks may have to prepay. Owners of smaller textile mills frequently have to personally guarantee payment. Prices are FOB the shipper's loading dock. The owner of the delivery truck used, or his insurance company, bears intransit liability.

Premiums and Discounts

Man-made fiber producers have institutionalized many standard price adjustments. Nine standard premium charges are:

1. packaging on cones, $0.05 per pound, instead of on returnable pirns;
2. plying filament yarns, $0.05 per pound;
3. twisting filament yarns on a turn per inch (TPI) basis:
   - $0.10 per pound for 2 TPI
   - $0.13 per pound for 3 TPI
   - $0.16 per pound for 4 TPI
   - $0.19 per pound for 5 TPI;
4. dyeability characteristics:
   - cationic dyeable fiber $0.15 per period above standard anionic
   - deep dyeable fiber $0.08 per pound above regular fiber;
5. small orders, that is, less than a truck load of about 6,000 pounds of fiber exclusive of packaging, $0.05 per pound;
6. bright luster fiber $0.10 per pound over semi-dull or dull prices;
7. multilobal cross-sections $0.10 per pound versus round fibrils or filaments;
8. producer-dyed fiber premiums vary by color (darker colors command greater prices), and dyeing process
   - packaged dyed yarns earn some $0.30 to $0.40 per pound over undyed fiber
   - solution-dyed fibers command $0.75 to $0.85 per pound more than undyed fiber;
9. producer textured yarns carry a premium of about $0.15 per pound over corresponding feed yarns.

Several distinct premium charges commonly apply simultaneously to a given order for a specific fiber. First-quality fiber sold with the producer's brand and bearing promotional support funds from or promotional activities by the producer merits a negotiated premium. That premium's size, total amount, how and when it will be spent, and who controls the spending are settled in intense bargaining sessions on a deal-by-deal basis. Promotional allowances often range from $0.25 to $0.50 per pound but may be as large as $1.00 per pound. Promotional "subsidies of up to 50 per cent have been common" [Tisdell and McDonald, 32].

Quality discounts are granted or demanded for both tangible defects and intangible ones. An unbranded, first-quality man-made fiber usually sells for $0.05 per pound under the price for spot delivery in truckload quantities for the same supplier's branded version of that item without promotional support. Second-grade fiber usually sells at least 10% below such first-quality, unbranded prices. Second-grade fiber may be discounted by another $0.20 per pound or more, depending on the nature and severity of its specific quality defect(s). Arbitrary downgrading of all or part of an order's quality also occurs either to save face or "justify" a discount to meet a key customer's needs or a rival's effort to buy entry or volume.

Order size discounts typically start at one million pounds and reappear at the three and five million pound levels. These discounts reportedly evoke progressive $0.05 per pound stepped cuts from the spot price. The large take-or-pay contracts discussed in Chapter 3 are extreme cases of order size discounts involving huge, irrevocable annual orders at correspondingly reduced prices.

Two common types of cumulative volume discounts exist. One applies to annual purchases of any specific product from a given supplier exceeding one, three, or five million pound totals. The other applies to similar total yearly purchases from a given supplier across generic fibers and forms. Both discounts reportedly offer a $0.05 per pound increment at each stage.

Estimated Average Net Price

The general effect of this elaborate structure of discounts and premiums on a firm's true net prices can be approximated. Two different methods were tried as cross-checks. The first approach involved developing two such estimates, termed Proxy I and Proxy II, from available 1975 data for acrylic staple, Type 6 nylon filament and staple, and PTA process polyester filament and staple.

Proxy I equated net selling prices to the average costs at mean plant sizes in the appended cost tables. Proxy I assumes that discounts might be granted until prices decline to the point at which normal profits would be eroded. Essentially, Proxy I represents the industry's view of its break-even price.

Proxy II's values further reduce those of Proxy I. Specifically, Proxy II's discounted prices equate to Proxy I's after eliminating both the 16% target returns on capital and half of the sales, administrative, and research expenses (SARE). This puts Proxy II closer to a true break-even figure.

List prices for 1975 were estimated because, for reasons stated above, they were no longer published. Those estimates of 1975 list prices were made by adding presumably constant differentials between the various 1971-72 average list prices and the average spot trading prices in the same time span to the corresponding 1975 average spot trading prices.

While the individual results of the first method's estimates range from a 2.8% apparent net premium to a 48.7% net discount, averages of Proxies I and II across the three genera and two forms conservatively show general net discounts of 25.7% and 40.0%, respectively. Historically, that is too conservative due to underestimation of list prices and the absolute size of the net discounts allowed.

Costs at mean plant sizes were used instead of either minimum costs at the largest plant size or the costs at the lower of the mean or modal plant sizes. The cost tables probably contain overstated components, except possibly the targeted returns, and so have potentially overstated totals; however, this systematic bias' size is unknown. The frequency of subsidies probably is less than 5% instead of the 10% figure used, and sales at spot trading prices probably are correspondingly rare. Thus, average discounts probably apply to 90% of real sales instead of the 80% figure used. Another potential bias arises from assuming 70 denier nylon filament's costs essentially are the same as 2,000 denier nylon filament for carpet for which average spot trading price data exist. As lower-denier yarns are disproportionately harder to make, they cost more to produce and so command much higher prices in order to maintain profit margins. Suitable corrections for this last point surely would enlarge the absolute discounts for nylon filament. The negative discount shown for Proxy I's nylon staple is but an alias for a premium. It signals that this item's cost estimates are overstated, if 1971-72 list prices are much below the estimated 1975 cost to manufacture this product. The approximate 30% differential between both Proxy I's and II's discounted values for polyester filament and staple suggest that the nylon staple figures should show much larger actual discounts. Furthermore, at the depths of a recent past recession, John N. Gregg, chairman of Avtex and one of the industry's most senior executives, publicly expressed his willingness to sell any Avtex fibers (acetate filament, polyester filament and staple, rayon filament and staple, and vinyon) at $0.50 per pound. Last, economic theory proves that marginal cost based prices are essential to optimize social welfare. That implies far lower effective prices than were estimated, since this industry's marginal costs were earlier shown to be much closer to zero than to Proxy II's values. The details and results of this first approximation method appear in Table 6-3.

Effective prices gain importance once list prices are recognized as merely crude first indications of a mid-point between promotional premiums and discounts when one ignores other possible adjustments. The second way to approximate general effective prices relies on a reasonable estimate of the output distribution sold at the "modal" 50% promotional premium, the mean 40% net discount, and at list price. Logic and experience indicate that discounts are common for at least 80% of all sales. While sales at premium and list prices are both rarer than discounts, absent better information, they are equally probable, according to Bayes' Theorem. Thus, the $1.032 per pound simple average imputed 1975 list price implies a 27% average net discount from list price, or an average effective price of $0.752 per pound, which is in good agreement with the effective price estimates on Table 6-3 of $0.612 to $0.767 per pound. Such discounts would generate potentially large economies of scale for price-sensitive textile mills.

Table 6-3

Estimated 1975 Net Percentage Discounts from List and Spot Prices

(U.S. current dollars per pound and percent)

| | Acrylic Staple | Type 6 Nylon | | PTA Polyester | | Row Averages |
		Filament	Staple	Filament	Staple	
1971-72 Prices						
List:	0.778	1.670	0.770	1.579	0.610	1.081
Average Spot:	0.560	0.937	0.525	1.378	0.340	0.748
Difference:	0.218	0.733	0.245	0.201	0.270	0.333
1975 Mean Costs or Prices						
Overall:	0.517	1.185	1.074	0.618	0.443	0.767
Breakeven (1):	0.350	0.840	0.798	0.419	0.288	0.539
Average Spot:	0.600	0.905	0.800	0.752	0.438	0.699
Net Price Estimators						
Proxy I (2):	0.517	1.185	1.074	0.618	0.443	0.767
Proxy II (3):	0.475	0.873	0.799	0.586	0.363	0.619
Imputed (4) 1975						
List Prices:	0.818	1.638	1.045	0.953	0.708	1.032

Average Percent Discounts from Imputed 1975 List Prices

	Acrylic Staple	Filament	Staple	Filament	Staple	Row Averages
Proxy I:	36.8%	27.7%	-2.8%	35.2%	37.4%	25.7%
Proxy II:	41.9%	46.7%	23.5%	38.6%	48.7%	40.0%

Sources: Appended cost tables, Johnson Redbook Service, Modern Textiles.

Notes: 1. Derived from appropriate cost tables by subtracting both the (16%) returns sought on all capital and half of SARE from the mean totals in the appropriate cost tables.
2. Identical to overall 1975 mean costs above.
3. Estimated as the mean of 1975 break-even costs and 1975 spot prices.
4. Estimated as the differences between 1971-72 average list and average spot prices plus 1975 average spot prices.

PRICE STRATEGIES

Markham reported dominant firm price leadership in his study of the rayon industry [Markham, 69-72]. Price leadership later evolved in the U.S. man-made fibers industry. By the 1960s, the larger man-made fiber producers had learned it was better to wait and confirm, or block, price changes proposed by smaller rivals, than to initiate price changes, especially increases.

Price leadership implies followers. Late entrants in the synthetic fibers arenas hoped to sell at prices set by the innovator, duPont. However, duPont obviously regarded pricing strategy as such an important element of its marketing [Green, 252-67] and strategic planning [Chandler, 63-137] and implementation to formally and carefully study both topics on an ongoing basis. DuPont eventually adapted a mixed pricing strategy.

DuPont integrated two forms of discriminatory pricing [Scherer, 315-34]--value-added pricing and price skimming [Dean, 419-21]--and applied them effectively for almost 40 years. Value-added pricing aims to set prices according to the customers' evaluation of a product's worth to them instead of as a function of the cost to manufacture and deliver it to the customer. DuPont found that small, often inexpensive improvements to or modifications of its fibers and services were prized so greatly by customers as to command very large price premiums and so were eminently worth doing. DuPont consciously and conspicuously shunned simplistic cost plus pricing, of which target return pricing is but a popular variant, for much of the U.S. man-made fibers industry. No other domestic fiber producer earned the privilege of pricing according to value added or did so as consistently and ably for even half as long.

DuPont also price skims with new products. Price skimming is a more dynamic strategy. It sets initial prices far above the supposedly competitive level for a truly new product. Price remains high until a new entrant begins commercial scale production and sales. Then price is reduced sharply. Further price reductions respond to later entries and may continue until a long-term competitive price is reached.

A price-skimming strategy has several simultaneous goals. First, it seeks to recoup investment as quickly as possible while imparting a luxury or prestige image to the product and reducing uncertainty as to the quantity demanded. Next, it tries to maximize economic profits in the interval between full recovery of investment and market entry by rivals. Third, it aims to mislead and then punish imitators to deter similar behavior in the future.

A price skimmer foresees the possibility, and maybe even hopes, that its new product's high initial price eventually will attract entrants. Entrants expect to profit from both the continuation of the original high price after entry and their avoidance or minimization of product and market research and development costs. Price skimming essentially lures such aggressive innocents into a financial ambush. Announcing a drastic reduction of the high original price just after the first entrant starts selling from its new plant springs the trap. Price cuts of at least 20% are common in such instances. Having failed to either anticipate the lagged retaliatory price cut or to accurately predict its size and timing, the entrant finds his financial forecasts overly optimistic. Specifically, a late entrant's investment recovery is prolonged, maybe by years, which defers and lowers profits, sometimes to unacceptable levels. That, in turn, inhibits any later or contingent expansion plans entrants may have had. It also warns them to act more circumspectly in the future. Naturally, the price skimmer can pass onto its clients some or all of its "newly established" cost savings, after updating its depreciation schedule, reserves, and so on. It also exploits any image enhancement arising from reducing price on a desirable product.

An earlier and somewhat different price skimming rationale received much support and attention within duPont's Textile Fibers Department. Many U.S. man-made producers learned about price skimming the hard way. A few gained that knowledge more gently, either via employees or consultants fresh from graduate school marketing courses or from literature searches as part of on-going competitor monitoring programs. Hence, the earlier price-skimming rationale is worth quoting.

> *In the chemical industry, pricing decisions, at least with respect to products in early growth stages, tend to be adaptive and reflect the asymmetry surrounding the ability to raise vs. lower prices in the future. That is, the strategy of price-skimming is frequently employed. Part of the rationale for this practice stems from the general belief that demand schedules are relatively inelastic in the early growth stages of a new chemical product. Perhaps just as importantly, however, is the judgment that setting a relatively high initial price preserves greater flexibility (in view of the asymmetrical nature of price increases vs. decreases) for making better future decisions as sales information accumulates. If the decision maker should overestimate the "best" price to charge for profit maximization, he may still be able to lower price at some future date, should sales response indicate its desirability. Contrast this situation to the case where the "best" price is underestimated. While full capacity of the plant might thereby be effected, the firm's output probe has resulted in some sales at least deferred to the future or perhaps irrevocably lost to competition. Lead times required for making capacity additions are substantially longer than those required for price changes, should the need arise through errors in demand estimation. In a sense, this behavior is a manifestation of Wroe Alderson's more general power principle, which states that present decisions should be made with a view to preserving the power to make better future decisions. [Green, 2-3]*

Further significant innovation or nearly immediate imitative market entry following a rival's innovation are the only effective responses to a price-skimming strategy. Either option calls for large investments, in both product and marketing, plus luck and self-confidence. Penetration pricing is the marketing alternative to a price-skimming strategy. A penetration pricing strategy has the innovator price at the low, long-term level from the outset to expand the market as fast as possible while deterring entry. Penetration pricing also calls for large and rapid investment in a period of great uncertainty; otherwise it too can be vitiated.

A mixed pricing strategy combining value-added pricing with price skimming is a far wiser option for an innovative U.S. man-made fibers' producer than some pure pricing strategy based on one of its components, a pure penetration pricing strategy, or no pricing strategy. Such a mixed strategy assuredly will adversely effect later entrants. However, there is no economic reason why any such firms should benefit from their own poor strategic planning, uncreative product and marketing development, faulty competitive assessment, or slow reflexes.

CONCLUSIONS

Secular declines in real fiber prices continued well into the late 1970s and sometimes into the 1980s. However, such declines are now seen to be associated with early product life-cycle stages when costs are falling rather than with fully mature or declining price-inelastic goods.

U.S. man-made fiber price behavior over their individually unique CUR cycles is complex and not yet fully understood. Each major man-made fiber's list and spot trading prices moved independently of any other's both over and between their own CUR cycles. As a generalization, although each particular man-made fiber's average spot trading prices are more flexible over its CUR cycle than are its list prices, both such price series clearly remain quite rigid in the shorter run as compared with competitively priced cotton. Man-made fibers' prices tend to drop after CURs have fallen below profitable levels for several consecutive months. That level probably is closer to 70% CUR than the 80% CUR level Bremer expected. Evidently, a small producer's higher sensitivity to losses eventually triggers a desperate attempt to buy volume despite the historic certainty of offsetting retaliation and, presumably, known price-inelasticity.

U.S. man-made fibers' list and spot trading prices poorly represent effective prices. A complex interactive structure of large net discounts limits any outsider's study of U.S. man-made fiber prices. That structure's complexity is so profound that even the parties to a given transaction cannot reliably predict or later determine their effective prices on individual products or product lines. As the U.S. man-made fibers industry not only survived but, as will be shown Chapter 8, earned profits for decades in such an environment, timely and exact effective price information either is not as important to normal operations as established economic theory suggests, or else periodically computed average prices, based on accounting data, suffice. The effect of all discounts, allowances, and subsidies on list prices was conservatively estimated to put average effective prices at least 25% and quite probably 40% or more below imputed list prices.

Three price strategies play important roles in this industry. Innovators have greater freedom to select a price strategy than do others. Integration of discriminatory value-added pricing and price skimming served duPont well since the late 1940s. Later entrants' reliance on easier-to-apply cost plus pricing left them at duPont's mercy.

A combination of practical considerations must have deterred duPont from crushing rivals, although it is renowned throughout the industry for the finest quality products, lowest costs, and ability to command premium prices. At first, duPont evidently was too busy expanding rapidly enough to keep pace with very fast growing demand to worry much about potential rivals who would have to bargain with it for a license, circumvent or await the lapse of its patents, or surpass its product innovations. Once domestic man-made fibers' supply came into reasonable equilibrium with demand in the early 1970s, competitive entry unquestionably would have affected established firms and new grounds for restraint were recognized at duPont. Those added restraints probably include antitrust concerns, better large investment prospects outside the mature U.S. man-made fibers industry, a wish to avoid the unenviably difficult role of sole supplier to cost-sensitive and hard-bargaining customers, and, perhaps, internal policy.

7

Nonprice Rivalry

Rivalry occurs among firms that vie for patronage by means aside from price competition. Competing solely on price makes sense only when the classical free enterprise model's premises, notably homogeneous goods and firms—both suppliers and customers—holds true. Although simpler analytically and more apt to yield definite equilibria, price competition seldom produces an even temporarily positive economic profit greater than zero. Hence, the few business executives aware of these facts are unlikely to try to deduce practical strategies from this model, while those less well informed are unlikely to learn how they erred. As a premise of un-differentiated goods and firms demonstrably does not fit the U.S. man-made fibers industry after 1948, the various sorts of rivalry used by the firms composing this industry, either instead of or to supplement price competition, merit consideration.

Rivalry based on nonprice activities resists assessment. Its effects are extremely hard to quantify in both theory and practice. Such efforts also are often inherently subjective in character and therefore notoriously hard to evaluate objectively. The crucial matter of the direction of causality is so uncertain as to often be indeterminate. For instance, one intuitively expects advertising to produce sales, and not the reverse. But what is causality's true direction if, as often happens, this year's advertising budget is set as a fixed proportion of sales one, two or more calendar years ago? Then, either sales cause advertising or both are inextricably interdependent. Un-certainty about the timing and the effects of nonprice activities further complicates the problem of evaluation. Nevertheless, an attempt was made to understand and quantify rivalry in the U.S. man-made fibers industry including its trade-offs with price. This originally was done to better understand and predict price versus nonprice trade-offs in the U.S. man-made fibers industry. Only later was the question raised about whether the method has general merit. This chapter's first major section treats these issues.

Economists theoretically know how to optimize any mix of price and nonprice activities. In theory, one need only do four things. First, ratio each input's--includ-ing nonprice activities--marginal physical product to its price. Second, track those marginal physical products over time. This often poses an insuperable task in practice. Third, cope with previously unrecognized indivisibilities while reallocating the mix to attain the optimum balance--another very arduous chore. Fourth, equate these fractions both to one another and to the reciprocal of the price of the good made from the inputs. While easy to state, this principle remains extremely difficult to apply. However, these four conceptually easy steps pale into insignificance when compared with the ensuing political turf battles.

One is therefore compelled at least to recognize the dilemma created by these intractabilities and perhaps sympathize with executives trying to optimize rivalrous practices in U.S. man-made fibers industry. On the one hand, price competition not only is inappropriate but easily detected and neutralized in the U.S. man-made fibers industry. But nonprice rivalry's efficacy, timing, and costs are, on the other hand, subject to enormous uncertainties, although logic and profit potential make it the only sensible approach. Those uncertainties nullify one's ability to rationally determine correct levels of a fitting mix of nonprice actions and the timing and duration of each.

This dilemma forces decision-makers to consider and commit to a position on a strategy spectrum for multiple periods as compared with pure price competition's implicitly single-period time horizon. Reducing nonprice activities to a bare minimum of effort, especially in cases of unavoidable differentiation, represents one end of this strategy spectrum. The rationale behind this option is rooted in the notions that if it either cannot be measured or does not assuredly yield superior results over price competition, then it is not worth doing. Advocates of this view are highly averse to uncertainty. American Hoechst apparently favored this strategy spectrum end-point before buying Celanese. DuPont pioneered the opposite end of this strategic spectrum. DuPont devoted greater intensity of effort to more forms of nonprice rivalry than any other U.S. man-made fiber producer, as described in earlier chapters, and has been outstandingly successful in doing so.

Two other families of nonprice behavior deserve mention. A wide middle ground lies between the polar strategies cited above. Obviously, most merchant man-made fiber manufacturers operate along that nonprice strategy spectrum instead of at an end point. As those, primarily marketing, strategies were also presented earlier, they can be ignored here. The remaining options aim to either moderate to tolerable levels, if not entirely eliminate, the uncertainties normally associated with nonprice rivalry, or to sow confusion, that is, to increase that uncertainty for rivals so as to lower one's own. Uncertainty-reducing strategies are used frequently enough within the U.S. man-made fibers industry to merit attention and so are covered in the second major section of this chapter. A final section examines the relevant effects, particularly as a source of uncertainty, of strategic planning by some U.S. man-made fibers producers.

RIVALRY QUANTIFIED

Demand for U.S. man-made fibers is realistically modeled by integrating the economic concepts of the kinked oligopoly demand curve [Scherer, 164-68] and inert areas [Leibenstein, 130-34]. The proposed revisions extend the familiar price and quantity demanded graphs into a third dimension to incorporate nonprice activity, and blur traditionally sharp lines into bands. The first extension is discussed next and is followed by descriptions of the adaptations to the price and quantity dimensions, respectively, before explaining the reasons for and consequences of blurring the lines.

U.S. man-made fiber firms within any common subindustry are both heterogeneous suppliers and producers of differentiated goods. Firms with essentially the same total level, but not necessarily the same kind(s), of heterogeneity were grouped together, as explained in prior chapters. Progressively more differentiated clusters of firms are assigned cumulative ranks to reflect this increasing heterogeneity, beginning with captive firms.

Undifferentiated firms, captive producers, were assigned a zero level of heterogeneity. Demand for captive fiber manufacturers' output appears only in the familiar price and quantity plane. However, truly differentiated groups of firms were assigned non-zero heterogeneity ranks. Successively more differentiated groups presumably appear as one moves away from the cluster of captive firms. Hence, heterogeneity ranks were devised to rise at an ever increasing pace by assigning them as the sum of the two immediately preceding ones, that is, a Fibonacci series.

A given U.S. man-made fiber's spot prices progressively decrease, by nickel multiples per pound, across heterogeneous groups. The most differentiated firm, duPont, generally enjoys a $0.20 per pound premium over the cluster of its closest rivals. Such discounts reflect the market's relative valuation of adjacent heterogeneous clusters and normally decrease sharply as a customer scans down its list of potential suppliers from the most desirable to the last option of becoming a captive producer. U.S. man-made fiber producers within any given cluster command essentially the same price, while rivals in the next higher (that is, more differentiated, cluster earn a premium. Correspondingly, the less well-differentiated firms in the next lower cluster sell at a common but discounted price. Only the firms constituting a particular cluster really appear to vie on primarily on price.

These discounts are automatically but tacitly applied by all experienced fiber producer sales executives and textile mill fiber buyers. Occasional attempts to buy at an atypically low price or sell at an unusually high price alert interested parties to review their fiber producer ratings and hence the discount structure. Such rare events normally result from a conscious attempt by someone to exercise market power. A fiber producer wants to exploit any significant development of any facets of its marketing mix while every textile mill wants to save on raw materials. If the market responds favorably to a fiber producer's improvement, then that firm advances into a more distinguished cluster, where it can sell more at higher prices. If the market is unimpressed by the offer, the firm remains in its current cluster. However, a strongly negative market reaction to the new development drops the firm into a less desirable cluster, where it suffers losses from reduced price and smaller real demand, lower priority, and loss of credibility as an innovator. Hence, the U.S. man-made fibers industries enjoys large lasting rewards for successful innovations and endures similar penalties for failures.

Differentiation can earn a producer both priority status for real volume and a premium price over less well differentiated rivals. Thus, the more heterogeneous a man-made fiber manufacturer appears to be the sooner its output sells as demand grows and the longer it can sell as demand contracts. This insight enables one to logically sequence clusters of firms along the quantity dimension.

Our three-dimensional model distinguishes kinds of behavior in a given strategic group or cluster from that across such groups. In effect, firms composing a cluster eschew price competition to stress individualized features of interest to different clients or end-uses. Such price competition as exists inside a group is constrained by pressures from firms in adjacent clusters. Firms in the next lower, or less well-differentiated, cluster tend to be more price-sensitive for two reasons. They price closer to the next lower group so that their price changes are more apt to be felt sooner by such rivals than by more differentiated ones. Also, less heterogeneous firms have smaller margins owing to higher costs. Firms in the next higher, or more distinguished, cluster are disinclined to automatically accept potentially disruptive entry. Enlarging this group might considerably reduce individual real sales, margins, or evoke other changes in accepted practices.

Each cluster in this model presumably occupies a three-dimensional space or arena. Each cluster space was first visualized as a hollow box. The box delimiting the primary arena for its constituent firms has a familiar vertical price dimension (P) and a familiar horizontal quantity dimension (Q) but an unfamiliar depth dimension (Z) for total nonprice efforts. Three as yet unresolved questions remain.

First, where do the firms within a given cluster operate? Theoretically, the triple maximization corner should be preferred. However, in practice, one settles for reasonable proximity to that ideal as, for reasons given later, that ideal position is indeterminate.

Second, how are the clusters connected? Figure 7-1A provides the best initial answer. However, other intercluster connection sites are possible. An extreme situation would show proximate but isolated clusters. Partial overlaps in either or both the price or nonprice dimensions are more realistic possibilities.

Third, what is a more precise representation of the spacial structures initially approximated by boxes on Figure 7-1A? Four basic adjustments are necessary to depict rivalry in U.S. man-made fibers industry with enough precision for practical decision-making. The net effect of these refinements appears as Figure 7-1B.

Adjustment one displaces slightly to the right the higher Z valued end of the higher Q valued PZ plane. This displacement shows that some elasticity of differentiation exists with respect to quantity demanded. Adjustment two slopes the top of each box so that price moves directly in association with differentiation.

Figure 7-1
Rivalry Space

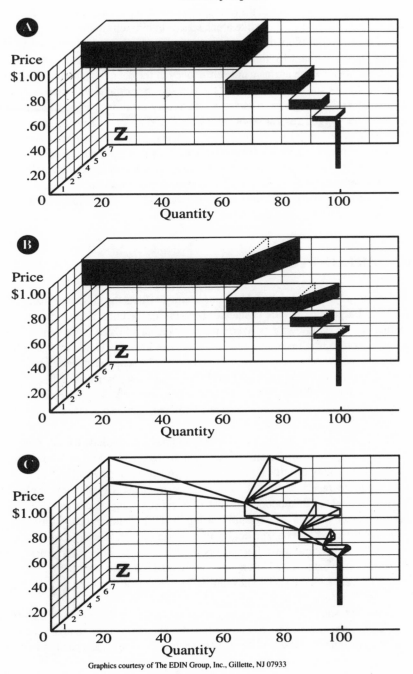

Graphics courtesy of The EDIN Group, Inc., Gillette, NJ 07933

Pragmatically, one initially linearizes this correction, although it almost surely is nonlinear and probably somewhat discontinuous.

Adjustment three removes the now idle or shunned part of each arena. This final excision pares the original boxlike arena spaces into much smaller wedges.

Adjustment four blurs the boundaries to these wedges of nonprice rivalry. This blurring is represented by thicker boundary lines in Figure 7-1C. Blurring the boundaries denotes the intrinsic indeterminacy of the data, the inherent uncertainties of the trade-offs, the reluctance of the firms to experiment with drastic changes or their general willingness to accept a satisfactory result instead of striving for an optimal one, lagged responses of the system, and so on. U.S. man-made fiber producers are not only loath to meddle with an acceptable practice until compelled to do so but prefer not to risk triggering retaliatory acts by rivals. Hence, firms in this industry have strong incentives not to vie as strenuously as possible unless very sure of an extremely favorable result. "Demand functions that are bands and that reflect degrees of inertia make it less risky for some sellers to experiment with pricing procedures involving price discrimination" [Leibenstein, 196].

UNCERTAINTY-REDUCING STRATEGIES

Uncertainty, both as risk and true uncertainty, afflicts the U.S. man-made fibers industry. Large bureaucratic businesses account for the bulk of the industry. Such entities have been known risk-averters since Machiavelli's day. One must expect their reaction to true uncertainty to be even more intense. U.S. man-made fibers producers use two sets of strategies to ameliorate the inescapable uncertainties facing them, aside from either ignoring or exploiting reality as described earlier. Various so-called strategic alliances form one set of uncertainty-reducing strategies. Various forms of collusion are the other, more traditional response. These two sets are examined next.

Strategic alliances of U.S. man-made fiber producers include backup contracts, joint ventures, licensing arrangements, and mergers. Backup contracts aim to stabilize availability of critical materials in the event of an external shock.

Only three facets of backup contracts are germane. First, they are routine practice throughout the chemical industry. Second, strong shocks can overwhelm these insurance devices, as happened during the OPEC embargoes. Third, negotiating and implementing backup contracts opens and formalizes a potentially significant dialogue, or communications channel, between supposedly independent firms.

Some joint ventures by U.S. man-made fibers producers can be traced through annual TO issues. Some such joint ventures focused on the domestic market. Others concerned overseas markets.

Four domestic joint ventures merit attention as they involved major man-made fiber producers. Two of these clearly failed. The two others clearly succeeded, according to a survivor test, and by many other criteria were at least partly successful.

Chemstrand was the earliest significant post-World War II joint venture in the U.S. man-made fibers industry. Chemstrand began in 1949 [Forrestal, 121] as a joint venture of Monsanto and American Viscose Corporation (A.V.C.). Monsanto had created its acrylic fiber, Acrilan, before 1941 but did not try to commercialize it during World War II.

> *Why did Monsanto tie in with Viscose instead of going it alone? Two principal reasons: The investment was, of course cut in half, and Viscose, as a fibers company (mainly rayon) knew the market. Monsanto's only related experience had been in making and applying various chemicals to improve the properties of natural fibers. This experience in fibers and in textiles, alongside Viscose's, was meager. . . . "All of a sudden we were hearing a foreign language containing such words as throwsters, dyers, converters, cutters and greige goods."*
>
> *Monsanto didn't have the time to get educated from scratch, particularly in light of DuPont's head start with nylon and Orlon. [Forrestal, 122-23]*

Surprisingly, the original Acrilan process yielded defective fiber.

> *Not until it was made in quantity at Chemstrand's first plant . . . did Acrilan reveal its basic flaw: susceptibility to fibrillation.*
>
> *What's fibrillation? Well, the fibers scaled; they ruptured. . . . the fibers would break down at a crucial point . . . This was disconcerting--and embarrassing.*
>
> *Also, the product wasn't as soft and woollike as DuPont's Orlon. It was somewhat rougher and fuzzier. Its "hand," or "feel," left something to be desired. . . . So it was back to the drawing board, under stress and duress . . . Ultimately a process improvement materialized . . . to eliminate . . . fibrillation. But, meantime, the giant new Acrilan plant . . . had been closed down.*
>
> *Naturally, neither the Monsanto board nor the Viscose board nor the Chemstrand board was happy. For almost two years the "bouncing, new baby" gave every indication of remaining a delinquent--requiring more research, more testing, more time, more dollars, more patience. . . .*
>
> *No one knew or guessed that fibrillation, plus start-up problems . . . plus delays in market penetration would ultimately result in Acrilan's causing . . . a $20-million loss over . . . nearly ten years. [Forrestal, 123-24]*
>
> *The other partner, Viscose, had sleepless nights. It hadn't reckoned on the foibles of fibrillation (neither had Monsanto). . . . Viscose needed Chemstrand's success. Viscose had nothing of substantial promise in its labs; its 50 percent stake in Chemstrand was its principal asset. . . .*

> *Viscose wanted out. And, of course, that's what happened in 1961,*
> *when Monsanto acquired Viscose's ... equity...for 3,540,000 shares*
> *of Monsanto common stock. [Forrestal, 128-29]*

Chemstrand eventually became a major domestic man-made producer. However, as a joint venture, Chemstrand was devastated by unforeseen problems before its intended risk/uncertainty-reducing features could come into play.

Monsanto's second and last domestic man-made fibers joint venture was the Polythane Company. The name Polythane connoted that the product, spandex fiber, is made from urethane, an acrylonitrile derivative. Polythane Company started in 1962 with a spandex technology from Peteco Corporation, the co-venturer, and Chemstrand's developing marketing expertise and funding. Polythane's spandex product and process, unfortunately and unforeseeably, were not commercially viable. The fiber lacked tensile strength and also was overly sensitive to ultraviolet degradation. Furthermore, Polythane's process could not be adapted to meet evolving requirements for finer denier and higher tenacity spandex fibers.

Monsanto had bought a copy of a study of U.S. spandex potential from a major consultant to the fibers industry before engaging in this joint venture. That report accurately foresaw limited demand and a shift to lower deniers. In retrospect, it is fair to say that some strategies (doing nothing; diversifying into polyester, olefins, or some other specialty fiber, none of which could be made from acrylonitrile; or expanding its acrylic and nylon capacities) were insufficiently considered and others were too arbitrarily and hastily rejected. Polythane ended as a joint venture 1964. The June 1965 TO listed Polythane as a Monsanto subsidiary; the June 1967 TO listed it as "idle;" but after that Polythane was not listed.

Both of the two more successful joint ventures into the U.S. man-made fibers market involved experienced foreign man-made fiber manufacturers. Fiber Industries (FI) was the first, and from some perspectives the more successful, of these joint ventures.

FI began as a 1959 joint venture of Celanese Corporation, a U.S. man-made fiber producer, and ICI, or Imperial Chemical Industries of England. Celanese had prior ties to ICI. FI was to produce and market polyester fibers in the United States based on British technology. By 1961, FI polyester was being sold domestically by Celanese under the Fortrel brand. By the 1960s FI was a Celanese subsidiary and the second largest U.S. polyester fiber manufacturer. A jump into a bit of licensing history is now necessary to better understand the FI joint venture.

A British company, Calico Printers, had discovered and patented a way to make stable polyester fiber in the late 1930s. Carothers' research team at duPont had created polyester but were unable to stabilize it for fiber production. Commercialization of nylon, a prior discovery of the Carothers' team, evidently took priority in research efforts, which reduced the urgency of, but by no means ended, duPont's interest in polyester fiber. ICI bought Calico Printers and then negotiated a cross-licensing deal with duPont. Reportedly, ICI sold a multi-year, exclusive license of

U.S. rights to its polyester technology starting after World War II in exchange for immediate access to duPont's nylon technology.

Dow Badische was the last U.S. man-made fiber joint venture of any consequence. It started in 1967. Dow Chemical Company had been struggling since 1958 to produce commercial acrylic, nylon, and saran fibers for the U.S. markets. Apparently Dow licensed the acrylic and Type 6 nylon technology from Badische. This joint venture ceased manufacturing saran fibers, which Dow then licensed to others, particularly overseas, and concentrated on acrylic, nylon, and polyester fibers.

Dow's original acrylic, Zefran, did not evenly absorb dye. After much unsuccessful effort to correct this critical problem, some executive(s) decided to exploit this quirk until it could be corrected. So Zefran became the first ring-dyeing fiber at a propitious time because heather-like yarns were gaining popularity.

In 1979 Dow Badische became a wholly owned subsidiary of BASF America. BASF America, in turn, was entirely owned by BASF. The former Dow Badische joint venture changed its name to Badische Corporation to reflect this change in ownership.

Many primarily U.S. man-made fiber producers had joint ventures and licensing deals in other lands with foreign man-made fiber producers. American Cyanamid and PPG had such arrangements for the Spanish market with AKZO of Holland. Hercules and Montefiber of Italy agreed to produce for the Italian market. OCF made fiberglass in South Africa with Pilkington Brothers of the United Kingdom and in Japan with Asahi Chemical Industries. DuPont also had ties to Japanese fiber manufacturers, notably Toray, but it is unclear whether these truly were joint ventures or technology licenses.

Technology licensing is a common, but not universal, practice in the man-made fiber industry both within the United States and across international boundaries. Since technology licenses are neither reported to nor published by a central agency in any consistent manner or depth, they are difficult to track and even harder to analyze. This reality forces reliance on anecdotes.

> *[I]n the Monsanto 1950 Annual Report: "The company is negotiating with ... du Pont ... for a license to manufacture and and sell nylon."*
> *[J. R.] Rusty Wilson [a Monsanto patent attorney, chemist, chemical engineer, chief negotiator in this situation] tells the pursuit-of-the-DuPont-license story ... like this:*
>
>> *In 1950, an antitrust suit had recently been filed against DuPont by the Department of Justice, alleging DuPont and ICI . . . had an agreement under which they would not compete against each other in nylon.*
>> *DuPont wanted an arm's length arrangement with an American licensee for nylon for two reasons: 1) It wanted a competitor to remove the sting of having a U.S. monopoly on nylon,*

*and 2) it wanted a yardstick to measure what DuPont should
rightfully charge for the knowhow, if and when the day would
ever come when an antitrust decree would require DuPont
to make nylon know-how and patents available to others.*

*During the forties DuPont had been contacted by many
companies, each requesting to be considered if the day might
ever dawn when DuPont would be willing to discuss licensing its nylon know-how and patents. Monsanto was on such
a list and so was American Viscose--long prior to the
Monsanto-Viscose association in Chemstrand.*

*Yet DuPont initiated its first contact with Eastman Kodak.
And Eastman said no. . . . Eastman declined to negotiate
 . . . not because of the potential of nylon but because
Eastman had a policy of not incurring a debt of the magnitude which would be required to get into the nylon business.
Considering Monsanto and Viscose were both on the DuPont
list and . . . were now united in the Chemstrand venture, it
is easy to see how DuPont was able to kill two birds with one
rock in agreeing to enter into preliminary discussions with
Chemstrand. . . .*

*[T]he first few months everything went rather smoothly. It
was a fact-finding expedition of unusual complexity. All
parties cooperated nicely. But by early 1951 the road had become
rocky. At one point negotiations were terminated. . . .*

*In June of 1951 a complicated formula for payment, accept-
able to both Chemstrand and DuPont, emerged. It provided
Chemstrand payments to DuPont based not only on the cost
of manufacture of nylon but also on such factors as inflation,
labor rates, raw materials prices, pretax return on investment, construction costs and selling prices.*

*DuPont wanted--and got--about $120 million for its know-
how and for establishing the operation of a Chemstrand
nylon plant geared to make 50 million pounds per year. This
was paid over a 15-year period. As it turned out, during the
period of licensing Chemstrand got its nylon plant up close
to 200 million pounds a year. Even so, the know-how
payments to DuPont remained in the $120-million range.*

*There are several reasons why it turned out this way, the chief
one relating to "product mix." . . . Almost immediately
Chemstrand decided to expand rapidly in the heavier-denier
continuous filament for the tire industry. Because it was a
less expensive product to make and sell, Chemstrand gained
under terms of the DuPont formula.*

The 1951 pact, based largely on the complicated formula, made DuPont responsible for actually setting the Pensacola plant into operation. There was also a patent license in- volved--a license for a wide variety of 17-year DuPont patents. ... More than 300 individual patents were involved. The agreement even gave Chemstrand a license on those DuPont nylon patents which would be issued for the ensuing five years after 1951. Royalty fees for patent licensing ranged from 4 to 6 percent over a 10-year period. Yet this was not totally an "extra fee" beyond the know-how formula, since a part of the royalty payments was covered in the know-how agreement.

In 1953 Chemstrand cranked up what would become--and still is--the world's largest integrated nylon plant combining both chemical and fiber manufacturing operations. In 1954 capacity went from 50 million to 58 million pounds. With gratifying smoothness. [Forrestal, 124-28]

Mergers are another well-known device to reduce risk and uncertainty. Five significant mergers have occurred in the U.S. man-made industry since 1948. They are discussed next in chronological order.

Food Machinery Corporation (FMC) bought the moribund American Viscose Corporation (A.V.C.) after A.V.C. withdrew from Chemstrand. FMC later acknowl- edged its inability to turn around A.V.C. and in the late 1970s spun off this asset to A.V.C. executives via a leveraged buy-out. That spin-off, known as Avtex, floundered for almost another decade. Rayon's waning demand, pollution control expenses and liabilities, and related forces have once again made Avtex's demise imminent.

In the mid-1970s Monsanto decided to expand into polyester filament quickly and cheaply by buying Rohm and Haas' facilities. MTC convinced the Federal Trade Commission (FTC) that it was rescuing terminally ill plants and would expand them. Those purchased facilities were later closed when MTC acknowledged that they could neither be expanded nor saved.

Amoco, starting in the late 1970s, began to acquire U.S. olefin fiber producers, typically captive manufacturers. It quietly accumulated a substantial olefin capacity base and has begun to explore other fibers, notably nylon, too.

Two major man-made fiber mergers happened in the middle to late 1980s. BASF America decided to expand Badische when AKZO wanted to sell its American Enka fiber subsidiary. American Hoechst, a wholly owned subsidiary of Hoechst A.G., tested the waters by buying some exotic-fiber producing facilities from Celanese. Hoechst then decided to think big and save investment banking fees; it bought all the rest of Celanese to form Hoechst-Celanese Corporation (HCC). The FTC, however, forced HCC to divest some of its enlarged polyester capacity as part of the price of allowing the complete merger. American Hoechst and Celanese, via FI, both made polyester fiber before they merged. That mandatory divestment delayed the HCC merger for nearly two years and reincarnated Fiber Industries as an independent firm. The mergers of American Enka into Badische and Celanese into Hoechst-Celanese seemingly involve complementary product lines. But it simply is too soon to tell if these new entities will satisfy their original aims and make economic sense in the long run.

A cartel is another uncertainty-reducing strategy. A British economic historian devoted over 60 pages of his second volume about Courtaulds' social and economic history before World War II to this topic. The details about the international rayon consortia and cartels between 1906 and 1940 came primarily from Courtaulds' internal records.

> *The main items of agreement were: (1) avoidance of competition in each other's territory; (2) establishment of technical collaboration . . .; (4) undertaking to refrain from engaging, without prior consultation and agreement, any employee who left any of the constituent companies. . . . [Coleman, 79]*
>
> *Third, a control committee was to be established. Its duties would include the . . . fixing of prices, and the allotment of production quotas. [Coleman, 92]*

Participation in these consortia and cartels by American Viscose Corporation (A.V.C.), then Courtaulds' U.S. subsidiary, and some of its leading U.S. rivals also was documented.

> *In fact DuPont initiated the price change but it was agreed between Yerkes [of duPont] and Salvage [of A.V.C.] that A.V.C. should announce it first. One cannot help wondering how many other leads and lags as given in Markham, pp. 82-83, were "fixed." [Coleman, 401]*

The prior existence of cartels influencing U.S. man-made fibers surely is of historic interest. However, the relevant concern is whether such an entity continued to function in the U.S. man-made fibers industry after 1948. Available indications are highly suggestive but not as conclusive as Coleman's evidence.

The existence of man-made fiber producer cartels in both Western Europe and their equivalent in Japan's Ministry of International Trade and Industry (MITI) is a matter of record. U.S. man-made producers can be trichotomized for purposes of this analysis. Some are subsidiaries of European firms active in the present European cartel. Others, headquartered in the United States, operate subsidiaries producing and selling in Western Europe or have strategic alliances with Western European man-made fiber firms as cited above. A residual group also exists of independent producers operating strictly within U.S. borders.

Some communications linkages that could facilitate a cartel's operation were identified earlier. Others established expressly for that purpose before 1948 have never been dismantled. Continuation of such message channels implies that they either still serve their original functions, at least significantly if not exclusively, or have assumed other duties. TEB is a notable example.

U.S. man-made fiber producers' antitrust vulnerability is hard to establish in the current permissive period. The introduction of "documents retention programs," to minimize accumulation of potential evidence, and similar devices to protect firms' images from taint by improper employee conduct is amenable to many inter-pretations. These acts could merely be a simple combination of cost cutting and caution in disposing of unnecessary documents that might be misconstrued. Alter-natively, they could be the destruction of papers that later might become evidence and then illegal to destroy. Evil, like beauty, is somewhat in the eye of the beholder. These measures' use implies enhanced fear of antitrust prosecution. By the late 1970s the larger U.S. man-made producers were less cavalier about antitrust viola-tions. Many of their parent organizations had been subjected to antitrust suits. Circumspection is not a crime. Neither is it equivalent to innocence, and there are reasons to be suspicious.

Restoring a sullied reputation is no easy task; it is hard to imagine what U.S. man-made fiber producers might do if they thought further steps advisable. Effec-tive prophylaxis, instead of political palliatives and lip service, could have interest-ing consequences. What would happen, for instance, if firms truly and publicly encouraged employees to balk at any order the employee suspected of violating the antitrust laws at least until an independent legal opinion was rendered at company expense? Since the employee will suffer first and disproportionately in an antitrust suit and is the firm's first line of defense, it seems reasonable for the employer to recognize that it bears such costs. What would happen if a law mandating extremely harsh penalties for any supervisor tolerating, let alone encouraging, a potential antitrust violation existed and were enforced? What would happen if managers had to be licensed to qualify for employment and could have their license permanently revoked by an independent agency for antitrust involvement? Society imposes similar strictures on vehicle operators and such professionals as doctors, lawyers, engineers, and accountants. Those licensed occupations rarely could harm as many as severely as one unlicensed willful senior executive at a major firm.

STRATEGIC PLANNING

Formal strategic planning is the last important and distinctive kind of nonprice rivalry engaged in by some major U.S. man-made fiber producers. Strategic planning is a resource allocation device appropriate to situations involving dramatic change and severe market imperfections, including market failure or non-existence.

DuPont pioneered in strategic planning long before its rivals seriously explored the possible benefits of such a discipline [Chandler, 63-137]. Having diligently created, refined, and institutionalized strategic planning over almost 65 years, duPont serves as a yardstick to measure the efficacy of rival man-made fiber producers' strategic planning.

Two examples of duPont's business strategy in the U.S. man-made fibers industry show its relative mastery of this arcane discipline. A strategic decision by duPont to invest in true research in some exotic fields paid off in polymer chemistry. Sponsorship of Carothers' research team led to nylon and many other valuable synthetic materials. DuPont's roughly $30 million investment to create and commercialize nylon generated billions in return. Discovery of nylon also freed duPont from subservience to A.V.C. and the European-based man-made fibers cartel. Thoughtful exploitation of its new-found opportunities enabled duPont to dominate at least the U.S. man-made industry for almost 50 years. Clearly, this was a dominant strategy according to the definition of Von Neumann and Morgenstern. DuPont is one of the few firms known to have ever devised and implemented a truly dominant strategy. It has twice applied dominant strategies to the U.S. man-made fibers industry. The second instance is sketched below.

Most U.S. man-made fibers producers did little, if any, formal strategic planning until the late 1960s, some 40 years after duPont was on record as innovating in this field, beyond paying lip service to the art of strategy. Once aware of their weakness in strategic planning or simply because it had become fashionable, domestic man-made fiber producers seeking to catch up with and then surpass duPont often hired a strategy consultant.

Unfortunately, those advisers' methodologies usually were incompatible with the U.S. man-made fiber industry's innate characteristics, as various firms' managements learned at great cost in time, money, effort, and credibility. The so-called strategic planning systems advocated by consultants failed to recognize and deal with the U.S. man-made fibers industry's price inelasticity, cyclicality, and so on. Technically, optimizing in this situation calls for nonlinear multiperiod goal programming. Internal political considerations and lack of data and computer power prevented the use of such advanced methods. Valid satisficing techniques were not considered; they were generally unknown at the time.

Celanese retained McKinsey & Company, hiring many senior executives from that consulting organization. Celanese essentially sought to stabilize profits in the face of fluctuating demand by varying employment. Emphasizing short-term financial stability cost Celanese dearly. Both momentum and customer goodwill were unintentionally sacrificed. Costs also were raised in two ways. Wage premiums were needed to attract desirable new employees who, by various means, knew there was far less job security at Celanese than at its rivals. Second, Celanese's workforce was less productive, due to cyclical morale problems and periodic efforts to seek jobs elsewhere instead of concentrating on their duties.

Chemstrand originally relied on executives' experienced-based intuition, not strategic planning. The latter was regarded as overly mechanistic, inflexible, long-term, demanding, and an infringement on the executive prerogative to be arbitrary and whimsical. One leading Chemstrand executive of the time was entranced by Field Marshall Irwin Rommel's North African campaign. That devotee stressed a militaristic world view and tried to operate accordingly in the U.S. man-made fibers industry. His zeal was eventually squelched by a colleague with military planning expertise and field experience. When pressed in public for an opinion the real expert quietly made two statements. "Rommel lost. Only amateurs get enthusiastic about imitation." It took a new CEO to revive interest in strategic planning at Monsanto.

John Hanley, formerly of Procter & Gamble, retained two strategy consultants, Bain and Company and Schleh Associates, to explore the strange chemical industry starting with the U.S. man-made fibers business. Few at Monsanto or among its advisers knew and cared that these strategy approaches were incompatible. Bain and Schleh posited theories as to how business can and should be done that disagreed radically as to the source(s) of profit and espoused quite different goals, time horizons, and techniques. At this stage Monsanto executives found suboptimization an unfamiliar, hard to understand and unimportant concept.

Results began to appear about three years after the strategy consultants started helping Monsanto in general and MTC in particular. First, multimillion dollar bills for consulting and related travel expenses were incurred and paid. Second, interested outsiders quickly became aware of the consultants' presence, efforts, methods, and likely strategies. Third, Rohm and Haas' plants were bought as described above. Next, many bright, to date loyal and productive Monsanto employees reacted. Some sought employment elsewhere, especially those who were both personally aggressive and predisposed to and knowledgeable about nonprice rivalry. Others, vested in the retirement program, began "soldiering on the job" to silently protest the perceived undesirable presence and management acceptance of these consultants. Fifth, implementing the strategic planning process and its plans did not go as well or as quickly as management had hoped. Finally, a preemptive strike was made against MTC.

MTC's evolving strategic planning process was based on many markedly erroneous assumptions about the U.S. man-made fibers industry. Supposedly, both goods and competitors were undifferentiated. Price supposedly was elastic, and constantly so. Competitors supposedly would ignore a rival's new strategy. Supposedly there were neither fashion nor business cycles in the U.S. man-made fibers industry, or the consultants could predict them accurately enough so that management would have enough lead time to neutralize them. Furthermore, the lowest cost fiber supposedly would capture and hold any market. Therefore, price cuts should be made to buy market share and so achieve cost savings from economies of scale and experience. The antitrust risk of per se predatory pricing either went unrecognized or was ignored. MTC's strategic fantasizing was disrupted just before implementation by a brief repeated signal from duPont.

DuPont convincingly signalled its intention to raise its prices if MTC cut price. That news stunned MTC's strategists. It impugned their strategy's basic premises at the psychologically worst time.

MTC was pinned. Its newly devised strategy was not quite ready for implementation. That strategy's efficacy now was in doubt. Such doubts, in turn, deterred lower level's acceptance of the new strategy, making fast, aggressive execution unlikely. Conversely, the sheer amount of middle and senior management effort, reputation, and ego invested precluded prompt rejection of the now demonstrably inferior strategy and switching to a viable alternative. In sum, MTC could not advance as planned. Retreat also was impossible; prior successful strategies had been ridiculed and spurned. No contingency plans had been developed. MTC drifted for years before resolving its strategic quandary. By then it was too late to regain its place in the industry's hierarchy.

DuPont's threat of a retaliatory price hike derived from a complex rationale. The primary aim apparently was to insulate duPont from any accusation of trying to improperly monopolize the industry. The probable secondary goal was to minimize market disruption by partly protecting MTC from the folly of price cutting to buy volume. Third, this counterstroke bolstered duPont's reputation and leadership by crushing MTC's aspirations. In planners' terms, duPont had again unleashed a dominant strategy in the U.S. man-made fibers industry.

Strategic planning strongly influenced both nonprice behavior and the performance of the firms vying in the U.S. man-made fibers industry. DuPont's strategic planning clearly was very successful in this industry. All others' strategic planning systems produced at best vulnerable and all too often truly inferior strategies. Those without a sound strategic planning process were increasingly at the ever less tender mercies of rivals in the face of an increasingly difficult environment. Inane or myopic strategies needlessly churned the industry and the markets it served. Every strategy, even an unplanned or inferior one, has lasting consequences or time-binding effects in the real world.

Vulnerable strategies significantly enhance uncertainty. A vulnerable strategy's efficacy always depends on many things holding true simultaneously. The actual state of nature has to be at least neutral, and preferably favorable. Implementation must be feasible, swift, and correctly done in secret. Only secrecy can defer detection, evaluation, and development of an effective counter until retaliation would be too late.

CONCLUSIONS

Nonprice rivalry generally resists objective evaluation. It is inherently complex, imprecise, and without smooth convertibility into price equivalents. Those traits simultaneously challenge analysts and rivals. Progress has been made in devising a model of aggregate rivalry within the U.S. man-made fibers industry. This model is amenable to tolerably precise quantification. It also is both generalizable to other industries and decomposable to handle specific forms of nonprice activities.

Between 1948 and the mid-1980s, the U.S. man-made fibers industry explored many forms of nonprice activities with varying degrees of success. Those nonprice behaviors either intended to decrease or increase the uncertainties of doing business within the industry.

Uncertainty-reduction efforts were rather tactical or short-term in character. Those devices generally were neither outstandingly effective nor outstandingly ineffective. Some useful lessons can, however, be drawn from them.

First, at least in this industry, joint ventures only succeeded when all parties concerned knew the markets and the technology involved. Joint ventures between those bringing partial knowledge to the venture did not endure and yielded low and temporary profits at best. Plainly, although psychologically uncomfortable, it is better to struggle alone to gain the requisite knowledge and skills than to try to accelerate learning with another also impaired by a lack of different knowledge. Coordinating small parts of two large organizations to a common goal poses grave managerial challenges because firms do not learn. Individuals may learn, but there is little assurance that they learn the right things at the proper pace. Also, there is even less likelihood that any learning will be effectively shared. If this industry's experience is representative, then a high-tech industry is not the place to simultaneously attempt to combine cross-cultural technology transfers with self-education.

Second, mergers were no more likely to succeed in the U.S. man-made fibers industry than in general. Buying suboptimal-sized plants to form a firm with high total capacity did not work any better in this industry than elsewhere.

Accelerating market entry via joint ventures and mergers is demonstrably inappropriate in particular environments. Although such devices can accelerate market entry, this industry's experience shows that the resulting firm is less viable in the longer term. These simple legal and financial devices readily succumb to pressures imposed by advanced technology, multiple end-use market operations, fashion, large multiproduct lines with differing life cycles, erratic business cycles, diverse nonprice rivalry, and so on.

The U.S. man-made industry was cartelized until 1940. During World War II, it was subject to extensive government control. Was this industry cartelized after 1945? The evidence is inconclusive but suggestive. Many prewar cartel communications channels remain open and active. Moreover, a Western European man-made fiber cartel exists. Some of those European firms have subsidiaries spinning man-made fiber in the United States. Some United States based man-made fiber firms have European subsidiaries undoubtedly influenced by that European fiber cartel. Japanese man-made operations also constitute a cartel under MITI's direction. Many of the old cartels' aims continue to be met, for example, stable prices, minimal exchange of personnel, and so on. But apparent continuity is insufficient proof. If a U.S. man-made fibers industry cartel exists, then it assuredly would somewhat reduce members' uncertainty. However, which uncertainties would be alleviated and by how much are even less clear.

Formal strategic planning is another form of nonprice rivalry engaged in by U.S. man-made fibers manufacturers. Although obvious in retrospect, some important principles derive from this industry's experience with strategic planning. They may help executives in future growth industries. First, firms with soundly based and well-established strategic planning processes make formidable rivals. If you cannot annihilate them, do not antagonize them. Second, unless chance intervenes, a large organization needs at least five years to devise and install a strategic planning process compatible with its technologies, markets, and internal culture. Only late in that incubation period will useful results start becoming visible. Third, trying to accelerate or bypass the inception and incubation stages of strategic planning is counterproductive. It just exposes the firm to great risks. Next, strategy consultants can be very hazardous to the health and welfare of firms able to afford them, especially when advisers with inappropriate or conflicting paradigms are retained simultaneously. Fifth, strategic planning is an essential but perilous management task. Sixth, persistent use of a strategic planning system kept appropriate to the organization's circumstances enables a firm to do quite well over the long term, as duPont illustrates. Seventh, neglecting or just dabbling with strategic planning entrusts one's fate to the gods and rivals. Firms doing so may enjoy occasional periods of luck, as seemed to happen at Celanese and Monsanto, but not enduring success. Eighth, a strategic planning process incompatible with the firm's and/or the industry's character must produce inferior strategies. Adopting an inferior strategy not only exposes one to retaliation but can precipitate a devastating counter, as MTC discovered to its dismay.

Any chosen strategic planning process generates characteristic strategies for consideration. A strategy is a chosen course of action, that is, behavior. The three basic strategy classes call for distinctive behaviors to succeed. Specifically, it pays to: (1) announce a dominant strategy well before implementing it; (2) shun every inferior strategy; and (3) execute any vulnerable strategy quickly and quietly so rivals cannot react in time to defeat it. Generally, one should rely on a mixed, instead of a pure, strategy and have a full set of contingency plans ready when operating in an uncertain environment. The firm's choice of a strategic planning process clearly is crucial because some strategies not only are less robust than others but more dangerous to their proponents than is yet widely recognized.

The U.S. man-made fibers industry after 1948 was a complex, dynamic, and uncertain arena rife with nonprice rivalry. Thriving in such an environment clearly called for a sound, long-term, and well-balanced mixed strategy. Simply trying to apply the latest fashion in tactics did not even ensure survival. It clearly is far better to do the right things tolerably well, tolerably promptly and undramatically instead of doing the wrong things, let alone doing them fast, efficiently, and, worst of all, with enthusiasm discernible by rivals.

8

Performance

This chapter discusses five aspects of U.S. man-made industry performance in the following order. The first section sketches some little-recognized but widespread social benefits arising from the industry's existence and operations. The next section compares the industry's labor productivity with that of all U.S. manufacturing. A third section treats various facets of the industry's profits. A crucial fourth section characterizes the industry's workability. The final section examines the individual performances of the firms composing the industry.

GENERAL SOCIAL BENEFITS

The U.S. man-made fibers industry produces many social benefits. Some enhance the quality of life; others prolong life. Lower cost of living and improved national welfare are further social benefits attributable to this industry. Examples are cited to validate these claims, but measurement and evaluation of their individual and overall net benefits have been left to those more quantitatively adept.

Man-made fibers have contributed to the health of the population and to technical progress in medicine. As man-made fibers displaced cotton, they reduced the spread of byssinosis, or brown lung disease. A corresponding displacement of asbestos is under way and should similarly reduce lung cancer among those who otherwise would be exposed to asbestos dust.

Man-made fibers have also facilitated significant technical advances in at least two medical areas, namely, surgery and nephrology. Surgical progress has been promoted by the development of arterial grafts of duPont's Dacron polyester and improved sutures of man-made fibers. Hollow cellulosic fibers form the core of the blood filter essential to every patient undergoing dialysis on an artificial kidney.

Other life-saving devices totally depend on man-made fibers. Vehicle safety belts and air bags for automobiles and stunt work are but two obvious nonmilitary examples. Parachutes and light, flexible (Kevlar) body armor are more combat-related life-saving devices calling for man-made fibers.

Man-made fibers reduced the cost of many recreational activities while improving sports performance. Fiberglass, polyester, or carbon fibers not only reinforce plastic fishing rods, boats, tennis rackets, golf clubs, and other sports equipment but make them stronger, lighter, easier to produce, more durable, and far more affordable than earlier products.

Many other socially important products depend on the creation and growth of man-made fibers. Among those are modern radial tires, stealth aircraft, felt tip pens, fiber optic communication networks, stain-resistant carpets, high-temperature filter bags, fiberglass reinforced printed circuit boards, inflatable buildings, permanent press clothes and bedlinens, and disposable diapers. Modern carpets reduced the cost of housing. Permanent press apparel saves ironing time and prevents burns needing costly treatment. Fiber-reinforced structures save construction time, materials, and capital. Lighter fiber-reinforced plastic vehicles also conserve fuel.

A lower cost and higher standard of living undoubtedly results from using man-made fibers. Those changes' exact economic value remains unsettled, but their combined effect surely is positive and large.

LABOR PRODUCTIVITY

U.S. cellulosic and noncellulosic fibers' labor statistics were analyzed separately and are appended as Tables A5-1 and A5-2. Both tables present an index of output per hour for all employed persons (on a common 1977 = 100 base) for comparison with a similar index for all U.S. manufacturing.

The three comparable labor productivity series exhibit visibly distinct trends based on their respective values and compound annual (percentage) rate of growth (CAR) measured across all cyclical troughs over the 1958-82 period. All three labor productivity index series show a similar inverted V pattern but differ in size and timing. The cellulosic series clearly is the most cyclical.

Trough years identified by the National Bureau of Economic Research (NBER) and reported in the Statistical Abstracts of the United States were used in calculating labor productivity index-based CARs for U.S. cellulosic and noncellulosic fibers as well as for all U.S. manufacturing. Five trough-to-trough cycles happened between 1958 and 1982 (see Table 8-1). It was fortunate but pure coincidence that the 1958 and 1982 trough years bounded the period for which annual man-made fiber data were available. CARs were also calculated for the entire 1958-82 period and the fortuitously equally long 1958 to 1970 and 1970 to 1982 periods. The details appear in Table 8-1. Essentially, the 1958-82 overall CAR results of 2.2% for cellulosics, 2.8% for all U.S. manufacturing, and 6.6% for noncellulosics typify the details over shorter intervals. Cellulosic fibers' low CARs, as compared with those for all U.S. manufacturing, and the generally high corresponding CARs of noncellulosics, again relative to all U.S. manufacturing, probably result from these three industries'

Table 8-1

Growth of Output per Hour for All Employed Persons in

Selected U.S. Manufacturing Industries

(compound annual percentage growth rates between cyclical troughs)

	Cellulosic Fibers	Noncellulosic Fibers	All U.S. Manufacturing
	(%) [1]	(%) [2]	(%) [1]
1958 to 1961	7.9	0.0	3.5
1961 to 1970	8.5	7.0	3.5
1970 to 1975	-5.5	12.6	2.1
1975 to 1980	0.7	7.6	3.9
1980 to 1982	-9.0	-1.8	-2.1
1958 to 1970	8.4	5.2	3.5
1970 to 1982	-3.6	8.0	2.1
1958 to 1982	2.2	6.6	2.8

Sources: 1. Index Series on Table A5-1.
         2. Index Series on Table A5-2.

Note: According to the National Bureau of Economic Research,
      cyclical troughs happened in 1958, 1961, 1970, 1975,
      1980, and 1982, as reported in the Statistical Abstracts

      of the United States.

different product life cycle stages. As discussed earlier, Harrigan established that the U.S. cellulosics fibers industry entered a declining life cycle stage. The total U.S. manufacturing industry approximates a mature life cycle stage. Large-scale commercialization of many new noncellulosic fibers and marked capacity expansions for those since 1958 suggest that this subindustry was in the growth stage of its life cycle until 1966, and then in its mature stage at least from the mid-to-late 1970s until 1983.

PROFITS

Introduction

Pretax profits were estimated for the U.S. cellulosic and noncellulosic fibers industries (except fiberglass) annually from 1958 through 1982 by subtracting estimated total costs from sales revenues. Pretax, instead of post-tax, profits were estimated for two reasons. First, it is an easier calculation. Second and more important, the proper yearly tax rates for each subindustry were unknown and no authoritative source of guidance could be found. Total costs were estimated from Census of Manufactures data. The cost details appear on appended Tables A6-1 and A6-2 for cellulosic and noncellulosic fibers. Undeflated dollar sales revenue data on these two broadly defined man-made fibers industries also were obtained from the Census of Manufactures for the same years. Deflated pretax estimates of profits or deflated estimated earnings before taxes (DEEBT), were used to assess the cyclicality of profits.

It was possible to examine three aspects of these industries' profit performance once their pretax earnings were calculated. One issue involves the presence and persistence of profits. A second issue is profit cyclicality. A comparison of these industries' pretax returns on gross fixed assets with that of all U.S. manufacturing is the last profit-related issue. The data analyzed to address these issues appear on Tables A7-1 and A7-2 for cellulosic fibers and noncellulosic fibers, and Table A7-3 compares returns on assets.

Profits' Existence and Persistence

Man-made fibers' DEEBT figures disclose essentially profitable industries. As was shown in Chapter 5, the U.S. man-made fibers industry regards a 16% pretax return on assets as a normal return to be earned at an 80% CUR. Between 1958 and 1982, these industries' average CUR was 83.1% for cellulosic fibers and 83.2% for noncellulosic fibers as reported on appended Tables A7-1 and A7-2. If those CUR series had been normally distributed, profits would have been earned about 62% of the time by cellulosic fibers and 70% of the time by noncellulosic fibers.

Since profits were generated for decades, the pace of competitive profit erosion must be slow in this industry. Hence, profits are apt to persist for some time to come. How much of this industry's profits result from successful innovation instead of any other potential sources, including the exercise of oligopoly power, is unknown. However, the U.S. man-made fibers industry undoubtedly has generated financial profits over four decades and probably will continue doing so indefinitely.

Cyclicality of Profits

DEEBT proxy profit series' cyclicality is most apparent graphically. Each DEEBT and CUR series was converted into indexes of percentage deviation from its mean to graph with a common vertical axis, instead of two with different units of measure, that is, millions of 1972 dollars and percent CUR. The DEEBT and CUR indexes were plotted separately for cellulosic and noncellulosic fibers as Figures 8-1 and 8-2.

Three common aspects of both graphs are evident at the outset. First, the indexed DEEBT and CUR series are visibly quite cyclical. Next, although each indexed DEEBT series appears more sensitive to cyclical fluctuations than the associated indexed CUR series, that apparently greater sensitivity might result solely from the well-known volatility of any profit series. Third, both indexed DEEBT series have runs of low values for several consecutive years. Those multi-year runs at opposite ends of the time scale presumably arise from, on the one hand, cellulosic fibers being in the declining stage of their product life cycle, and, on the other hand, high start-up and expansion costs characteristic of the embryonic and growth stages of non-cellulosic fibers' product life cycle.

Why are man-made fiber DEEBT series sensitive to cyclical fluctuations in CUR? Changes in a man-made fiber industry's CUR logically are far more apt to directly influence current year's profits than vice versa. These industries have been shown to have mostly fixed costs, quite low marginal costs within a relatively wide band of normal CUR operations which rapidly increase outside that CUR range, pricing to recoup producers' estimates of full costs at an 80% CUR (as reflected in cost tables in Chapter 5), and relatively inflexible and inelastic short-run prices. Thus, operations at increasingly suboptimal CURs necessarily are disproportionately and increasingly unprofitable, while operations in the 70% to 90% optimal CUR range generate correspondingly elevated profits, as explained in Chapter 5's discussion of marginal costs. Optimal 70-80% CURs, by design, yield a profit about equal to break-even in the conventional economic view, which regards a normal profit as part of the cost of doing business.

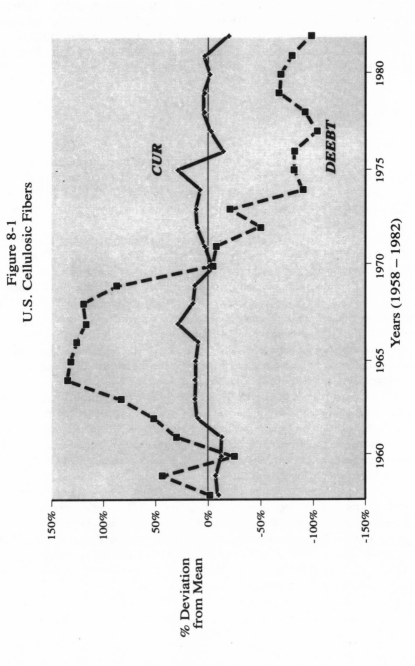

Figure 8-1
U.S. Cellulosic Fibers

% Deviation
from Mean

CUR

DEEBT

Years (1958 – 1982)

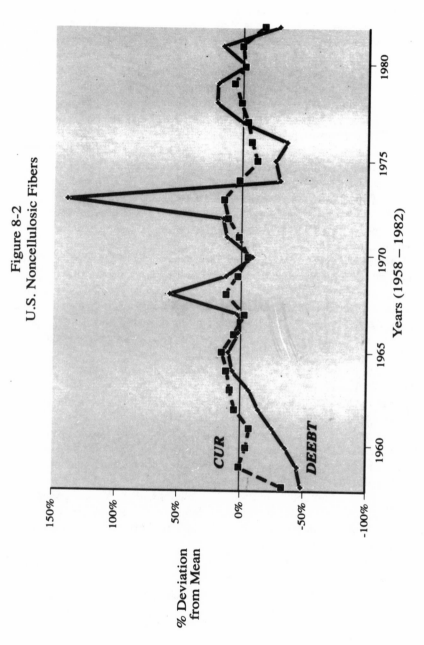

Figure 8-2
U.S. Noncellulosic Fibers

Pretax Returns on Gross Value of Fixed Assets

Data on pretax profits and gross value of fixed assets were obtained from various reports of the Bureau of the Census of the U.S. Department of Commerce and are reported on Table A7-3. Gross values for the U.S. cellulosic and noncellulosic fibers industries' fixed assets were found in Census of Manufactures reports and were the only non-inventory asset data available on these industries. It was necessary to develop a comparable series for all U.S. manufacturing as no such data could be found. Gross value of fixed assets for all U.S. manufacturing was thought equivalent to the year-end gross book value of depreciable assets in the Annual Survey of Manufactures reports of the U.S. Department of Commerce, Bureau of the Census. However, the data were unavailable before 1963 and in 1965 and 1966. Those missing data were estimated by applying link relative changes from another series, capital assets less reserves for all U.S. manufacturing, in the Historical Statistics of the United States Colonial Times to 1970 [1975].

These data were graphed to visually compare pretax returns on assets of U.S. noncellulosic and cellulosic fibers subindustries with all U.S. manufacturing. The result appears in Figure 8-3.

Figure 8-3 provides three comparisons. It shows that cellulosic fibers' pretax returns on the gross value of fixed assets occasionally exceeded that of all U.S. manufacturing between 1958 and 1968 but neither generally within that span nor at all from 1968 through 1982. Noncellulosic fibers' pretax returns generally, but not always, exceeded that of all U.S. manufacturing over the entire 1958-82 period. Noncellulosic fibers' annual pretax returns exceeded cellulosics' in all years except 1967, 1969, and 1970.

Average pretax returns on the gross value of fixed assets were calculated for the 1958-82 period and two equal subperiods, 1958-70 and 1970-82. The details appear at the bottom of appended Table A7-3. Cellulosic fiber's average return consistently was less than that of all U.S. manufacturing but noncellulosic fiber's return was only significantly lower after 1969. At first, noncellulosic's results were almost exactly the reverse of those for cellulosic fibers. Noncellulosic fibers' average pretax returns on gross value of fixed assets were higher, but not significantly so, than those of all U.S. manufacturing both overall (that is, between 1958 and 1982) and in the 1958-70 interval. Noncellulosic fibers' average pretax return for the 1970-82 period exceeded that of cellulosic fibers but was less than that of all manufacturing. Unlike cellulosics, this difference from all manufacturing was not statistically significant.

Figure 8-3
U.S. Pretax Returns on Assets

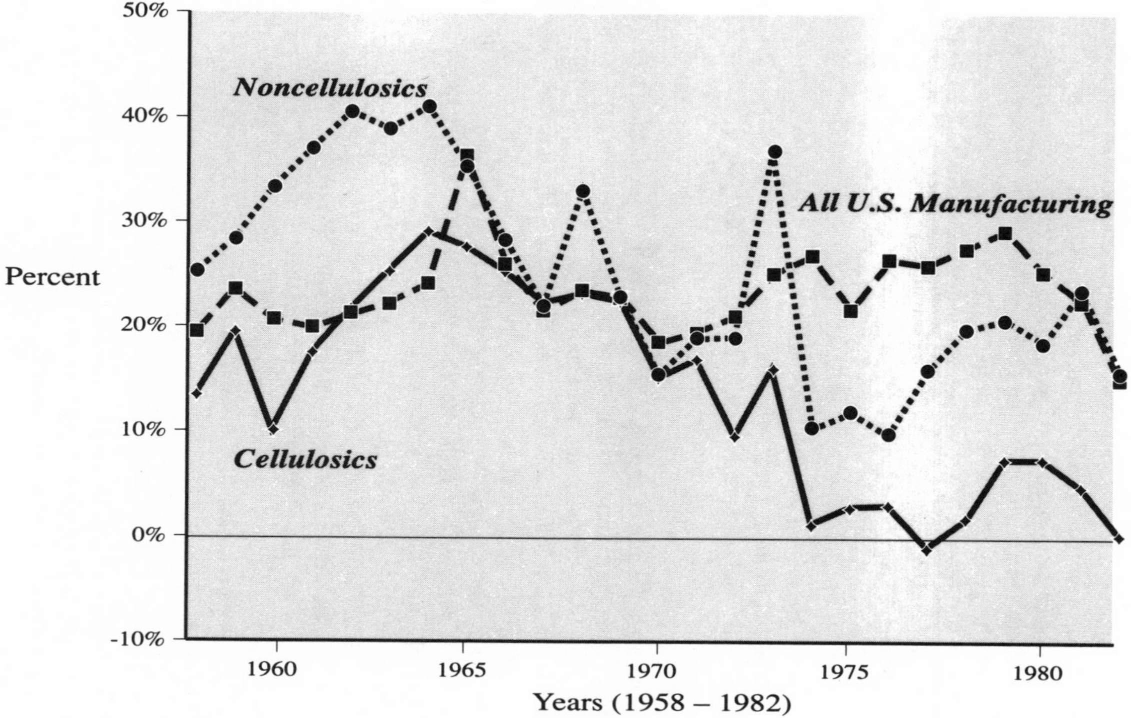

WORKABILITY OF COMPETITION

One cannot evaluate rivalry in the U.S. man-made fibers industries by a simple price competition norm as they are differentiated natural oligopolies with relatively rigid and inelastic shorter-run prices. The proper criterion, known as workability of competition, is far harder to apply because it lacks a clear, professionally accepted definition. Markham rated the U.S. rayon industry as workably competitive up to the late 1940s [Markham, 199-205] based on four tests. However, Markham also identified the crux of a critical problem: "At least any disagreement with this conclusion would evolve from placing a different construction upon such terms as rivalry, ... and the same commodity" [Markham, 201].

A practical means of coping with such problems was later proposed by Nobel Laureate George Stigler.

> *To determine whether any industry is workably competitive, there-fore, simply have a good graduate student write his dissertation on the industry and render a verdict. It is crucial to this test, of course, that no second graduate student be allowed to study the industry. [Stigler, 506]*

Although that advice creates a problem for any subsequent student, the passage of time, plus the commercialization of many new generic man-made fibers and forms, justify a view that the workability of a distinctly different industry than Markham's rayon industry is being assessed here. That invokes the questions of which norms to apply and how to evaluate them individually and, if necessary, collectively. Three collections of workability tests might be tried: the four Markham used; the 16 summarized by Scherer [Scherer, 42] from Sosnick [Sosnick, 380-423]; or the four Cox [Scherer, 43] later evaluated.

Markham first assessed the rayon industry's workability against J. M. Clark's criteria. That definition was: "Free option of the buyer to buy from a rival seller or sellers of what we think of as 'the same' product" [Markham, 200]. Since the U.S. man-made fibers industries and their constituent firms are heterogeneous within generic fibers and forms and often do not have comparable goods in their product lines, Clark's definition of the minimum standards for workability surely is not satisfied.

Markham next applied four criteria from Professor Stigler. Stigler's requirements for workable competition called for "a considerable number of firms selling closely related products in each important market area" which are not in collusion, and the stipulation that "the long-run average cost curve for a new firm is not materially higher than that for an established firm" [Markham, 201]. Although lacking quantified standards, and, hence, disputable, the requirements of a "considerable number of firms" and "closely related products" often were not met according to information presented earlier. It also is most unlikely that a new entrant ever had or eventually could even roughly match an efficient, established firm's long-run average cost curve. Whether collusion persisted in the industry after World War II probably is impossible to prove but not vital to showing that the U.S. man-made fiber industry could not pass Stigler's test of workability after 1948. However, the reasons to believe that such a cartel might still exist were presented in Chapter 7.

Markham's third test of rayon industry workability relied on seven standards proposed by Corwin Edwards [Markham, 202]. Some of these have already been found to have been either clearly or probably beyond the ability of the industries of interest to satisfy. Markham then devised and used an original test of the workability of competition in the rayon industry. His criterion was:

> *A possible alternative approach to the concept of workable competition, therefore, is one which shifts the emphasis from a set of specific structural characteristics to an appraisal of an industry's background of possible remedial action. A first approximation to the concept of workable competition when viewed along these lines might be as follows: An industry is workably competitive when, after its market characteristics and the dynamic forces which shaped them have been thoroughly examined, there is no clearly indicated change that can be effected through public policy measures which would result in greater social gains than social losses. [Markham, 204]*

Whether an industry passes Markham's proposed test plainly depends on the tester's creativity. Given the currently understood character of the overall U.S. man-made fibers industry and its subindustries, and ignoring all practical political problems of enacting or enforcing legislation, public policy changes are technically feasible to improve this industry's structural competitiveness. Generally, one might toughen existing merger regulations and enforcement. Alternatively, one could be more imaginative and aggressive in interpreting existing policy opportunities. For instance, the U.S. government's tax and tariff policy or its procurement powers could be applied to erode unduly high man-made fiber prices to correct chronic underutilization of capacity. In principle, national security-related powers also might be invoked to restructure the U.S. man-made fibers industry into a larger group of more independent, less vertically integrated firms, each with only one economic-sized plant in each form of each generic fiber. Obviously, such proposals would be unpalatable save perhaps in times of national emergency or rampant inflation. Such eventualities have happened frequently enough to show that the suggested policy changes are apt to be politically most acceptable just when most needed.

In sum, current information makes it impossible to regard the U.S. man-made fibers industry as workably competitive according to any currently recognized definition of that term. Part of this divergence from Markham's earlier finding of workability results from a reinterpretation of critical terms, as Markham anticipated. However, the grounds for those differences were exhaustively documented above.

INDIVIDUAL FIRMS' PERFORMANCE

Introduction

Assessing an industry's economic performance from financial data raises problems in fact and logic, as the existence of so many imperfect tests of competitive workability shows. One difficulty is that by unquestioningly accepting the preconditions to perfect competition as accurate descriptors of reality, the accounting and financial disciplines necessarily assume away many key facts needed to evaluate an industry's or a firm's economic performance. Reliance on those classical premises introduces a strong element of circularity into the analysis. Any nonprice rivalry further complicates the situation. A performance measure that is independent of the assumptions made about both the market structure and the behavior of the firms composing the industry of interest is needed. Ideally, such an instrument should also be easy to figure, call only for readily available data, and yield unambiguous results. One such device is called GREI.

GREI, an acronym for gross relative effectiveness indicator, was developed in the fall of 1973 by the author and a colleague, Alan W. Dickinson, Senior Science Fellow (statistics) at Monsanto, during our off hours. Although Dickinson never saw the raw data, his insights and statistical expertise were crucial to the development and testing of GREI.

GREI is a gross measure in at least two regards. First, it captures the combined results of all functional activities. Second, it can track performance at various levels, for example, the product, business unit, total enterprise, or for strategic groups of firms.

Method

A GREI is a dimensionless value condensed from four data series. The formula for GREI derives from three key premises. First, more economically effective units have higher average capacity utilization rates (ACURs) than less effective ones. Second, more economically effective units have smaller standard deviations (E) of their ACURs. Last, each unit struggles against an artificial coalition of all others in the industry.

GREI's first two premises are intuitively obvious and easy to apply with generally available data. Four statistical series on capacity and production for the unit of interest and for the rest of the industry are converted into ACURs and corresponding standard deviations. Those four numbers are condensed into two coefficients of variation (CV), via the usual formula--CV = E/ACUR, one for the unit of interest, denoted as F, and the other for the artificial coalition of all rivals, denoted as I.

Premise three calls for testing for statistically significant differences between F and I. Hence, one needs an overall standard error, S, and that means finding and combining the standard errors of F and I, S_f and S_i. The converging Taylor series used to establish S is:

$$S = [\{(F + 2F^3)^{0.5}/2N\}^2 + \{(I + 2I^3)^{0.5}/2N\}^2]^{0.5}$$

where N is the number of data pairs used.

GREI values are the t values from the above equation. GREI values may seem peculiar at first as the most economically effective unit will have the largest negative or smallest positive number while the least effective unit has the largest positive value. as a result of the interaction of GREI's key premises. Premise one gives the best firm the highest ACUR as its CV denominator, which ensures a low F value. Premise two also gives the best firm the smallest standard deviation as its CV numerator, which further assures it a low F value. Premise three mandates subtracting I from F, although I exceeds F, by definition, for economically superior performing entities. So, the best firm should have a small and even a negative t or GREI value.

GREI values enable objective comparison of any economic unit's performance with its rivals. Raw GREI figures can be evaluated to find the probability that F = I. They also can be rank ordered and tested accordingly against potentially causal variables.

Results

GREI values were calculated from annual production and capacity data between 1964 and 1973 for seven subindustries in terms of generic fiber and form across all U.S. man-made fiber producers after excluding captive producers and firms that ceased production by 1975. Those exclusionary guidelines precluded examination of the fiberglass and cellulosic subindustries. The cellulosic subindustries could only have been evaluated as a single entity, which would have been misleading. GREI data were ranked from 1 for the best firm in each instance to N for the worst and are presented on Table 8-2.

Several aspects of Table 8-2 deserve comment. First, many little-known and small U.S. man-made fiber producers earned better GREI ranks than bigger or more famous rivals. This conflicts with popular U.S. man-made fiber management beliefs that size, product diversification, and vertical integration are crucial to success. Many highly effective smaller producers of a single generic fiber and form were excluded because they were captive manufacturers. Second, among the larger and more diversified man-made fiber producers, only duPont and Eastman were consistently highly effective based on their GREI ranks. Next, duPont's seemingly poor nylon filament performance results from the inclusion of duPont's Aramid fibers' capacities and production in the raw data. If the effects of those, essentially start-up, Aramid operations were eliminated, duPont's GREI rank in nylon surely would improve markedly. Fourth, some man-made fiber producers' performances appar-

Table 8-2

Gross Relative Effectiveness Indicator Ranks

(1 = Best; and N = Worst)

	Acrylics and Modacrylics	Nylon		Olefin		Polyester	
		Filament	Staple	Filament	Staple	Filament	Staple
Akzona	-	2	7	-	-	13	9
Allied	-	1	3	3	-	4	6
American Cyanamid	3	-	-	-	-	11	-
Avtex	-	-	-	-	1	10	10
Badische	4	3	-	-	-	7	3
Beaunit	-	7	4	-	-	8	11
Celanese	-	10	5	-	-	12	4
Chevron	-	-	-	5	4	-	-
Courtaulds	-	9	-	-	-	-	-
duPont	1	5	1	-	-	1	1
Eastman	2	-	-	1	-	2	2
Hercules	-	-	-	2	2	-	-
American Hoechst	-	-	-	-	-	5	8
Monsanto	5	4	6	-	-	6	7
Phillips	-	6	-	4	3	9	5
Rohm & Haas	-	8	2	-	-	3	-
Number of Firms:	5	10	7	5	4	13	11

Source: Author.

ently were so grave and time-binding as to negate the possibility of recovery to an acceptable level because they eventually ceased making the particular item(s). MTC in polyester staple is the only visible example, but Beaunit, Rohm and Haas, and Union Carbide are three more cases in point that were excluded as having exited the industry by 1975. Last, if GREI is a reliable measure, why did some firms with relatively inferior ratings continue to operate?

That question has several possible answers. First, exit might be technically infeasible or, internally or externally, politically inconceivable or intolerable. Avtex seems to fit into this category. Second, corporate management may have strategic reasons for remaining in the man-made fibers business. American Cyanamid and MTC extrude man-made fibers in part to absorb excess acrylonitrile capacity from other divisions. Third, different firms might disagree on goals or use different time horizons when reviewing their commitments to the U.S. man-made fibers industry. Some of these possibilities were tested via Spearman rank correlations (Rs). Among them were: capacity as a proxy for size, domestic versus foreign ownership, public versus private ownership, autonomy of the fiber operation versus inclusion within a larger entity, number of man-made fiber product lines, traceable advertising expenditures, subjective ratings by textile mills, external shocks, and management stability.

Each firm was ranked, in descending order, in each of seven fiber industries on its GREI value and size, based on average annual capacity between 1964 and 1973, to test a null hypothesis that performance does not improve with absolute size. All Rs, Spearman rank correlation coefficients, were insignificant at an 0.05 level. Even less significant correlation results appeared when testing all but the last of the remaining potential causal variables. That leaves two possibilities. Either a ten-year, 1964-73, data base is statistically inadequate for this purpose, or these prospective independent variables were not causal.

Every U.S. man-made fiber producer experienced some common and uncommon shocks with long-lasting effects. How quickly and ably these organizations dealt with the opportunities and threats they were exposed to depends on their managements. Management can limit or increase a firm's exposure to needless or grave risks. Management can heighten or weaken a firm's resistance to shocks. Management also can enable a firm to promptly and fully exploit opportunities or to miss them in part or entirely. As a group, U.S. fiber company management illustrated a fairly complete spectrum of management influence on performance efficacy, with duPont by far the most consistently effective team. Arguably, firms that exited the industry were much less well served by their executives. That might be an unduly harsh statement if: (1) the team leading such a firm into the industry did so while protesting orders from above; or (2) the exit decision was made by a different group of executives than those who made the entry decision. Whether poor judgment, poor implementation, or bad luck caused the enterprise to end operations is irrelevant. Management's minimum obligation, if not fiduciary duty, to preserve the firm's tangible and intangible assets, is not excusable on grounds of misjudgment, poor execution, or even bad luck.

Management stability was interpreted as length of service of the head of the fibers operation and his immediate subordinates. U.S. man-made fibers manufacturers were thought stable if their senior executives averaged at least five years experience in the industry in a management role. An originally considered criterion of seven years per executive, instead of an average, had to be relaxed when it was found that few, if any, firms could satisfy it. Stable U.S. man-made fiber producers earned better GREI ranks than rivals with less seasoned executives, but not statistically significantly so. Obviously, there is no substitute for the coaching of a competent mentor in a dynamic and uncertain environment. Unfortunately, that insight will not greatly help future leaders until there is a general solution to the problems of identifying or creating and assuredly gaining the support of competent mentors.

CONCLUSIONS

This chapter yields some major conclusions about the U.S. man-made fibers industry's performance after 1948. First, the industry clearly has significantly enhanced social welfare by saving or prolonging life and improving the quality of life over many years, although it would be difficult to quantify those benefits. Second, those social gains were generated by an increasingly productive labor force especially in the newer, noncellulosics sector.

The industry has persistently generated profits. The noncellulosic sector of the industry, excluding fiberglass, had on average greater pretax returns on gross value of fixed assets than either the cellulosics or all U.S. manufacturing over the 1958-82 period. Both fiber sectors' estimated profits were visibly quite cyclical.

Having failed all established tests, the U.S. man-made fibers industry is not yet workably competitive. Available trends do, however, suggest that the industry is gradually approaching a more workably competitive state, due to growing pressures from imports, especially of downstream products, and an increasingly greater reliance on price competition over its more traditional nonprice rivalrous practices.

Recent trends in labor productivity and returns on assets seem to imply that the U.S. cellulosic fibers' outlook is bleak and deteriorating while that of noncellulosics fibers should continue to enjoy comparatively rosy prospects for some time to come.

Two conclusions above merit comment because they contradict Markham's earlier findings about the rayon industry. As this book focused on the post-1948 period, it might not agree with Markham's judgment that the pre-1948 rayon industry was workably competitive and had a promising future for three reasons. First, the U.S. man-made fibers industry could have had radically different economic traits in the separate periods which each of us, presumably correctly, assessed. Next, our conclusions might diverge because of legitimate differences in the definitions of critical terms, as clearly happened in the analysis of the industry's workability, although the logical rigor with which those terms were utilized presumably was impeccable. Last, the possibility of human error inevitably must be acknowledged even though it is improbable in so carefully reviewed a procedure as a doctoral dissertation on which both Markham's book and this work are based. The first of these explanations surely accounts for most of the reversal in the outlook for Markham's rayon industry; the shift in definitions between his rayon industry and the character of the post-1948 U.S. man-made fibers industry probably explains the remainder.

Last, merchant firms' performance varied across seven man-made fiber sub-industries in the 1964-73 period. Only duPont and Eastman had consistently effective performances, according to their GREI ranks. Thirteen other merchant U.S. man-made fiber producers generally showed far more erratic results or, worse, had uniformly weak performances across these subindustries. Courtaulds, MTC, and Phillips were among the latter group. No single, strong causal explanation of this variable performance by firm was discerned at a statistically significant level. However, producers led by experienced management teams apparently tended to outdo rivals lacking this intangible but apparently strategic resource. Rival firms' consistent and notable differences in performance over time are added proof of a heterogeneous industry.

Appendices

Table A1-1

U.S. Acetate Filament Capacity (1)

(millions of pounds at year-end November)

	1959	1960	1961	1962	1963	1964	1965	1966	1967	1968	1969	1970
Total Capacity:	301	317	228	327	346	381	451	468	459	488	496	497
Capacity by Firm												
Avtex (2)	65	65	65	70	75	80	85	85	85	85	85	85
Celanese (3)	145	155	155	155	165	187	245	265	250	260	275	270
duPont	35	35	3	40	40	40	45	45	45	50	45	45
Eastman	55	60	4	60	65	70	70	70	75	85	90	95
Imports	1	2	1	2	1	4	6	3	4	8	1	2
4 Firm Concentration Ratio (4):	0.997	0.994	0.996	0.994	0.997	0.990	0.987	0.994	0.991	0.984	0.998	0.996
Number of Suppliers (5):	5	5	5	5	5	5	5	5	5	5	5	5

Table A1-1 Continued

	1971	1972	1973	1974	1975	1976	1977	1978	1979	1980	1981	1982
Total Capacity:	492	486	465	450	385	412	332	347	361	329	335	324
Capacity by Firm												
Avtex (2)	85	85	80	80	65	70	60	60	60	50	50	50
Celanese (3)	260	260	255	250	210	225	200	215	235	215	220	210
duPont	50	50	50	45	40	40	-	-	-	-	-	-
Eastman	95	90	80	75	70	65	60	60	60	60	60	60
Imports	2	1	-	-	-	12	12	12	6	4	5	4
4 Firm Concentration Ratio (4):	0.996	0.998	1.000	1.000	1.000	0.971	1.000	1.000	1.000	1.000	1.000	1.000
			Max.			Min.						
Number of Suppliers (5):	5	5	4	4	4	5	4	4	4	4	4	4

Sources: Domestic capacity data estimated by the author.
Import data courtesy of the U.S. Department of Commerce.

Notes: 1 = Includes both diacetate and triacetate.
        2 = Successor to American Viscose Corporation.
        3 = Sole triacetate producer but also makes diacetate.
        4 = Includes imports as appropriate.
        5 = Includes imports.

Table A1-2

U.S. Acetate Staple Capacity (1)

(millions of pounds at year-end November)

	1959	1960	1961	1962	1963	1964	1965	1966	1967	1968	1969	1970
Total Capacity:	85	90	90	90	80	72	71	60	61	53	51	40
Capacity by Firm												
Avtex (2)	N	N	N	N	N	N	N	N	N	N	N	N
Beaunit	-	-	-	-	-	-	-	-	-	-	-	-
Celanese (3)	85	90	90	90	80	70	70	60	60	50	50	40
duPont	N	N	N	N	N	N	N	N	N	N	N	N
Eastman	N	N	N	N	N	N	N	N	N	N	N	N
Imports	-	-	-	-	-	2	1	-	1	3	1	-
4 Firm Concentration Ratio (4): Max.	1.000	1.000	1.000	1.000	1.000	1.000	1.000	1.000	1.000	1.000	1.000	1.000
Number of Suppliers (5):	4	4	4	4	4	5	5	4	5	5	5	4

169

Table A1-2 Continued

	1971	1972	1973	1974	1975	1976	1977	1978	1979	1980	1981	1982
Total Capacity:	30	30	30	30	20	20	10	10	10	10	5	5
Capacity by Firm												
Avtex (2)	N	N	N	N	N	N	N	N	N	N	N	N
Beaunit	-	-	N	N	N	-	-	-	-	-	-	-
Celanese (3)	30	30	30	30	20	20	10	10	10	10	5	5
duPont	N	N	N	N	N	-	-	-	-	-	-	-
Eastman	N	N	N	N	N	N	N	N	N	N	N	N
Imports	-	-	-	-	-	-	-	-	-	-	-	-
4 Firm Concentration Ratio (4):	1.000	1.000	1.000	1.000	1.000	1.000	1.000	1.000	1.000	1.000	1.000	1.000 Min.
Number of Suppliers (5):	4	4	5	5	5	3	3	3	3	3	3	3

Sources: Domestic capacity data estimated by the author.
Import data courtesy of the U.S. Department of Commerce.

Notes: 1 = Unadjusted for 'waste' capacity and excludes cigarette tow.
2 = Sucessor to American Viscose Corporation.
3 = Sole tracetate producer but also makes diacetate.
4 = Includes imports as appropriate.
5 = Includes imports.
N = Negligible, that is, less than 0.05 million pounds.

170

Table A1-3

U.S. Acrylic Staple Capacity (1)

(millions of pounds at year-end November)

	1959	1960	1961	1962	1963	1964	1965	1966	1967	1968	1969	1970
Total Capacity:	200	215	217	233	266	361	484	528	583	673	688	692
Capacity by Firm												
American Cyanamid (W)	5	5	5	10	20	35	50	55	60	90	100	110
BASF (W)	5	10	10	10	10	15	20	25	30	35	40	40
duPont	130	140	140	140	140	170	200	200	210	235	240	240
Eastman (W, M)	10	10	10	10	10	20	30	30	30	35	35	35
Monsanto (W)	45	45	45	45	70	95	140	180	200	210	220	220
Union Carbide (W, M)	5	5	5	10	10	10	10	15	15	15	15	15
Imports	-	-	2	8	6	16	34	23	38	53	38	32
4 Firm Concentration Ratio (2):	0.950	0.953	0.945	0.880	0.902	0.886	0.876	0.881	0.871	0.874	0.872	0.882
		Max.										
Number of Suppliers (3):	6	6	7	7	7	7	7	7	7	7	7	7

Table A1-3 Continued

	1971	1972	1973	1974	1975	1976	1977	1978	1979	1980	1981	1982
Total Capacity:	756	808	838	841	838	893	890	886	858	848	847	843
Capacity by Firm												
American Cyanamid (W)	115	120	125	125	125	125	125	125	120	120	120	120
BASF (W)	50	50	60	70	70	75	75	70	70	70	70	70
duPont	250	295	310	310	320	350	340	330	320	310	310	310
Eastman (W, M)	35	40	40	40	40	40	40	40	30	30	30	30
Monsanto (W)	230	230	230	250	270	280	290	300	300	300	300	300
Union Carbide (W, M)	20	20	20	20	-	-	-	-	-	-	-	-
Imports	56	53	53	26	13	23	20	21	18	18	17	13
4 Firm Concentration Ratio (2): Min.	0.861	0.864	0.865	0.898	0.937	0.929	0.933	0.931	0.944	0.943	0.945	0.949
Number of Suppliers (3):	7	7	7	7	6	6	6	6	6	6	6	6

Sources: Domestic capacity data estimated by the author.
Import data courtesy of the U.S. Department of Commerce.

Notes: 1 = Unadjusted for 'waste' capacity and includes modacrylics.
2 = Includes imports as appropriate.
3 = Includes imports.
W = Wet process only.
M = Modacrylic producer only.

Table A1-4

U.S. Fiberglass Capacity

(millions of pounds at year-end November)

	1959	1960	1961	1962	1963	1964	1965	1966	1967	1968	1969	1970
Total Capacity:	160	270	280	316	286	291	327	408	472	517	631	662
Capacity by Firm												
CertainTeed (1)	-	-	-	5	5	10	10	10	10	10	20	10
Fiberglass Industries	-	-	-	-	-	-	N	N	N	N	N	N
Kaiser (C)	-	-	-	-	-	N	N	-	-	1	5	5
Lundy	-	-	-	-	-	-	-	-	-	-	-	-
Manville (C)	10	20	20	20	20	20	20	20	25	30	30	40
Nicofibers	-	-	-	-	-	-	-	-	-	-	-	-
Oliver	-	-	-	1	1	1	1	1	1	1	1	1
Owens Corning Fiberglas	110	190	185	210	180	180	200	270	310	330	410	420
Pittsburgh Plate Glass	30	40	50	50	50	50	60	70	90	110	120	140
Reichhold	10	20	25	25	25	25	30	30	30	30	40	40
Stranglas	-	-	-	-	-	N	1	1	N	-	-	-
United Merchants (C)	-	-	-	5	5	5	5	5	5	5	5	5
Imports	-	-	-	-	-	-	-	1	1	-	-	1
Concentration Ratios (2)												
4 Firm:	1.000	1.000	1.000	0.965	0.962	0.945	0.948	0.956	0.964	0.967	0.951	0.967
8 Firm: Max.							1.000	0.998	1.000	1.000	1.000	0.998
Number of Suppliers (3):	4	4	4	6	6	9	10	10	10	9	9	10

173

Table A1-4 Continued

	1971	1972	1973	1974	1975	1976	1977	1978	1979	1980	1981	1982
Total Capacity:	693	730	754	832	919	909	1027	1137	1322	1491	1581	1727
Capacity by Firm												
CertainTeed (1)	-	-	-	-	-	-	40	50	70	110	170	190
Fiberglass Industries	N	-	-	-	-	-	-	-	-	-	N	10
Kaiser (C)	10	10	10	-	-	-	-	-	-	-	-	-
Lundy	-	-	-	-	-	-	-	-	-	-	N	N
Manville (C)	50	60	60	60	60	60	70	80	120	130	160	190
Nicofibers	-	-	-	-	5	5	5	5	5	5	5	5
Oliver	1	1	1	-	-	-	-	-	-	-	-	-
Owens Corning Fiberglas	425	425	425	475	520	510	540	570	690	790	780	860
Pittsburgh Plate Glass	160	180	200	240	280	280	300	360	370	380	390	400
Reichhold	40	40	40	40	40	40	50	50	50	60	60	60
Stranglas	-	-	-	-	5	-	-	-	-	-	-	-
United Merchants (C)	5	5	5	5	5	-	-	-	-	-	-	-
Imports	2	9	13	12	9	14	22	22	17	16	16	12
Concentration Ratios (2)												
4 Firm:	0.974	0.966	0.962	0.980	0.979	0.979	0.935	0.932	0.946	0.946	0.949	0.950
								Min.				
8 Firm:	1.000											
Number of Suppliers (3):	9	8	8	6	7	6	6	6	6	6	9	9

Sources: Domestic capacity data estimated by the author.
Import data courtesy of the U.S. Department of Commerce.

Notes: 1 = Includes 1959-70 operatons of Gustin Bacon, a predecessor organization.
2 = Includes imports as appropriate.
N = Negligible, that is, less than 0.05 million pounds.
C = Captive producer only.

Table A1-5

U.S. Nylon Filament Capacity (1)

(millions of pounds at year-end November)

	1959	1960	1961	1962	1963	1964	1965	1966	1967	1968	1969	1970
Total Capacity:	2377	2417	2518	2601	2680	2776	2926	3084	3190	3335	3427	3471
Capacity by Firm												
Albany Int'l. (2)	-	-	-	1	1	1	1	1	1	1	1	1
Allied	20	20	30	50	80	90	100	120	130	140	150	170
American Enka (3)	10	10	20	30	40	60	70	70	70	80	90	90
Ametek (2)	-	-	-	-	-	1	1	1	1	1	1	1
BASF (3)	-	-	-	-	-	-	-	-	-	30	30	30
Beaunit	-	-	1	1	5	5	10	40	40	40	40	40
Berkley (2, 3)	-	-	-	-	-	1	1	1	1	1	1	1
Camac (3)	-	-	-	-	-	-	-	-	-	-	-	-
Celanese (3)	-	-	-	-	N	1	40	60	70	70	70	80
Chevron (3)	-	-	-	-	-	-	-	-	-	20	30	30
Courtaulds (3)	-	-	-	-	5	5	5	5	5	5	5	5
duPont	250	280	320	360	360	410	450	520	550	580	630	630
Falk (2, 3)	-	-	-	-	N	N	1	1	1	5	5	5
Firestone (C, 3)	5	5	10	20	30	30	40	40	40	40	50	50
Gladding (2, 3)	-	-	-	-	-	-	-	-	-	-	-	-

Table A1-5 Continued

Capacity by Firm	1971	1972	1973	1974	1975	1976	1977	1978	1979	1980	1981	1982
Total Capacity:	3521	3673	3715	3804	3832	3866	3934	3988	4023	3945	3926	3909
Albany Int'l. (2)	-	1	1	1	1	1	1	1	1	1	1	1
Allied	170	170	170	190	200	220	220	220	220	220	220	220
American Enka (3)	100	110	120	120	120	120	140	150	150	150	150	150
Ametek (2)	-	1	1	1	1	1	1	1	1	1	1	1
BASF (3)	40	50	50	70	70	80	80	80	80	80	80	80
Beaunit	20	20	20	20	20	5	-	-	-	-	-	-
Berkley (2, 3)	1	1	1	1	1	1	1	1	1	1	1	1
Camac (3)	5	10	10	10	10	20	20	10	10	10	10	10
Celanese (3)	70	70	60	50	50	20	20	20	20	20	-	-
Chevron (3)	30	60	60	60	60	60	70	70	70	-	-	-
Courtaulds (3)	5	5	5	5	5	5	5	5	1	1	1	1
duPont	640	660	710	760	770	860	890	1020	1080	1110	1110	1080
Falk (2, 3)	5	5	5	5	5	5	5	5	5	5	5	5
Firestone (C, 3)	60	60	60	60	60	60	60	60	60	50	50	50
Gladding (2, 3)	-	-	-	-	-	N	N	N	-	-	-	-

176

	1959	1960	1961	1962	1963	1964	1965	1966	1967	1968	1969	1970
Guilford (C, 3)	-	-	-	-	-	-	-	-	-	5	5	5
Johnson Filament (2)	-	-	-	-	-	-	-	-	-	-	-	-
Kayser Roth (C, 4)	-	-	-	-	1	1	1	1	N	1	1	1
M & Q (2, 3)	-	-	N	N	N	-	N	N	N	-	-	-
Milliken (C, 2, 3)	-	-	-	-	-	-	-	-	-	N	-	-
Monofil Inc. (2, 4)	N	-	-	-	-	-	-	-	-	-	-	N
Monsanto (4)	130	140	170	170	190	200	230	240	280	280	280	280
Nylon Engineering (3)	-	-	-	-	-	-	-	-	-	1	1	5
Phillips (4)	-	-	-	-	-	-	-	-	-	20	30	30
Rohm & Haas	N	N	N	N	1	1	1	1	10	10	10	10
Shakespeare (2, 3)	-	-	-	-	-	-	1	1	1	1	5	5
Sunburst (4)	-	-	-	-	-	-	-	-	-	-	-	-
Uniroyal (C, 3)	-	N	N	N	N	N	N	N	N	N	N	N
Wellman (4)	-	-	-	-	1	1	1	5	10	10	10	10
Imports	3	2	5	7	4	5	8	11	12	26	13	22
Concentration Ratios (5)												
Four Firm:	0.172	0.186	0.214	0.235	0.250	0.274	0.290	0.308	0.323	0.324	0.336	0.337
		Max.										
Eight Firm:			0.221	0.246	0.266	0.290	0.324	0.357	0.374	0.365	0.379	0.380
Twenty Firm:										0.999	0.999	0.999
Number of Suppliers (6):	7	7	10	10	14	17	19	19	19	24	23	24

Table A1-5 Continued

	1971	1972	1973	1974	1975	1976	1977	1978	1979	1980	1981	1982
Guilford (C, 3)	5	5	5	5	5	5	5	5	5	5	5	5
Johnson Filament (2)	-	-	-	-	-	1	1	1	1	1	1	1
Kayser Roth (C, 4)	5	5	5	5	5	5	5	5	5	5	5	5
M & Q (2, 3)	-	-	-	-	-	-	-	-	-	-	-	-
Milliken (C, 2, 3)	-	-	-	-	-	-	-	-	-	-	-	-
Monofil Inc. (2, 4)	N	N	N	N	N	N	N	1	1	1	1	1
Monsanto (4)	280	290	290	300	300	300	300	290	290	260	260	270
Nylon Engineering (3)	5	5	5	-	-	-	-	-	-	-	-	-
Phillips (4)	30	50	50	60	70	-	50	-	-	-	-	-
Rohm & Haas	20	40	50	50	50	50	50	-	-	-	-	-
Shakespeare (2, 3)	5	5	5	5	5	5	5	5	5	5	5	5
Sunburst (4)	-	-	-	-	-	N	N	N	N	N	-	-
Uniroyal (C, 3)	N	N	N	N	N	N	N	N	N	N	N	N
Wellman (4)	20	30	30	30	30	30	30	30	30	30	30	30
Imports	32	48	29	22	19	36	48	30	8	9	9	11

Concentration Ratios (5)

	1971	1972	1973	1974	1975	1976	1977	1978	1979	1980	1981	1982
Four Firm:	0.338	0.335 Min.	0.347	0.360	0.363	0.388	0.394	0.421	0.433	0.441	0.443	0.440
Eight Firm:	0.383	0.395	0.406	0.426	0.431	0.453	0.460	0.481	0.492	0.487	0.487	0.484
Twenty Firm:	0.999	0.999	0.999	0.999	0.999	0.999	1.000	1.000	1.000	1.000	1.000	1.000

Number of
	1971	1972	1973	1974	1975	1976	1977	1978	1979	1980	1981	1982
Suppliers (6):	25	25	25	24	24	26	25	24	23	22	20	20

Sources: Domestic capacity data estimated by the author.
Import data courtesy of the U.S. Department of Commerce.

Notes: 1 = Includes Aramid fibers.   2 = Monofilament producer only.
3 = Type 6 only.   4 = Type 6, 6 only.
5 = Includes imports as appropriate.
6 = Includes imports.
N = Negligible, that is, less than 0.05 million pounds.

Table A1-6

U.S. Nylon Staple Capacity (1)

(millions of pounds at year-end November)

	1959	1960	1961	1962	1963	1964	1965	1966	1967	1968	1969	1970
Total Capacity:	45	47	48	59	76	97	116	161	183	234	279	298
Capacity by Firm												
Allied	1	1	1	5	5	10	20	20	20	20	60	60
American Enka (2)	1	1	1	1	1	1	5	5	5	5	5	10
BASF (2)	-	-	-	-	-	-	-	-	-	-	-	-
Beaunit	-	1	1	1	1	5	5	10	10	10	10	10
Celanese (3)	-	-	-	-	-	-	5	5	5	5	5	5
duPont	40	40	30	25	40	50	50	50	70	120	120	120
Firestone (C, 2)	-	-	-	-	-	-	-	-	-	-	-	-
Monsanto (3)	-	-	10	20	20	20	20	35	40	40	50	60
Nylon Engineering (2)	-	-	-	-	-	-	-	-	-	-	-	-
Rohm & Haas	-	-	-	-	-	-	-	-	-	-	-	-
Star Fibers (2)	-	-	-	-	-	-	-	-	-	-	-	-
Wellman (3)	-	-	-	-	1	1	1	10	10	10	10	15
Imports	3	4	5	7	8	10	10	26	23	24	19	18
Concentration Ratios (4)												
Four Firm: Max.	1.000	0.979	0.958	0.966	0.961	0.928	0.862	0.814	0.836	0.872	0.892	0.866
Eight Firm:							1.000	1.000	1.000	1.000	1.000	1.000
Number of Suppliers (5):	4	5	6	6	7	7	8	8	8	8	8	8

Table A1-6 Continued

	1971	1972	1973	1974	1975	1976	1977	1978	1979	1980	1981	1982
Total Capacity:	485	650	753	792	860	944	966	1041	1036	1004	1061	1021
Capacity by Firm												
Allied	120	120	130	150	170	180	200	200	200	200	220	220
American Enka (2)	40	40	60	80	100	100	100	100	100	100	100	100
BASF (2)	20	40	40	40	60	60	60	60	60	60	60	60
Beaunit	40	50	50	60	70	80	-	-	-	-	-	-
Celanese (3)	10	20	30	40	50	50	70	70	70	40	-	-
duPont	120	180	220	190	190	200	200	210	220	220	220	220
Firestone (C, 2)	-	-	-	10	10	10	10	10	-	-	-	-
Monsanto (3)	90	110	110	120	120	180	250	320	320	320	360	330
Nylon Engineering (2)	1	1	10	10	-	-	-	-	-	-	-	-
Rohm & Haas	-	5	5	5	5	5	5	-	-	-	-	-
Star Fibers (2)	1	10	20	20	20	20	20	20	20	20	20	20
Wellman (3)	20	30	30	30	30	30	30	30	30	30	30	30
Imports	23	44	48	37	35	29	21	21	16	14	51	41
Concentration Ratios (4)												
Four Firm:	0.763	0.708	0.691	0.707	0.674 Min.	0.699	0.776	0.797	0.811	0.837	0.848	0.852
Eight Firm:	0.975	0.945	0.914	0.905	0.924	0.932	0.964	0.971	0.985	0.986	1.000	1.000
Number of Suppliers (5):	11	12	12	13	12	12	11	10	9	9	8	8

Sources: Domestic capacity data estimated by the author.
Import data courtesy of the U.S. Department of Commerce.

Notes: 1 = Unadjusted for 'waste' capacity and includes Aramids.
2 = Type 6 only.
3 = Type 6, 6 only.
4 = Includes imports as appropriate.
5 = Includes imports.
C = Captive producer only.

Table A1-7

U.S. Olefin Filament Capacity (1)

(millions of pounds at year-end November)

	1959	1960	1961	1962	1963	1964	1965	1966	1967	1968	1969	1970
Total Capacity:	3936	3955	3969	3966	3980	3988	4026	4089	4134	4257	4259	4276
Capacity by Firm												
ACS Industries (C)	-	-	-	-	1	1	1	5	5	10	10	10
American Enka (F)	-	-	-	-	-	-	-	-	1	5	5	5
American Mfg. (2)	-	-	1	1	5	5	5	5	5	10	10	10
American Polyfibers (C)	-	-	-	-	-	-	-	-	-	-	-	-
Amoco	-	-	1	1	1	1	1	10	10	40	40	40
Andray (C, F)	-	-	-	-	-	-	-	-	-	-	-	-
Arlin (F)	-	-	-	-	-	-	-	-	-	-	N	N
Armstrong (C, F)	-	-	-	-	-	-	-	N	N	N	-	N
Avtex (4)	-	-	-	-	-	-	-	-	-	-	-	-
Beaunit	-	1	5	5	5	1	1	-	-	-	-	-
Bemis (C, F)	-	-	-	-	-	1	1	1	1	1	1	1
Berkley (C, 2)	-	-	-	-	-	1	1	1	1	1	1	1
Blue Mountain (C, F)	-	-	-	-	-	-	-	-	-	-	-	-
Bridon Cordage (C)	-	-	-	-	-	-	-	-	N	N	-	-
Buck (C, F)	-	-	-	-	-	-	-	-	-	-	-	-
Burlington Ind. (C, F)	-	-	-	-	-	-	-	-	1	5	5	5
Colorado F & I (C, 2)	-	1	1	-	1	-	5	-	5	-	N	N
Columbian Rope (C, 2)	-	-	-	1	1	1	5	5	5	5	5	5
Concorde Fibers	-	-	-	-	-	-	-	-	-	-	-	-
Consolidated (C, 2)	-	-	-	-	-	-	-	-	-	-	-	1

Table A1-7 Continued

	1971	1972	1973	1974	1975	1976	1977	1978	1979	1980	1981	1982
Total Capacity:	4308	4380	4454	4548	4778	4823	4856	4874	4880	4861	4948	5004
Capacity by Firm												
ACS Industries (C)	10	10	10	10	10	10	10	10	10	10	10	10
American Enka (F)	5	5	5	5	5	5	5	5	5	5	5	5
American Mfg. (2)	10	10	10	10	10	10	10	10	10	10	10	10
American Polyfibers (C)	-	N	N	-	-	-	-	-	-	-	-	-
Amoco	50	60	90	140	310	310	320	330	330	310	390	430
Andray (C, F)	-	1	1	1	1	1	1	1	1	-	-	-
Arlin (F)	-	-	-	-	1	1	1	1	1	1	1	1
Armstrong (C, F)	1	5	5	10	10	10	10	10	10	10	10	10
Avtex (4)	-	-	-	-	-	-	-	-	-	-	-	-
Beaunit	-	-	-	1	5	5	1	-	-	-	-	-
Bemis (C, F)	1	5	5	5	5	5	5	5	5	5	5	5
Berkley (C, 2)	1	1	5	5	10	10	10	10	10	10	10	10
Blue Mountain (C, F)	1	5	5	5	5	5	5	5	5	5	5	5
Bridon Cordage (C)	-	-	-	-	-	-	-	-	-	-	-	-
Buck (C, F)	-	-	-	-	-	-	-	-	-	-	-	-
Burlington Ind. (C, F)	-	-	-	-	-	-	-	-	-	-	-	-
Colorado F & I (C, 2)	N	N	-	-	-	-	-	-	-	-	-	-
Columbian Rope (C, 2)	10	10	10	10	10	10	10	10	10	10	10	10
Concorde Fibers	5	5	5	5	5	5	5	5	5	5	5	5
Consolidated (C, 2)	-	N	N	N	N	N	N	-	-	-	-	-

182

	1959	1960	1961	1962	1963	1964	1965	1966	1967	1968	1969	1970
Crowe Rope (C, 2)	-	-	-	-	-	-	-	-	1	1	1	1
duPont (C, S)	-	-	-	-	-	-	-	-	10	20	20	30
Duraplex (C)	-	-	-	-	-	-	-	-	-	N	-	-
Eastman (C, F)	-	-	-	-	-	-	-	15	15	15	15	15
Ensign-Bickford (C, F)	-	-	-	-	-	-	-	-	-	-	-	-
Exxon (C, 2)	5	5	5	-	-	-	-	-	-	-	-	-
Firestone (C)	1	1	1	1	1	1	1	1	-	-	-	-
FNT (C, 2, 3)	N	N	N	N	N	N	N	N	N	N	N	N
General Plastics	-	-	-	-	-	-	-	-	-	-	-	-
Georgia Synthetics (C)	-	-	-	-	-	-	-	-	-	-	-	-
H & L Industries (C)	-	-	-	-	-	-	-	-	-	-	-	-
Hercules	5	10	15	15	20	25	35	45	55	70	65	50
Hoover & Allison (C, F)	-	-	-	1	1	1	1	1	1	1	1	1
Keller Ind. (C, 2)	-	-	-	-	-	-	-	-	-	-	5	5
Kendall (C, F)	-	-	-	-	-	-	-	-	-	-	-	-
Kimberly Clark (C, S)	-	-	-	-	-	-	-	-	-	-	-	-
Lambeth Rope (C, 2)	-	-	-	1	1	1	1	1	1	1	1	1
Lorentzen (F)	-	-	-	-	-	-	-	-	-	-	-	-
Milliken (C, 2)	-	-	-	-	-	-	-	1	1	1	1	1
Mirafi (C)	-	-	-	-	-	-	-	-	-	10	10	5
Osterneck (F)	1	1	1	1	1	5	10	20	5	10	10	5
Phillips	-	1	1	1	1	5	10	20	20	20	20	20
Plant Industries (F)	-	-	-	-	-	-	-	-	-	-	-	-
Polyloom Corp. (F)	1	5	5	5	5	5	10	10	15	20	20	30
Polymer Int'l. (F)	-	-	-	-	-	-	-	-	-	-	N	N

Table A1-7 Continued

	1971	1972	1973	1974	1975	1976	1977	1978	1979	1980	1981	1982
Crowe Rope (C, 2)	1	1	1	1	1	1	1	1	1	1	1	1
duPont (C, S)	55	70	90	100	110	120	130	130	130	130	140	150
Duraplex (C)	-	-	-	-	-	-	-	-	-	-	-	-
Eastman (C, F)	15	15	15	15	15	15	15	15	-	-	-	-
Ensign-Bickford (C, F)	-	-	1	1	1	1	5	5	5	5	5	5
Exxon (C, 2)	-	1	5	5	10	10	10	10	10	10	10	10
Firestone (C)	-	-	-	-	-	-	-	-	-	-	-	-
FNT (C, 2, 3)	N	N	N	N	N	N	N	N	N	N	N	N
General Plastics	-	-	N	-	-	-	-	-	-	-	-	-
Georgia Synthetics (C)	-	-	-	1	5	10	10	10	10	10	10	10
H & L Industries (C)	-	N	N	-	-	-	-	-	-	-	-	-
Hercules	60	70	70	80	80	90	90	90	100	100	100	100
Hoover & Allison (C, F)	1	1	1	1	1	1	1	1	1	1	1	1
Keller Ind. (C, 2)	5	5	5	5	5	5	5	5	5	5	5	5
Kendall (C, F)	N	N	N	-	-	-	-	-	-	-	-	-
Kimberly Clark (C, S)	-	5	5	5	5	5	5	5	10	10	10	10
Lambeth Rope (C, 2)	1	1	1	1	1	1	1	1	5	5	5	5
Lorentzen (F)	-	-	-	-	1	1	5	5	5	5	5	5
Milliken (C, 2)	-	-	-	-	-	-	-	-	-	-	-	-
Mirafi (C)	5	5	5	5	5	5	5	5	5	5	5	5
Osterneck (F)	5	5	5	5	5	5	5	5	5	5	5	5
Phillips	20	20	20	20	20	20	20	30	30	30	30	30
Plant Industries (F)	-	-	5	5	5	5	5	5	5	5	-	-
Polyloom Corp. (F)	30	30	30	30	40	40	50	50	50	50	50	50
Polymer Int'l. (F)	-	-	-	-	-	-	-	-	-	-	-	-

	1959	1960	1961	1962	1963	1964	1965	1966	1967	1968	1969	1970
Prestwheel (C, 2)	-	-	-	-	N	N	N	N	N	N	N	N
Schegel (C, 2)	-	-	1	1	1	1	1	1	1	1	1	1
Shuford (F)	-	-	-	-	-	-	-	-	1	1	1	5
Sunshine Cordage (C)	-	-	-	-	-	-	-	-	1	1	1	1
Synthetic Fibers (2)	-	-	-	-	-	-	-	-	-	-	-	-
Synthetic Ind. (C, F)	-	-	-	-	-	-	-	-	1	5	5	5
3M Corp. (C)	-	-	-	-	-	-	-	-	-	-	-	-
Tubbs Cordage (C)	-	-	-	-	-	-	-	1	1	1	1	5
Twine Products (C)	-	-	-	-	-	-	-	1	1	1	1	1
Uniroyal (C)	-	-	1	1	1	1	10	20	20	30	30	30
Vogt Mfg. Corp. (4)	-	-	-	-	-	N	N	N	N	N	N	N
Waltrich Plastics (2)	-	-	-	1	1	1	1	1	1	1	5	5
Wayn-Tex	5	10	10	10	10	10	10	15	20	30	30	30
Wellington (C, 2)	-	-	-	-	-	-	-	-	1	5	5	5
Western Filament	-	-	-	-	-	-	-	-	-	-	-	1
Imports	-	-	-	-	-	-	3	-	-	-	-	-
Concentration Ratios (5)												
Four Firm:	0.004 Max.	0.008	0.009	0.009	0.010	0.011	0.016	0.024	0.028	0.040	0.039	0.035 Min.
Eight Firm:		0.009	0.011	0.010	0.012	0.013	0.022	0.034	0.040	0.058	0.056	0.057
Twenty Firm:								0.038	0.047	0.074	0.073	0.073
Number of Suppliers (6):	7	10	13	12	16	18	19	21	32	35	35	39

Table A1-7 Continued

	1971	1972	1973	1974	1975	1976	1977	1978	1979	1980	1981	1982
Prestwheel (C, 2)	-	-	-	-	-	-	-	-	-	-	-	-
Schegel (C, 2)	1	1	-	-	-	-	-	-	-	-	-	-
Shuford (F)	5	5	5	5	5	5	5	5	5	5	5	5
Sunshine Cordage (C)	1	1	1	1	1	1	1	1	1	1	1	1
Synthetic Fibers (2)	-	1	1	1	1	1	5	5	5	5	5	5
Synthetic Ind. (C, F)	10	15	15	15	20	20	20	20	20	20	20	20
3M Corp. (C)	-	N	-	-	N	N	N	-	-	-	-	-
Tubbs Cordage (C)	5	5	5	5	5	10	10	10	10	10	10	10
Twine Products (C)	10	10	10	10	10	10	10	10	10	10	10	10
Uniroyal (C)	-	-	-	-	-	-	-	-	-	-	-	-
Vogt Mfg. Corp. (4)	N	N	N	-	-	-	-	-	-	-	-	-
Waltrich Plastics (2)	5	5	5	5	5	5	5	5	5	5	5	5
Wayn-Tex	30	40	50	60	60	60	60	60	60	60	60	60
Wellington (C, 2)	5	5	5	10	10	20	20	20	20	20	20	20
Western Filament	1	1	1	1	1	1	1	-	-	-	-	-
Imports	1	1	-	-	14	11	4	2	2	2	2	6
Concentration Ratios (5)												
Four Firm:	0.045	0.055	0.067	0.084	0.117	0.120	0.124	0.125	0.127	0.123	0.139	0.148
Eight Firm:	0.063	0.073	0.085	0.101	0.133	0.141	0.146	0.150	0.152	0.148	0.164	0.172
Twenty Firm:	0.081	0.091	0.103	0.121	0.160	0.166	0.170	0.173	0.174	0.171	0.186	0.194
Number of Suppliers (6):	36	43	43	40	43	45	45	41	40	39	38	38

Sources: Domestic capacity data estimated by the author.
_____ Import data courtesy of the U.S. Department of Commerce.

Notes: N = Negligible, that is, less than 0.05 million pounds.
       C = Captive producer only.
       F = Most, if not all, of this firm's output is in the form
           of slit or split film.
       S = Includes significant amounts of captive production of
           spunbonded products.
       1 = Also includes saran and vinyon as well as film and/or
           spunbonded products.   3 = Includes saran.
       2 = Monofilament producer only.
       4 = Also produces vinyon.
       5 = Includes imports as appropriate.   6 = Includes imports.

Table A1-8

U.S. Olefin Staple Capacity (1)

(millions of pounds at year-end November)

	1959	1960	1961	1962	1963	1964	1965	1966	1967	1968	1969	1970
Total Capacity:	12	13	15	21	17	33	31	62	87	112	124	118
Capacity by Firm												
ACS Industries (C)												
Amoco	-	-	-	-	-	-	-	-	-	1	5	10
Avtex (2)	5	5	5	5	5	5	5	5	5	5	-	-
Beaunit	5	5	5	5	5	5	-	-	-	-	5	5
Chevron	-	-	-	-	-	10	10	25	25	25	25	30
Hercules	-	1	5	5	5	5	5	10	15	15	15	15
Keowee (3)	-	-	-	-	-	N	5	-	-	-	-	-
Phillips	-	-	-	-	-	5	5	10	30	45	50	50
Imports	2	2	-	6	2	3	6	12	12	21	24	8
4-Firm Concentration Ratio (4):	1.000	1.000	1.000	1.000	1.000	0.758	0.839	0.919	0.943	0.946	0.919	0.890
	Max.					Min.						
Number of Suppliers (5):	3	4	3	4	4	7	5	5	5	6	6	6

	1971	1972	1973	1974	1975	1976	1977	1978	1979	1980	1981	1982
Total Capacity:	112	118	126	136	136	141	140	153	145	135	266	271
Capacity by Firm												
ACS Industries (C)	10	5	5	5	5	5	5	5	5	5	5	5
Amoco	-	-	-	10	15	15	20	20	35	40	65	70
Avtex (2)	5	5	5	5	5	5	5	5	5	5	5	5
Beaunit	-	-	-	-	10	5	-	-	-	-	-	-
Chevron	15	15	15	10	10	10	10	10	10	10	10	10
Hercules	15	20	25	25	25	30	25	40	40	25	130	130
Keowee (3)	-	-	-	-	-	-	-	-	-	-	-	-
Phillips	55	60	55	50	50	50	50	50	50	50	50	50
Imports	12	13	21	31	16	21	25	23	-	-	1	1
4-Firm Concentration												
Ratio (4):	0.866	0.915	0.921	0.853	0.779	0.823	0.857	0.869	0.931	0.926	0.959	0.959
Number of												
Suppliers (5):	6	6	6	7	8	8	7	7	6	6	7	7

Sources: Domestic capacity data estimated by the author.
Import data courtesy of the U.S. Department of Commerce.

Notes: 1 = Unadjusted for 'waste' capacity and includes vinal and vinyon.
2 = Successor to American Viscose Corporation and sole vinyon producer.
3 = Sole vinal producer.
4 = Includes imports as appropriate.
5 = Includes imports.
C = Captive producer only.
N = Negligible, that is, less than 0.05 million pounds.

Table A1-9

U.S. Polyester Filament Capacity

(millions of pounds at year-end November)

	1959	1960	1961	1962	1963	1964	1965	1966	1967	1968	1969	1970
Total Capacity:	1994	2000	2003	2012	2020	2035	2067	2118	2184	2302	2463	2688
Capacity by Firm												
Albany Int'l. (1)	-	-	-	-	-	-	-	-	-	-	-	-
Allied	-	-	-	-	-	-	-	-	-	-	-	-
American Cyanamid	-	-	-	-	-	1	5	5	5	5	20	20
American Enka	-	-	-	-	-	5	5	10	20	25	25	30
Ametek (1)	-	-	-	-	-	-	-	-	-	-	-	-
Avtex (2)	-	-	-	-	-	5	5	5	10	15	20	50
BASF	-	-	-	-	-	-	-	-	-	-	10	20
Beaunit	-	-	1	5	5	5	10	15	15	30	50	50
Celanese/ICI (3)	-	-	-	5	5	5	20	45	60	110	180	200
duPont	35	40	40	40	45	50	55	65	90	120	140	180
Eastman	-	-	-	-	-	-	-	-	-	-	-	-
Falk Fibers	-	-	-	-	-	-	-	-	-	-	-	-
Firestone (C)	-	-	-	-	-	-	-	-	-	-	1	5
Gladding (1)	-	-	-	-	-	-	-	-	-	-	-	-
Goodyear (C)	-	-	-	-	-	-	1	5	5	5	5	5
Hoechst	-	-	-	-	-	-	-	-	-	-	10	20
Johnson Filament (1)	-	-	-	-	-	-	-	-	-	-	-	-
Monofil. Inc. (1)	-	-	-	-	-	-	-	-	-	-	-	-
Monsanto (4)	-	-	-	-	-	-	-	-	-	-	-	20
Omega Yarns	-	-	-	-	-	-	-	-	-	-	-	-

Table A1-9 Continued

	1971	1972	1973	1974	1975	1976	1977	1978	1979	1980	1981	1982
Total Capacity:	2974	3406	3595	3798	3961	4142	4157	4083	4129	4024	3784	3593
Capacity by Firm												
Albany Int'l. (1)	1	1	1	1	1	1	1	1	1	1	1	1
Allied	20	20	30	45	50	80	80	80	80	90	90	100
American Cyanamid	30	40	45	50	50	50	50	50	50	-	-	-
American Enka	50	80	110	110	130	130	120	110	110	110	110	110
Ametek (1)	-	-	1	1	1	1	1	1	1	1	1	1
Avtex (2)	50	50	50	50	70	70	70	70	70	70	70	70
BASF	30	40	50	60	60	60	20	20	20	-	-	-
Beaunit	50	50	50	50	20	20	-	-	-	-	-	-
Celanese/ICI (3)	245	280	320	360	370	450	500	480	460	440	420	400
duPont	280	405	450	540	640	630	610	680	780	750	520	570
Eastman	10	30	30	60	70	90	100	110	120	120	130	130
Falk Fibers	5	5	5	5	10	10	10	10	10	15	15	15
Firestone (C)	5	5	20	30	30	30	40	40	40	40	40	40
Gladding (1)	-	-	-	-	-	1	1	1	1	1	1	1
Goodyear (C)	20	20	20	20	20	20	20	20	20	20	20	20
Hoechst	50	90	100	110	120	120	120	80	80	80	80	80
Johnson Filament (1)	-	-	-	-	-	1	1	1	1	1	1	1
Monofil. Inc. (1)	-	-	1	1	1	1	1	1	1	1	1	1
Monsanto (4)	30	50	60	80	100	130	140	215	230	230	230	-
Omega Yarns	-	20	30	40	50	50	50	50	50	50	50	50

Table A1-9 Continued

	1959	1960	1961	1962	1963	1964	1965	1966	1967	1968	1969	1970
Phillips	-	-	-	-	-	-	1	1	5	5	10	10
Rohm & Haas (4)	-	-	-	-	-	-	-	-	-	-	-	-
Shakespeare (1)	-	-	-	-	-	-	-	-	-	-	-	-
Tolaram Fibers	-	-	-	-	-	-	-	-	-	-	-	-
Wellman	-	-	-	-	-	-	-	-	-	-	-	-
Imports	-	-	-	-	2	-	-	1	7	18	23	108
Concentration Ratios (5)												
Four Firm:	1.000 Max.	1.000	1.000	1.000	1.000	0.032	0.044	0.064	0.085	0.124	0.160	0.200
Eight Firm:								1.000	0.998	0.997	0.989	0.978
Twenty Firm:												
Number of Suppliers (6):	1	1	3	3	4	6	8	9	9	10	12	13

192

Table A1-9 Continued

	1971	1972	1973	1974	1975	1976	1977	1978	1979	1980	1981	1982
Phillips	20	50	70	70	90	50	50	50	-	-	-	-
Rohm & Haas (4)	-	20	60	70	70	140	140	-	-	-	-	-
Shakespeare (1)	-	-	-	-	1	1	5	5	5	5	5	5
Tolaram Fibers	-	-	-	-	10	10	10	10	10	10	10	10
Weltman	-	-	-	-	-	-	-	-	-	-	1	1
Imports	107	178	119	71	22	20	40	20	10	9	7	6

Concentration Ratios

	1971	1972	1973	1974	1975	1976	1977	1978	1979	1980	1981	1982
Four Firm:	0.229	0.280	0.278	0.295 (Min.)	0.318	0.326	0.334	0.364	0.385	0.383	0.344	0.337
Eight Firm:	0.953	0.347	0.356	0.372	0.401	0.427	0.435	0.457	0.463	0.470	0.436	0.420
Twenty Firm:			1.000	1.000	0.999	0.999	0.999	0.999	1.000	1.000	1.000	1.000

Number of

	1971	1972	1973	1974	1975	1976	1977	1978	1979	1980	1981	1982
Suppliers (6):	17	19	21	21	23	25	24	23	22	20	21	19

Sources: Domestic capacity data estimated by the author.
          Import data courtesy of the U.S. Department of Commerce.

Notes: 1= Monofilament producer only.
       2 = Successor to American Viscose Corporation.
       3 = Joint Venture known as Fiber Industries.
       4 = Monsanto bought Rohm & Haas' idled facility in 1978.
       5 = Includes imports as appropriate.
       6 = Includes imports.
       C = Captive producer only.

Table A1-10

U.S. Polyester Staple Capacity (1)

(millions of pounds at year-end November)

	1959	1960	1961	1962	1963	1964	1965	1966	1967	1968	1969	1970
Total Capacity:	80	105	150	160	215	276	377	624	818	971	1191	1447
Capacity by Firm												
Allied	-	-	-	-	-	-	-	-	-	5	10	10
American Enka	-	-	-	-	-	-	-	5	5	30	40	50
Avtex (2)	-	-	-	-	-	-	-	20	30	30	30	50
BASF	-	-	-	-	-	-	-	-	-	-	20	10
Beaunit	5	10	10	10	20	25	30	30	30	30	30	30
Celanese/ICI (3)	-	5	20	20	25	40	80	180	210	250	260	350
duPont	75	80	110	120	150	180	190	240	310	330	430	430
Eastman	N	10	10	10	20	30	60	100	140	170	250	270
Hoechst	-	-	-	-	-	-	-	-	20	30	40	70
Monsanto (4)	-	-	-	-	-	-	1	10	40	50	60	80
Phillips	-	-	-	-	-	-	1	10	20	20	10	10
Rohm & Haas (4)	-	-	-	-	-	-	-	-	-	-	-	-
Wellman	-	-	-	-	-	-	-	-	1	5	5	10
Imports	-	-	-	-	-	1	15	29	12	21	6	77
Concentration Ratios (5)												
Four Firm:	Max.	1.000	1.000	1.000	1.000	0.996	0.955	0.881	0.856	0.824	0.840	0.781 Min.
Eight Firm:								0.992	0.978	0.947	0.957	0.952
Number of Suppliers (6):	3	4	4	4	4	5	7	9	11	12	13	13

	1971	1972	1973	1974	1975	1976	1977	1978	1979	1980	1981	1982
Total Capacity:	1403	1583	1722	1911	2028	2372	2472	2568	2681	2762	2844	2724
Capacity by Firm												
Allied	10	10	10	10	-	-	-	-	-	-	-	-
American Enka	30	30	30	20	10	5	5	5	5	5	5	5
Avtex (2)	50	50	40	40	40	40	40	10	-	-	-	-
BASF	5	5	-	-	-	-	-	-	-	-	-	-
Beaunit	30	30	20	10	5	5	-	-	-	-	-	-
Celanese/ICI (3)	350	380	420	510	590	700	750	770	770	780	780	780
duPont	430	500	580	670	700	800	820	820	910	940	970	970
Eastman	300	360	360	360	360	370	380	410	420	430	430	430
Hoechst	70	90	120	140	170	280	300	350	370	400	450	450
Monsanto (4)	90	90	90	90	100	100	120	130	130	130	130	-
Phillips	1	-	-	-	-	-	-	-	-	-	-	-
Rohm & Haas (4)	-	5	5	5	5	5	-	-	-	-	-	-
Wellman	20	20	30	40	40	50	50	60	70	70	70	70
Imports	17	13	17	16	8	17	7	13	6	7	9	19
Concentration Ratios (5)												
Four Firm:	0.834	0.840	0.859	0.879	0.897	0.906	0.910	0.915	0.921	0.923	0.925	0.965
Eight Firm:	0.962	0.967	0.970	0.979	0.991	0.994	0.998	0.998				
Number of												
Suppliers (6):	13	13	12	12	11	11	9	9	8	8	8	7

Sources: Domestic capacity data estimated by the author.
Import data courtesy of the U.S. Department of Commerce.

Notes: 1 = Unadjusted for 'waste' capacity.
2 = Successor to American Viscose Corporation.
3 = Joint venture known as Fiber Industries.
4 = Monsanto bought Rohm & Haas' idled facility in 1978.
5 = Includes imports as appropriate.
6 = Includes imports.
N = Negligible, that is, less than 0.05 million pounds.

Table A1-11

U.S. Rayon Filament Capacity (1)

(millions of pounds at year-end November)

	1959	1960	1961	1962	1963	1964	1965	1966	1967	1968	1969	1970
Total Capacity:	546	536	476	476	426	436	456	436	399	402	378	357
Capacity by Firm												
American Cyanamid	80	70	60	60	60	60	60	60	60	60	50	40
American Enka	140	140	120	100	100	100	120	120	110	110	100	100
Avtex (2)	130	130	110	110	110	120	130	130	130	140	140	140
Celanese	10	10	10	10	10	10	10	10	-	-	-	-
duPont (3)	60	60	50	50	-	-	-	-	-	-	-	-
Fair Haven Mills	N	N	N	N	N	N	N	N	N	N	N	N
Mohasco	5	5	5	5	5	5	5	5	5	5	5	5
North Am. Rayon (4)	120	120	120	140	140	140	130	110	90	80	80	70
Imports	1	1	1	1	1	1	1	1	4	7	3	2
4-Firm Concentration Ratio (5):	0.861	0.858	0.861	0.861	0.962	0.963	0.965	0.963	0.977	0.970	0.979	0.980
		Min.										
Number of Suppliers (6):	9	9	9	9	8	8	8	8	7	7	7	7

	1971	1972	1973	1974	1975	1976	1977	1978	1979	1980	1981	1982
Total Capacity:	343	240	238	179	109	103	102	93	85	72	73	69
Capacity by Firm												
American Cyanamid	40	-	-	-	-	-	-	-	-	-	-	-
American Enka	100	90	90	50	-	-	-	-	-	-	-	-
Avtex (2)	140	90	90	80	60	50	50	40	40	30	30	30
Celanese	-	-	-	-	-	-	-	-	-	-	-	-
duPont (3)	-	-	-	-	-	-	-	-	-	-	-	-
Fair Haven Mills	N	N	-	-	-	-	-	-	-	-	-	-
Mohasco	-	N	-	-	-	-	-	-	-	-	-	-
North Am. Rayon (4)	60	50	40	40	40	40	40	40	35	35	35	35
Imports	3	10	18	9	9	13	12	13	10	7	8	4
4-Firm Concentration Ratio (5):	0.991	1.000	1.000	1.000	1.000	1.000	1.000	1.000	1.000	1.000	1.000	1.000 Max.
Number of Suppliers (6):	6	5	4	4	3	3	3	3	3	3	3	3

Sources: Domestic capacity data estimated by the author.
Import data courtesy of the U.S. Department of Commerce.

Notes: 1 = Entirely viscose process.
2 = Successor to American Viscose Corporation.
3 = High wet modulus (HWM) only.
4 = Bought plant from Beaunit and began operations in 1975. HWM only.
5 = Includes imports as appropriate.
6 = Includes imports.
N = Negligible, that is, less than 0.05 million pounds.

Table A1-12

U.S. Rayon Staple Capacity (1)

(millions of pounds at year-end November)

	1959	1960	1961	1962	1963	1964	1965	1966	1967	1968	1969	1970
Total Capacity:	648	587	576	613	748	856	827	876	864	912	899	901
Capacity by Firm												
American Cyanamid	-	-	-	-	-	-	-	20	20	20	20	20
American Enka	50	60	60	70	100	100	100	100	100	100	100	100
Avtex (2)	390	370	360	340	370	420	430	440	450	470	480	490
Beaunit	10	10	10	10	10	10	20	20	20	20	20	20
Celanese	5	5	5	10	10	10	10	10	10	-	-	-
Courtaulds	70	80	100	130	140	200	190	170	180	180	190	190
Hartford Fibers Co.	N	N	N	N	-	-	-	-	-	-	-	-
North Am. Rayon (3)	-	-	-	-	-	-	-	-	-	-	-	-
Imports	123	62	41	53	118	116	77	116	84	122	89	81
4-Firm Concentration Ratio (4):	0.977	0.974	0.974	0.967	0.973	0.977	0.964	0.943	0.942	0.956	0.956	0.956
									Min.			
Number of Suppliers (5):	7	7	7	7	6	6	6	7	7	6	6	6

	1971	1972	1973	1974	1975	1976	1977	1978	1979	1980	1981	1982
Total Capacity:	836	806	812	764	773	738	714	701	685	518	525	522
Capacity by Firm												
American Cyanamid	-	-	-	-	-	-	-	-	-	-	-	-
American Enka	100	100	100	110	110	110	110	110	110	110	110	110
Avtex (2)	470	480	480	400	390	350	320	320	320	190	190	190
Beaunit	5	5	5	5	5	5	5	-	-	-	-	-
Celanese	-	-	-	-	-	-	-	-	-	-	-	-
Courtaulds	180	170	180	210	230	230	220	220	230	200	200	200
Hartford Fibers Co.	-	-	-	-	-	-	-	10	10	10	10	-
North Am. Rayon (3)	-	-	-	-	-	-	-	10	10	10	10	10
Imports	81	51	47	39	38	43	59	41	15	8	15	12
4-Firm Concentration Ratio (4): Max.	0.994	0.994	0.994	0.993	0.994	0.993	0.993	0.986	0.985	0.985	0.981	0.981
Number of Suppliers (5):	5	5	5	5	5	5	5	5	5	5	5	5

Sources: Domestic capacity data estimated by the author.
Import data courtesy of the U.S. Department of Commerce.

Notes: 1 = Unadjusted for 'waste' capacity; entirely viscose process.
2 = Successor to American Viscose Corporation.
3 = Bought plant from Beaunit and began operations in 1975.
4 = Includes imports as appropriate.
5 = Includes imports.
N = Negligible, that is, less than 0.05 million pounds.

Table A1-13

Total U.S. Man-Made Fibers' Capacity (1)

(millions of pounds at year-end November)

	1959	1960	1961	1962	1963	1964	1965	1966	1967	1968	1969	1970
Total Capacity:	2548	2712	2814	3026	3268	3746	4299	5050	5566	6384	7011	7567

Total Capacity by Firm (1)

	1959	1960	1961	1962	1963	1964	1965	1966	1967	1968	1969	1970
Allied	21	21	31	55	85	100	120	140	150	165	220	240
American Cyanamid	85	75	65	70	80	96	115	140	145	175	190	190
American Enka	201	211	201	201	241	266	300	310	311	355	365	385
Amoco	-	-	1	1	1	1	1	10	10	40	40	40
Avtex (2)	590	570	540	525	560	630	655	685	710	745	760	820
BASF	5	10	10	10	10	15	20	25	30	65	100	100
Beaunit (3)	130	137	143	167	181	186	186	205	185	190	210	200
Celanese (4)	245	265	281	290	295	323	480	635	665	745	840	945
CertainTeed (5)	-	-	-	5	5	10	10	10	10	10	10	10
Chevron	-	-	-	-	-	10	10	25	25	45	55	60
Courtaulds	70	80	100	130	145	205	195	175	185	185	195	195
duPont (6)	625	675	725	775	775	900	990	1120	1285	1455	1625	1675
Eastman	65	80	80	80	95	120	160	215	260	305	390	415
Firestone	6	6	11	21	31	31	41	41	40	41	51	55
Goodyear	-	-	-	-	-	-	1	5	5	5	5	5
Hercules	5	11	20	20	25	30	40	55	70	85	80	65
Hoechst	-	-	-	-	-	-	-	-	20	30	50	90
Kimberly Clark	-	-	-	-	-	-	-	-	-	-	-	-
Manville	10	20	20	20	20	20	20	20	25	30	30	40
Mohasco	5	5	5	5	5	5	5	5	5	5	5	5

	1971	1972	1973	1974	1975	1976	1977	1978	1979	1980	1981	1982
Total Capacity:	8069	9027	9610	10189	10739	11459	11692	11969	12299	12099	12291	12084

Total Capacity by Firm (1)

	1971	1972	1973	1974	1975	1976	1977	1978	1979	1980	1981	1982
Allied	320	320	340	395	420	480	500	500	500	510	530	540
American Cyanamid	185	160	170	175	175	175	175	175	170	120	120	120
American Enka	425	455	515	535	475	470	480	480	480	480	480	480
Amoco	50	60	90	150	325	325	340	350	365	350	455	500
Avtex (2)	800	760	745	655	630	585	545	505	495	345	345	345
BASF	145	185	190	240	260	275	235	230	230	210	210	210
Beaunit (3)	200	200	190	181	170	160	41	50	45	45	45	45
Celanese (4)	965	1040	1115	1240	1290	1465	1550	1565	1565	1505	1425	1395
CertainTeed (5)	-	-	-	-	-	-	40	50	70	110	170	190
Chevron	45	75	75	70	70	70	80	80	80	10	10	10
Courtaulds	185	175	185	215	235	235	225	225	231	201	201	201
duPont (6)	1825	2160	2410	2615	2770	3000	2990	3190	3440	3460	3270	3300
Eastman	455	535	525	550	555	580	595	635	630	640	650	650
Firestone	65	65	80	100	100	100	110	110	100	90	90	90
Goodyear	20	20	20	20	20	20	20	20	20	20	20	20
Hercules	75	90	95	105	105	120	115	130	140	125	230	230
Hoechst	120	180	220	250	290	400	420	430	450	480	530	530
Kimberly Clark	-	5	5	5	5	5	5	5	10	10	10	10
Manville	50	60	60	60	60	60	70	80	120	130	160	190
Mohasco	-	-	-	-	-	-	-	-	-	-	-	-

Table A1-13 Continued

	1959	1960	1961	1962	1963	1964	1965	1966	1967	1968	1969	1970
Monsanto	175	185	225	235	280	315	391	465	560	580	610	660
Owens Corning Fiberglas	110	190	185	210	180	180	200	270	310	330	410	420
Omega	-	-	-	-	-	-	-	-	-	-	-	-
Phillips	1	1	1	1	1	10	17	41	75	110	120	120
Pittsburgh Plate Glass	30	40	50	50	50	50	60	70	90	110	120	140
Reichhold	10	20	25	25	25	25	30	30	30	30	40	40
Rohm & Haas (6)	-	-	N	-	1	1	1	1	10	10	10	10
Union Carbide	5	5	5	10	10	10	10	15	15	15	15	15
Uniroyal	-	-	1	1	1	1	10	20	20	30	30	30
WaynTex	5	10	10	10	10	10	10	15	20	30	30	30
Weltman	-	-	-	-	2	2	2	15	21	25	25	35
Imports of MMF (7)	133	73	55	84	142	158	161	223	198	303	218	351
Unadjusted Concentration Ratios (8)												
Four Firm:	0.652	0.635	0.629	0.603	0.584	0.579	0.585	0.575	0.579	0.552	0.547	0.542
	Max.											
Eight Firm:	0.867	0.853	0.853	0.837	0.813	0.802	0.790	0.777	0.772	0.755	0.745	0.749
Twenty Firm:	1.760	1.712	1.687	1.636	1.592	1.504	1.434	1.358	1.314	1.256	1.228	1.207
Number of Suppliers (9)	28	30	34	36	40	48	51	52	64	69	70	74
Imports of Man-Made Fiber Manufactures (10):	37	32	29	34	39	50	77	113	137	184	255	263
Imports of Man-made Fiber and Man-Made Fiber Manufactures:	170	105	84	118	181	208	238	336	335	487	473	614
Revised Grand Totals:	2585	2744	2843	3060	3307	3796	4376	5163	5703	6568	7266	7830

	1971	1972	1973	1974	1975	1976	1977	1978	1979	1980	1981	1982
Monsanto	720	770	780	840	890	990	1100	1255	1270	1260	1300	900
Owens Corning Fiberglas	425	425	425	475	520	510	540	570	690	790	780	860
Omega	-	20	30	50	50	50	50	50	50	50	50	50
Phillips	126	180	195	200	230	120	120	130	80	80	80	80
Pittsburgh Plate Glass	160	180	200	240	280	280	300	360	370	380	390	400
Reichhold	40	40	40	40	40	40	50	50	50	60	60	60
Rohm & Haas (6)	20	70	120	130	130	200	195	-	-	-	-	-
Union Carbide	20	20	20	20	-	-	-	-	-	-	-	-
Uniroyal	-	-	-	-	-	-	-	-	-	-	-	-
WaynTex	30	40	50	60	60	60	60	60	60	60	60	60
Wellman	60	80	90	100	100	115	110	120	130	130	131	131
Imports of MMF (7)	336	426	365	263	183	239	270	218	108	94	140	129
Unadjusted Concentration Ratios (8)												
Four Firm:	0.534	0.524	0.525	0.525	0.520 Min.	0.527	0.533	0.555	0.566	0.580	0.551	0.534
Eight Firm:	0.738	0.728	0.716	0.717	0.703	0.705	0.710	0.727	0.737	0.754	0.729	0.718
Twenty Firm:	1.188	1.164	1.138	1.131	1.118	1.108	1.103	1.106	1.108	1.107	1.106	1.107
Number of Suppliers (9)	71	78	78	72	74	79	80	76	76	75	75	74
Imports of Man-Made Fiber Manufactures (10):	566	494	465	367	399	471	512	631	528	542	656	703
Imports of Man-made Fiber and Man-Made Fiber Manufactures:	902	920	830	630	582	710	782	849	636	636	796	832
Revised Grand Totals:	8635	9521	10075	10556	11138	11930	12204	12600	12827	12641	12947	12787

Table A1-13 Continued

	1959	1960	1961	1962	1963	1964	1965	1966	1967	1968	1969	1970
Adjusted Concentration Ratios (11)												
Four Firm:	0.643	0.627	0.623	0.596	0.578	0.571	0.575	0.563	0.565	0.537	0.528	0.524
Eight Firm:	0.869	0.852	0.844	0.828	0.814	0.799	0.788	0.782	0.778	0.762	0.753	0.758
Twenty Firm:	1.749	1.704	1.680	1.629	1.585	1.497	1.427	1.350	1.307	1.249	1.220	1.200

	1971	1972	1973	1974	1975	1976	1977	1978	1979	1980	1981	1982
Adjusted Concentration Ratios (11)												
Four Firm:	0.499	0.497	0.501	0.507	0.501	0.506	0.511	0.527	0.543	0.555	0.523	0.505
Eight Firm:	0.755	0.742	0.729	0.714	0.692	0.697	0.705	0.720	0.719	0.734	0.717	0.704
Twenty Firm:	1.176	1.155	1.132	1.127	1.114	1.104	1.098	1.101	1.103	1.102	1.100	1.101

Sources: Domestic capacity data estimated by the author.
Import data courtesy of the U.S. Department of Commerce.

Notes: 1 = Excludes proprietary products not publicly reported, which may add as much as 150 million pounds to the subtotal and total.
2 = Successor organization to American Viscose Corporation.
3 = Combines Beaunit and North American Rayon Corporation.
4 = Includes polyester joint venture with ICI known as Fiber Industries.
5 = Includes predecessor organization, Gustin Bacon.
6 = Excludes proprietary products not publicly reported such as Lycra spandex, Anidex, and so on.
7 = MMF is an acronym for man-made fiber(s).
8 = Includes MMF imports as appropriate in the numerator and always in the denominator.
9 = Counts each supplier only once regardless of how many different generic fibers and forms it produces and imports as appropriate.
10 = Includes imported yarn, fabric, and finished products of man-made fibers.
11 = Includes imports of MMF and MMF manufactures as appropriate in the numerators and always in the denominators.
N = Negligible, that is, less than 0.05 million pounds.

204

Table A2-1

Merchant 100 Denier Multifilament Acetate (Diacetate Process) Costs

(1975 U.S. dollars per pound)

Number of Merchant Plants: 156	Minimum Efficient Module	Smallest	Merchant Plants 1959-82 - - - Averages - - -			Largest
			Mean	Mode	Median	
Plant Size (Millions of Pounds/Year)	20	26	49	44	44	93
Doublings from Minimum Efficient Module:		0.38	1.29	1.14	1.14	2.22
Fixed Capital Needed						
per Pound	0.600	0.540	0.419	0.438	0.438	0.324
Total (Millions)	12.00	14.05	20.54	19.26	19.26	30.18
Cost Components						
Ingredients	0.325	0.325	0.325	0.325	0.325	0.260
Conversion Costs						
Labor	0.060	0.055	0.045	0.047	0.047	0.037
Energy	0.019	0.016	0.012	0.011	0.013	0.009
Maintenance	0.027	0.024	0.017	0.018	0.018	0.013
Taxes, Insurance, and Overhead	0.027	0.024	0.017	0.018	0.018	0.013
Depreciation	0.030	0.027	0.021	0.022	0.022	0.016
Sales, Administration, and Research	0.089	0.078	0.057	0.060	0.060	0.041
16% Pretax Return on Capital	0.188	0.174	0.141	0.150	0.150	0.114
Totals:	0.765	0.723	0.603	0.651	0.653	0.502
Capital-to-Labor Ratio:	11.26	11.57	12.00	12.26	12.28	12.45
Total Costs' Change from Minimum:	34.4%	30.6%	16.7%	23.0%	23.1%	0.0%

Source: Author.

Table A2-2

Merchant Staple Acrylic (Wet Process) Costs

(1975 U.S. dollars per pound)

Number of Merchant Plants: 96	Minimum Efficient Module	Smallest	Merchant Plants 1959-82 Averages			
			Mean	Mode	Median	Largest
Plant Size (Millions of Pounds/Year)	35	4	114	125	102	325
Doublings from Minimum Efficient Module:		-3.13	1.70	1.84	1.54	54
Fixed Capital Needed						
per Pound	0.810	1.929	0.505	0.487	0.528	0.332
Total (Millions)	28.35	7.70	57.58	60.85	53.86	107.95
Cost Components						
Ingredients	0.220	0.220	0.220	0.198	0.220	0.176
Conversion Costs						
Labor	0.043	0.086	0.029	0.029	0.030	0.021
Energy	0.024	0.071	0.013	0.011	0.014	0.008
Maintenance	0.034	0.101	0.019	0.018	0.020	0.011
Taxes, Insurance, and Overhead	0.034	0.101	0.019	0.018	0.020	0.011
Depreciation	0.041	0.096	0.025	0.024	0.026	0.017
Sales, Administration, and Research	0.103	0.305	0.057	0.055	0.060	0.034
16% Pretax Return on Capital	0.209	0.465	0.0142	0.134	0.147	0.098
Totals:	0.708	1.445	0.525	0.487	0.538	0.375
Capital-to-Labor Ratio:	13.85	12.18	15.32	15.05	15.16	16.09
Total Costs' Change from Minimum:	47.0%	74.0%	28.5%	23.0%	30.3%	0.0%

Source: Author.

Table A2-3

Merchant Multifilament and Staple Fiberglass Costs

(1975 U.S. dollars per pound)

	Minimum Efficient Module	Smallest	Merchant Plants 1959-82 - - - Averages - - -			
			Mean	Mode	Median	Largest
Number of Merchant Plants: 124						
Plant Size (Millions of Pounds/Year)	20	1	67	84	37	200
Doublings from Minimum Efficient Module:		-4.32	1.74	2.07	0.89	3.32
Fixed Capital Needed						
per Pound	1.560	5.171	0.962	0.879	1.220	0.621
Total (Millions)	31.20	5.17	64.44	73.81	45.13	124.21
Cost Components						
Ingredients	0.110	0.110	0.11	0.099	0.110	0.088
Conversion Costs						
Labor	0.059	0.155	0.040	0.037	0.048	0.028
Energy	0.062	0.277	0.034	0.027	0.046	0.020
Maintenance	0.041	0.183	0.022	0.020	0.030	0.013
Taxes, Insurance, and Overhead	0.041	0.183	0.022	0.020	0.030	0.013
Depreciation	0.078	0.259	0.048	0.044	0.061	0.031
Sales, Administration, and Research	0.122	0.546	0.067	0.060	0.090	0.039
16% Pretax Return on Capital	0.332	1.101	0.209	0.190	0.262	0.136
Totals:	0.845	2.814	0.552	0.497	0.676	0.368
Capital-to-labor Ratio:	17.28	16.10	17.81	17.71	17.53	17.98
Total Costs' Change from Minimum:	56.5%	86.9%	33.4%	26.0%	45.7%	0.0%

Source: Author.

Table A2-4

Merchant 70 Denier Multifilament Nylon (Type 6) Costs

(1975 U.S. dollars per pound)

Number of Merchant Plants: 204	Minimum Efficient Module	Smallest	Merchant Plants 1959-82 Averages			Largest
			Mean	Mode	Median	
Plant Size (Millions of Pounds/Year)	15	1	34	54	35	110
Doublings from Minimum Efficient Module:		-3.91	1.18	1.85	1.22	2.87
Fixed Capital Needed						
per Pound	1.250	3.693	0.901	0.749	0.891	0.563
Total (Millions)	18.75	3.69	30.64	40.44	31.17	61.97
Cost Components						
Ingredients	0.597	0.597	0.597	0.597	0.597	0.478
Conversion Costs						
Labor	0.078	0.187	0.060	0.052	0.059	0.041
Energy	0.013	0.050	0.009	0.006	0.009	0.005
Maintenance	0.064	0.248	0.043	0.034	0.042	0.024
Taxes, Insurance, and Overhead	0.064	0.248	0.043	0.034	0.042	0.024
Depreciation	0.063	0.185	0.045	0.037	0.045	0.028
Sales, Administration, and Research	0.191	0.740	0.127	0.101	0.125	0.071
16% Pretax Return on Capital	0.170	0.951	0.292	0.248	0.289	0.197
Totals:	1.240	3.205	1.214	1.049	1.208	0.867
Capital-to-Labor Ratio:	13.21	10.69	14.78	15.20	14.84	16.15
Total Costs' Change from Minimum:	43.0%	73.0%	28.6%	17.3%	28.2%	0.0%

Source: Author.

Table A2-5

Merchant 70 Denier Multifilament Nylon (Type 6, 6) Costs

(1975 U.S. dollars per pound)

	Minimum Efficient Module	Smallest	Merchant Plants 1959-82 Averages			
			Mean	Mode	Median	Largest
Number of Merchant Plants: 266						
Plant Size (Millions of Pounds/Year)	20	1	66	25	68	143
Doublings from Minimum Efficient Module:		-4.32	1.72	0.32	1.77	2.84
Fixed Capital Needed						
per Pound	1.160	3.845	0.720	1.061	0.711	0.528
Total (Millions)	23.20	3.84	47.49	26.52	48.35	75.52
Cost Components						
Ingredients	0.620	0.620	0.620	0.558	0.620	0.496
Conversion Costs						
Labor	0.080	0.210	0.054	0.074	0.054	0.042
Energy	0.011	0.049	0.006	0.009	0.006	0.004
Maintenance	0.060	0.268	0.033	0.54	0.033	0.022
Taxes, Insurance, and Overhead	0.058	0.268	0.033	0.54	0.033	0.022
Depreciation	0.058	0.192	0.036	0.053	0.036	0.026
Sales, Administration, and Research	0.178	0.796	0.098	0.159	0.097	0.067
16% Pretax Return on Capital	0.356	1.000	0.256	0.323	0.254	0.193
Totals:	1.421	3.404	1.137	1.284	1.131	0.874
Capital-to-labor Ratio:	13.17	10.28	15.47	13.12	15.54	15.95
Total Costs' Change from Minimum:	38.5%	74.3%	23.1%	32.0%	22.8%	0.0%

Source: Author.

Table A2-6

Merchant Staple Nylon (Type 6) Costs

(1975 U.S. dollars per pound)

	Minimum Efficient Module	Merchant Plants 1959-82				
			- - - - Averages - - - -			
		Smallest	Mean	Mode	Median	Largest
Number of Merchant Plants: 159						
Plant Size (Millions of Pounds/Year)	25	1	27	32	21	110
Doublings from Minimum Efficient Module:		-4.64	0.11	0.36	-0.25	2.14
Fixed Capital Needed						
per Pound	0.530	1.921	0.514	0.480	0.568	0.293
Total (Millions)	13.25	1.92	13.88	15.37	11.93	32.23
Cost Components						
Ingredients	0.597	0.597	0.597	0.597	0.597	0.478
Conversion Costs						
Labor	0.038	0.107	0.037	0.035	0.040	0.024
Energy	0.012	0.060	0.012	0.010	0.013	0.006
Maintenance	0.042	0.210	0.040	0.037	0.046	0.020
Taxes, Insurance, and Overhead	0.026	0.210	0.040	0.037	0.046	0.020
Depreciation	0.027	0.096	0.026	0.024	0.028	0.015
Sales, Administration, and Research	0.126	0.630	0.121	0.111	0.137	0.060
16% Pretax Return on Capital	0.224	0.613	0.222	0.203	0.236	0.146
Totals:	1.091	2.523	1.095	0.995	1.144	0.768
Capital-to-labor Ratio:	13.84	9.08	14.20	14.01	13.55	17.06
Total Costs' Change from Minimum:	29.6%	69.6%	29.9%	22.8%	32.9%	0.0%

Source: Author.

Table A2-7

Merchant Staple Nylon (Type 6, 6) Costs

(1975 U.S. dollars per pound)

Number of Merchant Plants: 223	Minimum Efficient Module	Smallest	Merchant Plants 1959-82 Averages			
			Mean	Mode	Median	Largest
Plant Size (Millions of Pounds/Year)	35	1	31	32	24	185
Doublings from Minimum Efficient Module:		-5.13	-0.18	-0.13	-0.54	2.4
Fixed Capital Needed						
per Pound	0.510	2.114	0.535	0.529	0.593	0.262
Total (Millions)	17.85	2.11	16.60	16.92	14.23	48.47
Cost Components						
Ingredients	0.620	0.620	0.620	0.558	0.620	0.496
Conversion Costs						
Labor	0.039	0.123	0.041	0.040	0.044	0.023
Energy	0.011	0.065	0.012	0.010	0.013	0.005
Maintenance	0.038	0.225	0.040	0.040	0.046	0.017
Taxes, Insurance, and Overhead	0.031	0.225	0.040	0.040	0.046	0.017
Depreciation	0.026	0.106	0.027	0.026	0.030	0.013
Sales, Administration, and Research	0.114	0.674	0.121	0.119	0.138	0.050
16% Pretax Return on Capital	0.222	0.664	0.230	0.218	0.245	0.141
Totals:	1.101	2.702	1.131	1.052	1.181	0.760
Capital-to-labor Ratio:	14.46	9.03	14.20	13.66	13.55	18.51
Total Costs' Change from Minimum:	30.9%	71.9%	32.0%	27.7%	35.6%	0.0%

Source: Author.

Table A2-8

Merchant 1,000 Denier Multifilament Polypropylene (Resin Process) Costs

(1975 U.S. dollars per pound)

Number of Merchant Plants: 169	Minimum Efficient Module	Smallest	Merchant Plants 1959-82 - - - Averages - - -			
			Mean	Mode	Median	Largest
Plant Size (Millions of Pounds/Year)	15	1	36	6	22	113
Doublings from Minimum Efficient Module:		-3.91	1.26	-1.32	0.55	2.91
Fixed Capital Needed						
per Pound	1.070	3.161	0.754	1.544	0.918	0.477
Total (Millions)	16.05	3.16	27.14	9.26	20.20	53.91
Cost Components						
Ingredients	0.244	0.244	0.240	0.244	0.244	0.195
Conversion Costs						
Labor	0.076	0.182	0.057	0.102	0.067	0.040
Energy	0.008	0.031	0.005	0.011	0.007	0.003
Maintenance	0.039	0.151	0.025	0.062	0.032	0.014
Taxes, Insurance, and Overhead	0.036	0.151	0.025	0.062	0.032	0.014
Depreciation	0.054	0.158	0.038	0.077	0.046	0.024
Sales, Administration, and Research	0.126	0.488	0.081	0.199	0.104	0.046
16% Pretax Return on Capital	0.264	0.731	0.193	0.368	0.232	0.130
Totals:	0.847	2.135	0.644	1.125	0.764	0.466
Capital-to-Labor Ratio:	11.89	10.72	12.30	11.41	12.17	12.98
Total Costs' Change from Minimum:	45.0%	78.2%	27.7%	56.6%	39.0%	0.0%

Source: Author.

212

Table A2-9

Merchant Staple Polypropylene (Resin Process) Costs

(1975 U.S. dollars per pound)

Number of Merchant Plants: 169	Minimum Efficient Module	Smallest	Merchant Plants 1959-82 Averages			Largest
			Mean	Mode	Median	
Plant Size (Millions of Pounds/Year)	25	2	13	6	8	131
Doublings from Minimum Efficient Module:		-3.64	-0.94	-2.06	-1.64	2.39
Fixed Capital Needed						
per Pound	0.470	1.291	0.611	0.832	0.741	0.242
Total (Millions)	11.75	2.58	7.94	4.99	5.93	31.74
Cost Components						
Ingredients	0.244	0.244	0.220	0.244	0.244	0.195
Conversion Costs						
Labor	0.031	0.070	0.038	0.049	0.045	0.018
Energy	0.008	0.028	0.011	0.015	0.014	0.003
Maintenance	0.024	0.085	0.033	0.049	0.042	0.010
Taxes, Insurance, and Overhead	0.036	0.085	0.033	0.049	0.042	0.010
Depreciation	0.024	0.065	0.031	0.042	0.037	0.012
Sales, Administration, and Research	0.073	0.258	0.101	0.149	0.129	0.032
16% Pretax Return on Capital	0.146	0.340	0.172	0.229	0.207	0.084
Totals:	0.586	1.175	0.640	0.825	0.761	0.366
Capital-to-labor Ratio:	13.48	10.68	12.13	11.56	11.85	15.36
Total Costs' Change from Minimum:	37.5%	68.9%	42.8%	55.7%	51.9%	0.0%

Source: Author.

Table A2-10

Merchant 150 Denier Multifilament Polyester (DMT Process) Costs

(1975 U.S. dollars per pound)

Number of Merchant Plants: 351	Minimum Efficient Module	Merchant Plants 1959-82 Averages				
		Smallest	Mean	Mode	Median	Largest
Plant Size (Millions of Pounds/Year)	15	1	44	23	40	140
Doublings from Minimum Efficient Module:		-3.91	1.55	0.62	1.42	3.22
Fixed Capital Needed						
per Pound	1.210	3.575	0.787	1.020	0.817	0.495
Total (Millions)	18.15	3.57	34.62	23.46	32.69	69.33
Cost Components						
Ingredients	0.306	0.306	0.275	0.306	0.306	0.245
Conversion Costs						
Labor	0.085	0.203	0.060	0.074	0.062	0.041
Energy	0.014	0.054	0.008	0.010	0.009	0.005
Maintenance	0.052	0.201	0.030	0.042	0.032	0.017
Taxes, Insurance, and Overhead	0.073	0.201	0.030	0.042	0.032	0.017
Depreciation	0.061	0.179	0.039	0.051	0.041	0.025
Sales, Administration, and Research	0.155	0.600	0.091	0.125	0.095	0.051
16% Pretax Return on Capital	0.313	0.851	0.211	0.267	0.223	0.143
Totals:	1.058	2.596	0.746	0.918	0.799	0.544
Capital-to-labor Ratio:	12.03	10.57	12.54	12.22	12.73	13.41
Total Costs' Change from Minimum:	48.6%	79.1%	27.1%	40.8%	32.0%	0.0%

Source: Author.

214

Table A2-11

Merchant 150 Denier Multifilament Polyester (PTA Process) Costs

(1975 U.S. dollars per pound)

Number of Merchant Plants: 95	Minimum Efficient Module	Smallest	Merchant Plants 1959-82 Averages			Largest
			Mean	Mode	Median	
Plant Size (Millions of Pounds/Year)	25	1	78	77	80	125
Doublings from Minimum Efficient Module:		-4.64	1.64	1.62	1.68	2.32
Fixed Capital Needed						
per Pound	0.990	3.588	0.628	0.631	0.622	0.520
Total (Millions)	24.75	3.59	48.99	48.61	49.74	65.01
Cost Components						
Ingredients	0.244	0.244	0.244	0.244	0.220	0.195
Conversion Costs						
Labor	0.072	0.203	0.050	0.050	0.050	0.043
Energy	0.010	0.050	0.006	0.005	0.006	0.004
Maintenance	0.038	0.190	0.022	0.022	0.021	0.017
Taxes, Insurance, and Overhead	0.060	0.190	0.022	0.022	0.021	0.017
Depreciation	0.050	0.179	0.031	0.032	0.031	0.026
Sales, Administration, and Research	0.178	0.089	0.101	0.101	0.100	0.080
16% Pretax Return on Capital	0.263	0.885	0.176	0.177	0.171	0.144
Totals:	0.914	2.832	0.651	0.653	0.619	0.527
Capital-to-Labor Ratio:	10.20	8.54	10.99	10.98	10.77	10.91
Total Costs' Change from Minimum:	42.4%	81.4%	19.2%	19.3%	14.9%	0.0%

Source: Author.

Table A2-12

Merchant Staple Polyester (DMT Process) Costs

(1975 U.S. dollars per pound)

Number of Merchant Plants: 277	Minimum Efficient Module	Smallest	Merchant Plants 1959-82 - - - Averages - - -			Largest
			Mean	Mode	Median	
Plant Size (Millions of Pounds/Year)	25	1	73	3	68	450
Doublings from Minimum Efficient Module:		-4.64	1.55	-3.06	1.44	4.17
Fixed Capital Needed						
per Pound	0.540	1.957	0.352	1.261	0.362	0.170
Total (Millions)	13.50	1.96	25.68	3.78	24.61	76.47
Cost Components						
Ingredients	0.306	0.306	0.275	0.306	0.306	0.245
Conversion Costs						
Labor	0.038	0.107	0.027	0.075	0.028	0.015
Energy	0.013	0.065	0.008	0.034	0.008	0.003
Maintenance	0.029	0.145	0.017	0.084	0.018	0.007
Taxes, Insurance, and Overhead	0.028	0.145	0.017	0.084	0.018	0.007
Depreciation	0.027	0.098	0.018	0.063	0.018	0.008
Sales, Administration, and Research	0.088	0.440	0.051	0.254	0.053	0.021
16% Pretax Return on Capital	0.171	0.522	0.122	0.346	0.130	0.076
Totals:	0.700	1.828	0.535	1.245	0.578	0.382
Capital-to-labor Ratio:	13.04	9.97	14.52	10.68	14.94	18.76
Total Costs' Change from Minimum:	45.5%	79.1%	28.7%	69.3%	33.9%	0.0%

Source: Author.

Table A2-13

Merchant Staple Polyester (PTA Process) Costs

(1975 U.S. dollars per pound)

Number of Merchant Plants: 100	Minimum Efficient Module	Smallest	Merchant Plants 1959-82 Averages			Largest
			Mean	Mode	Median	
Plant Size (Millions of Pounds/Year)	40	15	131	198	130	218
Doublings from Minimum Efficient Module:		-1.42	1.71	2.31	1.70	2.45
Fixed Capital Needed						
per Pound	0.450	0.666	0.280	0.237	0.281	0.228
Total (Millions)	18.00	9.99	36.68	46.99	36.51	49.79
Cost Components						
Ingredients	0.244	0.244	0.244	0.220	0.244	0.195
Conversion Costs						
Labor	0.033	0.045	0.023	0.020	0.023	0.019
Energy	0.009	0.015	0.005	0.004	0.005	0.004
Maintenance	0.021	0.034	0.012	0.009	0.012	0.009
Taxes, Insurance, and Overhead	0.025	0.034	0.012	0.009	0.012	0.009
Depreciation	0.023	0.033	0.014	0.012	0.014	0.011
Sales, Administration, and Research	0.062	0.101	0.034	0.028	0.034	0.027
16% Pretax Return on Capital	0.139	0.188	0.100	0.086	0.100	0.080
Totals:	0.555	0.695	0.443	0.388	0.443	0.355
Capital-to-labor Ratio:	13.54	12.24	15.71	16.01	15.69	15.51
Total Costs' Change from Minimum:	36.1%	49.0%	19.9%	8.6%	20.0%	0.0%

Source: Author.

Table A2-14

Merchant 150 Denier Multifilament Rayon (Viscose Process) Costs

(1975 U.S. dollars per pound)

Number of Merchant Plants: 147	Minimum Efficient Module	Smallest	Merchant Plants 1959-82 Averages			Largest
			Mean	Mode	Median	
Plant Size (Millions of Pounds/Year)	20	3	33	30	36	70
Doublings from Minimum Efficient Module:		-2.74	0.72	0.58	0.85	1.81
Fixed Capital Needed						
per Pound	0.670	1.431	0.548	0.570	0.530	0.406
Total (Millions)	13.40	4.29	18.10	17.09	19.07	28.41
Cost Components						
Ingredients	0.295	0.295	0.295	0.295	0.266	0.236
Conversion Costs						
Labor	0.055	0.101	0.047	0.048	0.046	0.037
Energy	0.027	0.070	0.021	0.020	0.020	0.014
Maintenance	0.016	0.041	0.012	0.013	0.012	0.009
Taxes, Insurance, and Overhead	0.016	0.041	0.012	0.013	0.012	0.009
Depreciation	0.034	0.072	0.027	0.028	0.026	0.020
Sales, Administration, and Research	0.070	0.181	0.054	0.057	0.052	0.037
16% Pretax Return on Capital	0.189	0.357	0.163	0.167	0.154	0.123
Totals:	0.702	1.158	0.633	0.642	0.588	0.485
Capital-to-Labor Ratio:	13.14	11.64	13.75	13.59	13.45	13.85
Total Costs' Change from Minimum:	30.9%	58.1%	23.3%	24.5%	17.5%	0.0%

Source: Author.

Table A2-15

Merchant Staple Rayon (Viscose Process) Costs

(1975 U.S. dollars per pound)

	Minimum Efficient Module	Smallest	Merchant Plants 1959-82 Averages			
			Mean	Mode	Median	Largest
Number of Merchant Plants: 185						
Plant Size (Millions of Pounds/Year)	50	1	88	2	106	236
Doublings from Minimum Efficient Module:		-5.64	0.82	-4.64	1.08	2.24
Fixed Capital Needed						
per Pound	0.600	2.869	0.479	2.174	0.444	0.323
Total (Millions)	30.00	2.87	42.11	4.35	47.09	76.12
Cost Components						
Ingredients	0.295	0.295	0.295	0.295	0.266	0.236
Conversion Costs						
Labor	0.048	.169	0.040	0.135	0.038	0.029
Energy	0.022	0.156	0.017	0.099	0.015	0.010
Maintenance	0.013	0.092	0.010	0.065	0.009	0.006
Taxes, Insurance, and Overhead	0.013	0.092	0.010	0.065	0.009	0.006
Depreciation	0.030	0.143	0.024	0.109	0.022	0.016
Sales, Administration, and Research	0.041	0.290	0.031	0.205	0.028	0.019
16% Pretax Return on Capital	0.170	0.657	0.145	0.504	0.133	0.103
Totals:	0.632	1.894	0.571	1.477	0.519	0.425
Capital-to-labor Ratio:	15.50	13.07	16.31	13.24	16.05	16.72
Total Costs' Change from Minimum:	32.7%	77.5%	25.5%	71.2%	18.1%	0.0%

Source: Author.

Table A3-1

U.S. Cellulosic Fibers' Estimated Short-Run Marginal Costs and Capacity Utilization Rates

Year	Cost of Materials and Fuels (mill. $) (a, 1)	Total Payroll (mill. $) (a)	Year-End Inventories (million $) (a)	Estimated Total Variable Cost (mill. $) (2)	GNP Deflator (1975=100) (b)	Deflated Estimated Total Variable Cost (mill. $) (3)	Change in Estimated Total Variable Cost from Prior Year (mill. $)	Production (mill. lbs.) (c)	Change in Production from Prior Year (mill. lbs.)
1957									
1958	322.3	211.5	108.1	544.6	53.3	1021.0		1034.9	
1959	344.2	211.3	114.7	567.0	54.2	1045.8	24.8	1166.8	131.9
1960	324.6	211.0	119.0	547.5	55.1	993.9	-51.9	1028.5	-138.3
1961	268.3	171.7	92.5	449.3	55.8	805.1	-188.8	1005.2	-23.3
1962	315.0	183.8	99.1	508.7	56.4	901.3	96.2	1272.1	266.9
1963	320.0	167.0	81.6	495.2	57.2	866.4	-34.9	1348.8	76.7
1964	353.5	182.9	90.9	545.5	58.0	939.7	73.3	1431.8	83.0
1965	393.8	198.0	90.2	600.8	59.1	1015.9	76.2	1527.0	95.2
1966	395.2	208.8	120.2	616.0	61.0	1009.1	-6.8	1519.0	-8.0
1967	383.3	198.2	108.8	592.4	62.9	942.1	-67.0	1788.1	269.1
1968	445.2	228.1	143.8	687.7	65.6	1048.6	106.5	1594.3	-193.8
1969	384.5	190.7	139.3	589.1	69.0	853.8	-194.8	1576.2	-18.1

220

Year	Preliminary Estimate of Deflated Marginal Costs (1975 $/lb.) (4)	Estimated Positive Deflated Marginal Costs (1975 $/lb.)	Estimated Positive Deflated Marginal Costs when CUR Is Less than 80% (1975 $/lb.)	Positive Deflated Marginal Costs when CUR Exceeds 80% but not 90% (1975 $/lb.)	Estimated Positive Deflated Marginal Costs when CUR Exceeds 90% (1975 $/lb.)	November Year-End Capacity (mill. lbs.) (c)	Average Annual Capacity (mill. lbs.)	Capacity Utilization Rate (CUR) (percent) (5)
1957						1152.0		
1958						1651.0	1401.5	73.8%
1959	0.188	0.188	0.188			1445.0	1548.0	75.4%
1960	0.375	0.375	0.375			1453.0	1449.0	71.0%
1961	8.103	8.103	8.103			1421.0	1437.0	70.0%
1962	0.360	0.360	0.360	0.360		1453.0	1437.0	88.5%
1963	-0.455					1493.0	1473.0	91.6%
1964	0.883	0.883			0.883	1635.0	1564.0	91.5%
1965	0.800	0.800			0.800	1709.0	1672.0	91.3%
1966	0.854	0.854		0.854		1720.0	1714.5	88.6%
1967	-0.249					1686.0	1703.0	105.0%
1968	-0.550					1715.0	1700.5	93.8%
1969	10.761	10.761			10.761	1729.0	1722.0	91.5%

Table A3-1 Continued

Year	Cost of Materials and Fuels (mill. $) (a, 1)	Total Payroll (mill. $) (a)	Year-End Inventories (million $) (a)	Estimated Total Variable Cost (mill. $) (2)	GNP Deflator (1975=100) (b)	Deflated Estimated Total Variable Cost (mill. $) (3)	Change in Estimated Total Variable Cost from Prior Year (mill. $)	Production (mill. lbs.) (c)	Change in Production from Prior Year (mill. lbs.)
1970	299.6	142.0	104.3	452.0	72.7	621.5	-232.3	1373.2	-203.0
1971	331.3	149.8	133.0	494.4	76.3	647.9	26.4	1390.9	17.7
1972	327.8	135.2	97.4	472.7	79.5	594.7	-53.1	1394.3	3.4
1973	343.0	134.0	85.2	485.5	83.5	581.7	-13.1	1357.0	-37.3
1974	592.2	205.1	142.1	811.5	91.5	887.0	305.3	1198.8	-158.2
1975	516.3	178.5	127.3	707.5	100.0	707.5	-179.5	749.0	-449.8
1976	596.5	202.9	123.1	811.7	105.2	771.8	64.3	840.9	91.9
1977	683.2	213.7	110.8	908.0	111.4	815.3	43.5	887.7	46.8
1978	731.5	246.2	96.7	987.4	119.6	825.9	10.6	904.5	16.8
1979	788.5	269.8	103.6	1068.7	129.9	822.8	-3.1	929.8	25.3
1980	877.8	279.0	97.9	1166.6	141.8	822.6	-0.2	806.0	-123.8
1981	929.4	299.8	107.7	1240.0	155.5	797.5	-25.1	770.1	-35.9
1982	812.1	292.4	109.9	1115.5	164.9	676.6	-120.9	584.4	-185.7

Year	Preliminary Estimate of Deflated Marginal Costs (1975 $/lb.) (4)	Estimated Positive Deflated Marginal Costs (1975 $/lb.)	Estimated Positive Deflated Marginal Costs when CUR Is Less than 80% (1975 $/lb.)	Positive Deflated Marginal Costs when CUR Exceeds 80% but not 90% (1975 $/lb.)	Estimated Positive Deflated Marginal Costs when CUR Exceeds 90% (1975 $/lb.)	November Year-End Capacity (mill. lbs.) (c)	Average Annual Capacity (mill. lbs.)	Capacity Utilization Rate (CUR) (percent) (5)
1970	1.145	1.145	1.145			1713.0	1721.0	79.8%
1971	1.491	1.491		1.491		1615.0	1664.0	83.6%
1972	-15.626					1513.0	1564.0	89.1%
1973	0.351	0.351			0.351	1493.0	1503.0	90.3%
1974	-1.930					1273.0	1383.0	86.7%
1975	0.399	0.399	0.399			1239.0	1256.0	59.6%
1976	0.699	0.699	0.699			1193.0	1216.0	69.2%
1977	0.929	0.929	0.929			1063.0	1128.0	78.7%
1978	0.631	0.631		0.629		1086.0	1074.5	84.2%
1979	-0.122					1109.0	1097.5	84.7%
1980	0.001	0.001	0.001			909.0	1009.0	79.9%
1981	0.699	0.699		0.699		898.0	903.5	85.2%
1982	0.651	0.651	0.651			895.0	896.5	65.2%
Case 1 (6)								
Mean:	0.432	1.629	1.388	0.807	3.198			83.1%
t Ratio:	0.099	0.562	0.546	1.913	0.634			10.5%
N:	24	18	9	5	4			7.922
								24
Case 2 (7)								
Mean:		0.654	0.548	0.807	0.678			
t Ratio:		1.746	1.440	1.913	2.354			
N:		16	8	5	3			

223

Table A3-1 Continued

Sources: a. Censuses of Manufactures, United States Department of Commerce.
———— b. Statistical Abstracts of the United States.
         c. Textile Economics Bureau's Man-Made Fiber Producer' Handbooks.

Notes: 1. Includes purchased electric power.
       2. Equals sum of materials and fuels and total payroll plus 10% of year-end inventories.
       3. Equals estimated toal variable cost divided by GNP deflator values, which also were divided by 100.
       4. Equals change in deflated estimated total variable cost from prior year divided by change in production from prior year.
       5. Equals production times 100 divided by average annual capacity.
       6. Case 1 includes all short-run marginal cost values.
       7. Case 2 includes all positive short-run marginal cost values over $2.00 per pound.

224

Table A3-2

U.S. Noncellulosic Fibers' Estimated Short-Run Marginal Costs and Capacity Utilization Rates

Year	Cost of Materials and Fuels (mill. $) (a, 1)	Total Payroll (mill. $) (a)	Year-End Inventories (million $) (a)	Estimated Total Variable Cost (2)	GNP Deflator (1975 = 100) (b)	Deflated Total Variable Cost (mill. $) (3)	Change in Deflated Total Variable Cost from Prior Year (mill. $)	Production (mill. lbs.) (c)	Change in Production from Prior Year (mill. lbs.)
1957									
1958	243.7	102.7	48.6	351.3	53.3	659.0		490.5	
1959	333.7	129.6	68.9	470.2	54.2	867.5	208.5	645.3	154.8
1960	321.6	141.8	69.5	470.4	55.1	853.6	-13.9	677.2	31.9
1961	367.4	186.4	75.0	561.3	55.8	1005.9	152.3	750.9	73.7
1962	418.1	214.4	99.2	642.4	56.4	1139.0	133.1	972.9	222.0
1963	487.8	275.8	124.0	776.0	57.2	1356.6	217.6	1156.0	183.1
1964	540.0	304.6	130.0	857.6	58.0	1478.6	122.0	1406.7	250.7
1965	683.4	358.5	211.0	1063.0	59.1	1798.6	320.0	1780.1	373.4
1966	733.8	421.3	266.8	1181.8	61.0	1937.3	138.7	2082.8	302.7
1967	767.7	415.9	267.7	1210.4	62.9	1924.3	-13.1	2353.3	270.5
1968	891.9	480.3	303.8	1402.6	65.6	2138.1	213.8	3229.4	876.1
1969	1066.9	581.1	385.6	1686.6	69.0	2444.3	306.2	3527.9	298.5
1970	1198.0	642.6	455.8	1886.2	72.7	2594.5	150.2	3586.2	58.3
1971	1343.3	687.2	462.2	2076.7	76.3	2721.8	127.3	4292.8	706.6
1972	1588.3	759.5	444.5	2392.3	79.5	3009.1	287.3	5355.7	1062.9
1973	1655.8	837.9	392.6	2533.0	83.5	3033.5	24.4	6309.4	953.7
1974	2617.7	911.1	792.6	3608.1	91.5	3943.2	909.7	6223.6	-85.8

225

Table A3-2 Continued

Year	Preliminary Estimate of Deflated Marginal Costs (1975 $/lb.) (4)	Estimated Positive Deflated Marginal Costs (1975 $/lb.)	Estimated Positive Deflated Marginal Costs when CUR is Less than 80% (1975 $/lb.)	Positive Deflated Marginal Costs when CUR Exceeds 80% but not 90% (1975 $/lb.)	Estimated Positive Deflated Marginal Costs when CUR Exceeds 90% (1975 $/lb.)	November Year-End Capacity (mill. lbs.) (c)	Average Annual Capacity (mill. lbs.)	Capacity Utilization Rate (CUR) (percent) (5)
1957						1052.2		
1958	1.347	1.347		1.347		757.5	904.9	54.2%
1959	-0.435					808.7	783.1	82.4%
1960	2.066	2.066	2.066			910.7	859.7	78.8%
1961	0.600	0.600		0.600		1063.0	986.9	76.1%
1962	1.188	1.188		1.188		1214.0	1138.5	85.5%
1963	0.487	0.487			0.487	1395.0	1304.5	88.6%
1964	0.857	0.857			0.857	1667.0	1531.0	91.9%
1965	0.458	0.346		0.458		2101.0	1884.0	94.5%
1966	-0.048					2726.0	2413.5	86.3%
1967	0.244	0.244			0.244	3206.0	2966.0	79.3%
1968	1.026	1.026		1.024		3867.0	3556.5	91.3%
1969	2.576	2.576	2.576			4459.0	4163.0	84.7%
1970	0.180	0.180		0.180		4862.0	4660.5	76.9%
1971	0.270	0.270			0.270	5416.0	5139.0	83.5%
1972	0.026	0.026			0.026	6396.0	5906.0	90.7%
1973	-10.603					7040.0	6718.0	93.9%
1974						7772.0	7406.0	84.0%

Year	Cost of Materials and Fuels (mill. $) (a, 1)	Total Payroll (mill. $) (a)	Year-End Inventories (million $) (a)	Estimated Total Variable Cost (2)	GNP Deflator (1975 = 100) (b)	Deflated Total Variable Cost (mill. $) (3)	Change in Deflated Total Variable Cost from Prior Year (mill. $)	Production (mill. lbs.) (c)	Change in Production from Prior Year (mill. lbs.)
1975	2752.1	887.0	549.3	3694.0	100.0	3694.0	-249.2	5885.7	-337.9
1976	3092.9	942.3	587.8	4094.0	105.2	3891.6	197.6	6626.6	740.9
1977	3618.1	1086.1	661.8	4770.4	111.4	4282.2	390.6	7327.9	701.3
1978	3732.6	1170.0	740.3	4976.6	119.6	4161.1	-121.1	7783.0	455.1
1979	4823.2	1252.3	792.9	6154.8	129.9	4738.1	577.0	8436.6	653.6
1980	5181.8	1285.3	811.6	6548.3	141.8	4618.0	-120.1	7892.5	-544.1
1981	5804.2	1351.0	876.4	7242.8	155.5	4657.8	39.8	8005.9	113.4
1982	4768.4	1326.5	400.7	6135.0	164.9	3720.4	-937.4	6459.9	-1546.0

Table A3-2 Continued

Year	Preliminary Estimate of Deflated Marginal Costs (1975 $/lb.) (4)	Estimated Positive Deflated Marginal Costs (1975 $/lb.)	Estimated Positive Deflated Marginal Costs when CUR Is Less than 80% (1975 $/lb.)	Estimated Positive Deflated Marginal Costs when CUR Exceeds 80% but not 90% (1975 $/lb.)	Estimated Positive Deflated Marginal Costs when CUR Exceeds 90% (1975 $/lb.)	November Year-End Capacity (mill. lbs.) (c)	Average Annual Capacity (mill. lbs.)	Capacity Utilization Rate (CUR) (percent) (5)
1975	0.738	0.738	0.738			8436.0	8104.0	72.6%
1976	0.267	0.267	0.267			9132.0	8784.0	75.4%
1977	0.557	0.557	0.557			9368.0	9250.0	79.2%
1978	-0.266					9571.0	9469.5	82.2%
1979	0.883	0.883		0.883		9804.0	9687.5	87.1%
1980	0.221	0.221		0.221		9647.0	9725.5	81.2%
1981	0.351	0.351		0.351		9716.0	9681.5	82.7%
1982	0.606	0.606	0.606			9364.0	9540.0	67.7%
Case 1 (6)								
Mean:	0.150	1.094	0.906	1.557	0.375			83.2%
t Ratio:	0.063	0.518	1.005	0.515	1.200			12.57
N:	24	24	8	11	5			24
Case 2 (7)								
Mean:		0.681	0.548	0.807	0.377			
t Ratio:		1.088	1.220	0.593	1.200			
N:		23	4	9	5			

Sources: As for Table A3-1.

Notes: As for Table A3-1.

Table A4-1

Independent Variables Used in Regression Analysis
of
Man-Made Fibers' Cyclical Price Behavior

Label	Description

Cotton Price Related Independent Variables

	CCPRICE	= Deflated cotton price in current month
	HCP I	= Deflated cotton price in month i counting back in time from the current month
1.	DELTACP	= CCPRICE - HCP1
2.	HDIF1	= HCP1 - HCP2
3.	HDIF2	= HCP2 - HCP3
4.	HDIF3	= HCP3 - HCP4
5.	HDIF4	= HCP4 - HCP5
6.	ACCEL1	= DELACF - XDIF1
7.	ACCEL2	= HDIF1 - HDIF2
8.	ACCEL3	= HDIF2 - HDIF3
9.	ACCEL4	= HDIF3 - HDIF4
10.	THDIF1	= ACCEL1 - ACCEL2
11.	THDIF2	= ACCEL2 - ACCEL3
12.	THDIF3	= ACCEL3 - ACCEL4

Capacity Utilization Rate (CUR)-Related Independent Variables

	STUDYIDX	= CUR of man-made fiber of interest in current month
	HMMFC I	= STUDYIDX in month i counting back in time from the current month
13.	CDIF1	= STUDYIDX - HMMFC1
14.	CDIF2	= HMMFC1 - HMMFC2
15.	CDIF3	= HMMFC2 - HMMFC3
16.	CDIF4	= HMMFC3 - HMMFC4
17.	CDIF5	= HMMFC4 - HMMFC5
18.	CACCEL1	= CDIF1 - CDIF2
19.	CACCEL2	= CDIF2 - CDIF3
20.	CACCEL3	= CDIF3 - CDIF4
21.	DCML	= 1 IFF STUDYIDX < 80.0; otherwise = 0
22.	DCMU	= 1 IFF STUDYIDX > 90.0; otherwise = 0
23.	DP1ML	= 1 IFF HMMFC1 < 80.0; otherwise = 0
24.	DP2ML	= 1 IFF HMMFC2 < 80.0; otherwise = 0
25.	DP3ML	= 1 IFF HMMFC3 < 80.0; otherwise = 0
26.	DP4ML	= 1 IFF HMMFC4 < 80.0; otherwise = 0
27.	DP5ML	= 1 IFF HMMFC5 < 80.0; otherwise = 0
28.	DP1MU	= 1 IFF HMMFC1 > 90.0; otherwise = 0
29.	DP2MU	= 1 IFF HMMFC2 > 90.0; otherwise = 0
30.	DP3MU	= 1 IFF HMMFC3 > 90.0; otherwise = 0
31.	DP4MU	= 1 IFF HMMFC4 > 90.0; otherwise = 0
32.	DP5MU	= 1 IFF HMMFC5 > 90.0; otherwise = 0

Source: Author.

Table A4-2

Regression Results of Man-Made Fibers' Cyclical Price Behavior

I   Y: 55 Denier Acetate Filament Deflated Average Monthly Spot Trading Price
Y = -0.0061 - 0.0954 ACCEL4 + 0.0290 DCMU + 0.1311 ACCEL1 + 0.0011 CDIF3 + 0.0008 CDIF2 - 0.1712 XDIF3 + ...
            [0.0421]   [0.0400]   [0.0215]   [0.0191]   [0.0194]   [0.0205]
    + 0.0006 CDIF5
       [0.0017]

II Y: 150 Denier Acetate Filament Deflated Average Monthly Spot Trading Price
Y = 0.0009 - 0.0067 DCML - 0.0304 CP4MU + 0.0120 DP2MU + 0.0115 DP5MU + 0.0108 DP1MU + 0.0005 CDIF1 + ...
           [0.0483]   [0.0746]   [0.0432]   [0.0102]   [0.0085]   [0.0085]
    + 0.0004 CDIF5
       [0.0100]

III Y: 3 Denier Acrylic Staple Deflated Monthly List Price
Y = 0.0520 - 0.0006 CACCEL4 + 0.0143 DCMU - 0.0007 HMMFC2 - 0.0158 CP2ML - 0.0134 DP4MU - 0.0006 CDIF3
           [0.0196]   [0.0127]   [0.0189]   [0.0265]   [0.0161]   [0.0191]

IV Y: 70 Denier Nylon Filament Deflated Monthly List Price
Y = - 0.1569 + 0.0008 HMMFC5 - 0.0081 DP3MU + 0.0102 DP1ML + 0.0009 HMMFC3 + 0.0648 DELTACP - 0.0053 DP2MU
             [0.0808]   [0.0482]   [0.0187]   [0.0220]   [0.0200]   [0.0133]

V   Y: 40 Denier Type 6 Nylon Filament Deflated Average Monthly Spot Trading Price
Y = 0.0052 + 0.0043 CDIF1 - 0.1209 CP2ML + 0.0981 DP3ML + 0.3676 DELTACP
           [0.0261]   [0.0161]   [0.0170]   [0.0107]

VI Y: 2,000 Denier Type 6 Nylon Filament for Carpet Deflated Average Monthly Spot Trading Price
Y = 0.0091 + 0.0036 CDIF1 - 0.0341 CP1ML - 0.2038 XDIF4
           [0.0197]   [0.0149]   [0.0084]

VII Y: 15 Denier Nylon Staple Deflated Monthly List Price
$$Y = - 0.1935 - 0.0013\ CDIF3 + 0.0312\ CP3ML - 0.0205\ DP2ML - 0.0146\ CP1ML + 0.0234\ DP5MU - 0.0119\ DP4MU + \cdots$$
$$[0.0397]\qquad [0.0175]\qquad [0.0536]\qquad [0.0187]\qquad [0.0119]\qquad [0.0180]$$
$$+ 0.0124\ DP5ML$$
$$[0.0137]$$

VIII Y: Type 6 Nylon Staple for Carpet Deflated Average Monthly Spot Trading Price
$$Y = - 0.0177 + 0.0009\ HMMFC1 - 0.1237\ XDIF3 + 0.0145\ DP5ML - 0.0235\ DP2ML - 0.0006\ HMMFC3$$
$$[0.0439]\qquad [0.0227]\qquad [0.0180]\qquad [0.0136]\qquad [0.0102]$$

IX Y: 1.5 Denier Polyester Staple Deflated Monthly List Price
$$Y = - 0.2827 + 0.6339\ XDIF3 + 0.0017\ CACCEL2 - 0.1822\ THDIF3 - 0.0042\ CDIF5 + 0.0513\ DP5ML + 0.0033\ HMMFC5 - \cdots$$
$$[0.2493]\qquad [0.0467]\qquad [0.0627]\qquad [0.0181]\qquad [0.0110]\qquad [0.0243]$$
$$- 0.0308\ DP5MU - 0.0388\ DP2ML$$
$$[0.0165]\qquad [0.0627]$$

X Y: Polyester Staple Deflated Average Monthly Spot Trading Price
$$Y = - 0.0452 + 0.0014\ HMMFC1 - 0.0009\ HMMFC4 - 0.0699\ XDIF3 - 0.0003\ CACCEL1 + 0.0289\ THDIF1$$
$$[0.0882]\qquad [0.0585]\qquad [0.0115]\qquad [0.0098]\qquad [0.0100]$$

XI-A Y: 150 Denier Rayon Filament deflated Monthly List Price Using Acetate Filament's CUR
as a Proxy for Rayon's CUR
$$Y = 0.0017 + 0.9379\ DELTACP + 0.0011\ CDIF5 - 0.0183\ DP4MU + 0.0167\ DCMU + 0.1024\ XDIF3$$
$$[0.2692]\qquad [0.0062]\qquad [0.0034]\qquad [0.0081]\qquad [0.0034]$$

XI-B Y: 150 Denier Rayon Filament deflated Monthly List Price Using Nylon Filament's CUR
as a Proxy for Rayon's CUR
$$Y = 0.2638 - 0.0007\ CACCEL2 + 0.0313\ DP4MU - 0.0032\ HMMFC5 - 0.0206\ DF4ML + 0.0123\ DCMU + 0.1288\ DELTACP + \cdots$$
$$[0.0260]\qquad [0.0115]\qquad [0.0278]\qquad [0.0173]\qquad [0.0177]\qquad [0.0137]$$
$$+ 0.0543\ THDIF2 - 0.0008\ CDIF1$$
$$[0.0109]\qquad [0.0110]$$

Table A4-2 Continued

XI-C Y: 150 Denier Rayon Filament deflated Monthly List Price Using Polyester Filament's CUR
     as a Proxy for Rayon's CUR

Y = - 0.1327 + 0.0142 DP4MU + 0.0234 DP4ML - 0.0133 DP5ML - 0.0136 DP2ML + 0.0305 DCML + 0.0014 HMMFC1 + ...
            [0.0266]   [0.0199]   [0.0299]   [0.0149]   [0.0256]   [0.0619]

    + 0.1278 XDIF4
            [0.0140]

XII-A Y: 1.5 Denier Rayon Staple Deflated Monthly Average Spot Trading Price Using Acrylic Staple's CUR
     as a Proxy for Rayon's CUR

Y = - 0.0007 + 0.0116 DCMU - 0.0005 CDIF4 + 0.0513 THDIF3 - 0.0893 XDIF1 - 0.0067 DCML + 0.0078 DP3ML - ...
            [0.0464]   [0.01740]   [0.0150]   [0.0253]   [0.0119]   [0.0089]

    + 0.0059 DP2ML
            [0.0084]

XII-B Y: 1.5 Denier Rayon Staple Deflated Monthly Average Spot Trading Price Using Nylon Staple's CUR
     as a Proxy for Rayon's CUR

Y = - 0.0385 - 0.0196 DP4ML + 0.0147 DP5ML - 0.0736 XDIF1 + 0.0467 THDIF3 + 0.0089 DP2MU + 0.0232 DP1ML + ...
            [0.0427]   [0.0237]   [0.0132]   [0.0220]   [0.0110]   [0.0100]

    + 0.0004 HMMFC2 - 0.0005 CDIF5 + 0.0006 CACCEL1 + 0.0088 DCMU - 0.0087 DP2ML - 0.0078 DP1MU
            [0.0251]   [0.0121]   [0.0074]   [0.0083]   [0.0071]   [0.0089]

XII-C Y: 1.5 Denier Rayon Staple Deflated Monthly Average Spot Trading Price Using Polyester Staple's CUR
     as a Proxy for Rayon's CUR

Y = - 0.0012 + 0.0088 DP2MU - 0.0150 DP2ML 0.0405 THDIF3 - 0.0579 XDIF1 - 0.0004 CDIF4 + 0.0077 DP1ML
            [0.0504]   [0.0186]   [0.0161]   [0.0166]   [0.0102]   [0.0071]

Source: Author.

_____

Notes: 1. Definitions of independent variables appear on Table A4-1 and dependent variables on Table 6-2.
        2. Partial coefficients of determination (R squares) appear in brackets below their associated variables.
        3. Proxy CUR series were used in lieu of unobtainable rayon CUR data. X1-A, B, and C used acetate, nylon,
           and polyester filament CUR data, respectively. Similarly, XII-A, B, and C used acrylic, nylon, and
           polyester staple CUR data, respectively.

232

Table A5-1

U.S. Cellulosic Fibers' Labor Statistics

Year	Employment (Thousands)			Payroll (mil. of current $)			Production Hours Worked (millions) [a]	Hourly Production Wages (current $) [2]
	Total [a]	Production [a]	Other [1]	Total [a]	Production [a]	Other [1]		
1958	42.6	31.8	10.8	211.5	141.0	70.5	62.5	2.26
1959	41.5	32.2	9.3	211.3	145.4	65.9	64.0	2.27
1960	40.3	30.7	9.6	211.0	141.3	69.7	59.3	2.38
1961	33.1	25.6	7.5	171.7	118.1	53.6	50.1	2.36
1962	35.1	27.3	7.8	183.8	128.5	55.3	53.8	2.39
1963	30.1	24.0	6.1	167.0	120.5	46.5	48.1	2.51
1964	31.9	25.5	6.4	182.9	132.5	50.4	52.0	2.55
1965	34.0	27.2	6.8	198.0	141.8	56.2	54.3	2.61
1966	34.3	27.5	6.8	208.8	150.7	58.1	55.0	2.74
1967	31.9	25.3	6.6	198.2	141.1	57.1	50.0	2.82
1968	34.2	27.4	6.8	228.1	165.0	63.1	54.8	3.01
1969	29.3	24.2	5.1	190.7	148.7	42.0	49.1	3.03
1970	21.5	17.8	3.7	142.0	109.1	32.9	35.1	3.11
1971	20.2	17.1	3.1	149.8	119.1	30.7	33.6	3.54
1972	17.1	14.4	2.7	135.2	107.1	28.1	29.6	3.62
1973	16.7	14.3	2.4	134.0	107.1	26.9	29.7	3.61
1974	20.5	16.2	4.3	205.1	144.2	60.9	31.8	4.53
1975	15.9	12.0	3.9	178.5	119.3	59.2	22.9	5.21
1976	16.7	12.8	3.9	202.9	137.9	65.0	25.0	5.52
1977	16.0	12.6	3.4	213.7	151.8	61.9	25.2	6.02
1978	17.1	13.7	3.4	246.2	179.6	66.6	27.3	6.58
1979	17.0	13.6	3.4	269.8	195.8	74.0	26.9	7.28
1980	16.1	12.7	3.4	279.0	196.7	82.3	25.1	7.84

Table A5-1 Continued

Year	Hourly Production Wages (1972=100) [3]	GNP Deflator (1972=100) [b]	Production (mill. lbs.) [c]	Output per Production Hour Worked (1958 = 100) [4]	(pounds)
1958	3.36	67.1	1034.9	100.0	16.6
1959	3.33	68.2	1166.8	110.1	18.2
1960	3.44	69.3	1028.5	104.7	17.3
1961	3.36	70.2	1005.2	121.2	20.1
1962	3.36	71.0	1272.1	142.8	23.6
1963	3.48	71.9	1348.8	169.3	28.0
1964	3.49	73.0	1431.8	166.3	27.5
1965	3.51	74.4	1527.0	169.8	28.1
1966	3.57	76.8	1519.0	166.8	27.6
1967	3.57	79.1	1788.1	216.0	35.8
1968	3.65	82.5	1594.3	175.7	29.1
1969	3.49	86.8	1576.2	193.9	32.1
1970	3.40	91.5	1373.2	236.3	39.1
1971	3.69	96.0	1390.9	250.0	41.4
1972	3.62	100.0	1394.3	284.5	47.1
1973	3.43	105.0	1357.0	275.9	45.7
1974	3.94	115.1	1198.8	227.7	37.7
1975	4.14	125.8	749.0	197.5	32.7
1976	4.17	132.3	840.9	203.1	33.6
1977	4.30	140.1	887.7	212.7	35.2
1978	4.37	150.4	904.5	200.1	33.1
1979	4.45	163.4	929.8	208.7	34.6
1980	4.39	178.4	806.0	193.9	32.1

Year	Employment (Thousands)			Payroll (mil. of current $)			Production Hours Worked	Hourly Production Wages
	Total	Production	Other	Total	Production	Other	(millions)	(current $)
	[a]	[a]	[1]	[a]	[a]	[1]	[a]	[2]
1978	17.1	13.7	3.4	246.2	179.6	66.6	27.3	6.58
1979	17.0	13.6	3.4	269.8	195.8	74.0	26.9	7.28
1980	16.1	12.7	3.4	279.0	196.7	82.3	25.1	7.84
1981	15.6	12.2	3.4	299.8	209.0	90.8	24.5	8.53
1982	14.3	10.9	3.4	292.4	195.4	97.0	21.1	9.26
Mean:	25.7	20.4	5.4				40.4	4.22
t Ratio:	2.69	2.79	2.26				2.80	1.94
CAR [5]:	-4.4%	-4.4%	-4.7%				-4.4%	6.1%

Table A5-1 Continued

Year	Hourly Production Wages (1972=100) [3]	GNP Deflator (1972=100) [b]	Production (mill. lbs.) [c]	Output per Production Hour Worked (1958 = 100) [4]	(pounds)
1978	4.37	150.4	904.5	200.1	33.1
1979	4.45	163.4	929.8	208.7	34.6
1980	4.39	178.4	806.0	193.9	32.1
1981	4.36	195.6	770.1	189.8	31.4
1982	4.47	207.4	584.4	167.3	27.7
Mean:	3.77		1179.2	187.4	31.0
t Ratio:	9.08		3.69	3.86	3.86
CAR [5]:	1.2%		-2.4%	2.2%	2.2%

Sources: a. Censuses of Manufactures, U.S. Department of Commerce.
b. Statistical Abstracts of the United States.
c. Textile Economics Bureau's Man-Made Fiber Producers' Handbooks.

Notes: 1. Deduced by subtracting production data from total.
2. Equals production payroll divided by production hours worked.
3. Equals hourly production wages in current dollars divided by GNP deflator which in turn was divided by 100.
4. Equals production divided by production hours worked and then indexed to this series' 1958 value.
5. Equals annually compounded (percentage) rate of growth between 1958 and 1982.

Table A5-2

U.S. Noncellulosic [1] Fibers' Labor Statistics

| Year | Employment | | | Payroll | | | Production Hours Worked | Hourly Production Wages |
	Total (000s) [a]	Production (000s) [a]	Other (000s) [2]	Total (mill. $) [a]	Production (mill. $) [a]	Other (mill. $) [2]	(millions) [a]	(current $) [3]
1958	18.7	12.9	5.8	102.7	61.9	40.8	26.0	2.38
1959	22.2	16.3	5.9	129.6	82.2	47.4	32.2	2.55
1960	23.4	17.0	6.4	141.8	88.6	53.2	33.6	2.64
1961	29.0	20.4	8.6	186.4	111.8	74.6	40.2	2.78
1962	31.8	23.3	8.5	214.4	131.4	83.0	46.5	2.83
1963	41.4	28.4	13.0	275.8	161.0	114.8	57.2	2.81
1964	44.3	30.7	13.6	304.6	180.6	124.0	62.3	2.90
1965	51.5	36.5	15.0	358.5	216.4	142.1	73.6	2.94
1966	59.1	40.6	18.5	421.3	246.0	175.3	80.7	3.05
1967	57.2	40.7	16.5	415.9	257.9	158.0	80.9	3.19
1968	62.1	45.6	16.5	480.3	309.8	170.5	92.4	3.35
1969	70.2	50.9	19.3	581.1	367.4	213.7	101.7	3.61
1970	75.7	54.6	21.1	642.6	405.6	237.0	107.5	3.77
1971	75.2	55.2	20.0	687.2	438.7	248.5	108.5	4.04
1972	78.2	58.4	19.8	759.5	497.7	261.8	116.2	4.28
1973	81.8	61.5	20.3	837.9	556.5	281.4	122.3	4.55
1974	80.9	60.5	20.4	911.1	595.1	316.0	118.4	5.03
1975	70.2	51.0	19.2	887.0	556.9	330.1	97.3	5.72
1976	69.3	50.2	19.1	942.3	594.4	347.9	94.9	6.26
1977	74.0	54.8	19.2	1086.1	704.8	381.3	105.8	6.66
1978	72.4	53.6	18.8	1170.1	758.8	411.3	104.1	7.29
1979	70.8	52.7	18.1	1252.3	819.6	432.7	103.0	7.96
1980	65.3	47.7	17.6	1285.3	826.3	459.0	90.9	9.09

237

Table A5-2 Continued

Year	Hourly Production Wages (1972 = 100) [4]	GNP Deflator (1972 = 100) [b]	Production (mill. lbs.) [c]	Output per Production Hour Worked (1958 = 100) [5]	(pounds)
1958	3.55	67.1	490.5	100.0	18.9
1959	3.74	68.2	645.3	106.2	20.0
1960	3.81	69.3	677.2	106.8	20.2
1961	3.96	70.2	750.9	99.0	18.7
1962	3.99	71.0	972.9	110.9	20.9
1963	3.91	71.9	1156.0	107.1	20.2
1964	3.97	73.0	1406.7	119.7	22.6
1965	3.95	74.4	1780.1	128.2	24.2
1966	3.97	76.8	2082.8	136.8	25.8
1967	4.03	79.1	2353.3	154.2	29.1
1968	4.06	82.5	3229.4	185.3	35.0
1969	4.16	86.8	3527.9	183.9	34.7
1970	4.12	91.5	3586.2	176.8	33.4
1971	4.21	96.0	4292.8	209.7	39.6
1972	4.28	100.0	5355.7	244.3	46.1
1973	4.33	105.0	6309.4	273.5	51.6
1974	4.37	115.1	6223.6	278.6	52.6
1975	4.55	125.8	5885.7	320.6	60.5
1976	4.73	132.3	6626.6	370.1	69.8
1977	4.75	140.1	7327.9	367.1	69.3
1978	4.85	150.4	7783.0	396.3	74.8
1979	4.87	163.4	8436.6	434.2	81.9
1980	5.10	178.4	7892.5	460.2	86.8

Year	Employment			Payroll			Production Hours Worked	Hourly Production Wages
	Total	Production	Other	Total	Production	Other		
	(000s) [a]	(000s) [a]	(000s) [2]	(mill. $) [a]	(mill. $) [a]	(mill. $) [2]	(millions) [a]	(current $) [3]
1981	62.6	45.7	16.9	1351.0	868.7	482.3	86.7	10.02
1982	56.8	40.6	16.2	1326.5	832.9	493.6	74.6	11.16
Mean:	57.8	42.0	15.8				82.3	4.84
t Ratio:	2.93	2.82	3.20				2.85	1.91
CAR [6]:	4.47%	4.9%	4.4%				4.5%	6.7%

Table A5-2 Continued

Year	Hourly Production Wages (1972 = 100) [4]	GNP Deflator (1972 = 100) [b]	Production (mill. lbs.) [c]	Output per Production Hour Worked (1958 = 100) [5]	(pounds)
1981	5.12	195.6	8005.9	489.5	92.3
1982	5.38	207.4	6459.9	459.0	86.6
Mean:	4.31		4130.4	240.7	45.4
t Ratio:	8.94		1.48	1.80	1.80
CAR [6]:	1.8%		11.3%	6.6%	6.6%

Sources: As for Table A5-1.

Notes:
1. Excludes fiberglass.
2. Deduced by subtracting production from total.
3. Equals production payroll divided by production hours worked.
4. Equals hourly production wages in current dollars divided by GNP deflator which in turn was divided by 100.
5. Equals production divided by production hours worked and then indexed to this series' 1958 value.
6. Equals annually compounded (percentage) rate of growth between 1958 and 1982.

Table A6-1

U.S. Cellulosic Fibers' Estimated Total Costs and Capacity Utilization Rates

Year	Cost of Materials and Fuels (million $) [a, 1]	Total Payroll (million $) [a]	Gross Value of Fixed Assets (million $) [a, 2]	Depreciation (million $) [3]	Year-End Inventories (million $) [a, 4]	Nonproduction Employees' Payroll (million $) [a]
1957						
1958	322.3	211.5	583.9	29.2	108.1	70.5
1959	344.2	211.3	603.9	30.2	114.7	65.9
1960	324.6	211.0	624.4	31.2	119.0	69.7
1961	268.3	171.7	623.0	31.2	92.5	53.6
1962	315.0	183.8	618.4	30.9	99.1	55.3
1963	320.0	167.0	625.6	31.3	81.6	46.5
1964	353.3	182.9	710.7	35.5	90.9	50.4
1965	393.8	198.0	749.1	37.5	90.2	56.2
1966	395.2	208.8	800.8	40.0	120.2	58.1
1967	383.3	198.2	912.1	45.6	108.8	57.1
1968	445.2	228.1	963.4	48.2	143.8	63.1
1969	384.5	190.7	871.1	43.6	139.3	42.0
1970	299.6	142.0	614.3	30.7	104.3	32.9
1971	331.3	149.8	623.7	31.2	133.0	30.7
1972	327.8	135.2	611.1	30.6	97.4	28.1
1973	343.0	134.0	612.6	30.6	85.2	26.9
1974	592.2	205.1	877.5	43.9	142.1	60.9
1975	516.3	178.5	917.6	45.9	127.3	59.2

241

Table A6-1 Continued

Year	Estimated Total Cost (million $) [5]	Production (million $) [b]	November Year-End Capacity (mill. lbs.) [b]	Average Annual Capacity (mill. lbs.)	Capacity Utilization Rate (CUR) (percent) [6]
1957			1152.0		
1958	644.3	1034.9	1651.0	1401.5	73.8%
1959	663.1	1166.8	1445.0	1548.0	75.4%
1960	648.4	1028.5	1453.0	1449.0	71.0%
1961	534.0	1005.2	1421.0	1437.0	70.0%
1962	594.9	1272.1	1453.0	1437.0	88.5%
1963	572.9	1348.8	1493.0	1473.0	91.6%
1964	631.2	1431.8	1635.0	1564.0	91.5%
1965	694.5	1527.0	1709.0	1672.0	91.3%
1966	714.2	1519.0	1720.0	1714.5	88.6%
1967	695.1	1788.1	1686.0	1703.0	105.0%
1968	798.9	1594.3	1715.0	1700.5	93.8%
1969	674.7	1576.2	1729.0	1722.0	91.5%
1970	515.6	1373.2	1713.0	1721.0	79.8%
1971	556.3	1390.9	1615.0	1664.0	83.6%
1972	531.4	1394.3	1513.0	1564.0	89.1%
1973	543.0	1357.0	1493.0	1503.0	90.3%
1974	916.3	1198.8	1273.0	1383.0	86.7%
1975	812.6	749.0	1239.0	1256.0	59.6%

242

Year	Cost of Materials and Fuels (million $) [a, 1]	Total Payroll (million $) [a]	Gross Value of Fixed Assets (million $) [a, 2]	Depreciation (million $) [3]	Year-End Inventories (million $) [a, 4]	Nonproduction Employees' Payroll (million $) [a]
1976	596.5	202.9	818.5	40.9	123.1	65.0
1977	683.2	213.7	806.9	40.3	110.8	61.9
1978	731.5	246.2	799.2	40.0	96.7	66.6
1979	788.5	269.8	843.0	42.2	103.6	74.0
1980	877.8	279.0	884.0	44.2	97.9	82.3
1981	929.4	299.8	951.6	47.6	107.7	90.8
1982	812.1	292.4	992.7	49.6	108.9	97.0

Table A6-1 Continued

Year	Estimated Total Cost (million $) [5]	Production (million $) [b]	November Year-End Capacity (mill. lbs.) [b]	Average Annual Capacity (mill. lbs.)	Capacity Utilization Rate (CUR) (percent) [6]
1976	917.6	840.9	1193.0	1216.0	69.2%
1977	1010.2	887.7	1063.0	1128.0	78.7%
1978	1093.9	904.5	1086.0	1074.5	84.2%
1979	1184.8	929.8	1109.0	1097.5	84.7%
1980	1293.1	806.0	909.0	1009.0	79.9%
1981	1378.3	770.1	898.0	903.5	85.2%
1982	1262.1	584.4	895.0	896.5	65.2%

Sources: a. Census of Manufactures, U.S. Department of Commerce.
——— b. Textile Economics Bureau's Man-Made Fiber Producers' Handbooks.

Notes: 1. Includes electric power purchased.
2. Deduced for 1958-62 and 1977-82 by taking 95% of the prior year's value plus new capital expenditures in the current year.
3. Asumed to be 5% of current year's gross value of fixed assets.
4. Missing official data was estimated as average of 1958-1981 values.
5. Sum of materials and fuels, total payroll, depreciation, 10% interest carrying charge on year-end inventories, plus nonproduction employees' payroll as a proxy for the nonlabor component of SARE (sales, administrative, and research expense).
6. Equals production times 100 divided by average annual capacity.

244

Table A6-2

U.S. Noncellulosic Fibers' Estimated Total Costs and Capacity Utilization Rates

Year	Cost of Materials and Fuels (million $) [a, 1]	Total Payroll (million $) [a]	Gross Value of Fixed Assets (million $) [a, 2]	Depreciation (million $) [3]	Year-End Inventories (million $) [a, 4]	Nonproduction Employees' Payroll (million $) [a]
1957						
1958	243.7	102.7	915.9	45.8	48.6	40.8
1959	333.7	129.6	893.6	44.7	68.9	47.4
1960	321.6	141.8	894.6	44.7	69.5	53.2
1961	367.4	186.4	961.5	48.1	75.0	74.6
1962	418.1	214.4	1025.9	51.3	99.2	83.0
1963	487.8	275.8	1160.9	58.0	124.0	114.8
1964	540.0	304.6	1288.7	64.4	130.0	124.0
1965	683.4	358.5	1587.3	79.4	211.0	142.1
1966	733.8	421.3	1892.6	94.6	266.8	175.3
1967	767.7	415.9	2428.7	121.4	267.7	158.0
1968	891.9	480.3	2670.4	133.5	303.8	170.5
1969	1066.9	581.1	2977.8	148.9	385.6	213.7
1970	1198.0	642.6	3598.3	179.9	455.8	237.0
1971	1343.3	687.2	3839.1	192.0	462.2	248.5
1972	1588.3	759.5	4159.3	208.0	444.5	261.8
1973	1655.8	837.9	4603.7	230.2	392.6	281.4
1974	2617.7	911.1	4924.3	246.2	792.4	316.0
1975	2752.1	887.0	5491.8	274.6	549.3	330.1

245

Table A6-2 Continued

Year	Estimated Total Cost (million $) [5]	Production (million $) [b]	November Year-End Capacity (mill. lbs.) [b]	Average Annual Capacity (mill. lbs.)	Capacity Utilization Rate (CUR) (percent) [6]
1957			1052.2		
1958	437.9	490.5	757.5	904.9	54.2%
1959	562.3	645.3	808.7	783.1	82.4%
1960	568.3	677.2	910.7	859.7	78.8%
1961	684.0	750.9	1063.0	986.9	76.1%
1962	776.7	972.9	1214.0	1138.5	85.5%
1963	948.8	1156.0	1395.0	1304.5	88.6%
1964	1046.0	1406.7	1667.0	1531.0	91.9%
1965	1284.5	1780.1	2101.0	1884.0	94.5%
1966	1451.7	2082.8	2726.0	2413.5	86.3%
1967	1489.8	2353.3	3206.0	2966.0	79.3%
1968	1706.6	3229.4	3867.0	3536.5	91.3%
1969	2049.2	3527.9	4459.0	4163.0	84.7%
1970	2303.1	3586.2	4862.0	4660.5	76.9%
1971	2517.2	4292.8	5416.0	5139.0	83.5%
1972	2862.0	5355.7	6396.0	5906.0	90.7%
1973	3044.5	6309.4	7040.0	6718.0	93.9%
1974	4170.3	6223.6	7772.0	7406.0	84.0%
1975	4298.7	5885.7	8436.0	8104.0	72.6%

Year	Cost of Materials and Fuels (million $) [a, 1]	Total Payroll (million $) [a]	Gross Value of Fixed Assets (million $) [a, 2]	Depreciation (million $) [3]	Year-End Inventories (million $) [a, 4]	Nonproduction Employees' Payroll (million $) [a]
1976	3092.9	942.3	5875.9	293.8	587.8	347.9
1977	3618.1	1086.1	5920.6	296.0	661.8	381.3
1978	3732.6	1170.0	6112.1	305.6	740.3	411.2
1979	4823.2	1252.3	6255.2	312.8	792.9	432.7
1980	5181.8	1285.3	6445.6	322.3	811.6	459.0
1981	5804.2	1351.0	6567.8	328.4	876.4	482.3
1982	4768.4	1326.5	6662.5	333.1	400.7	496.6

Table A6-2 Continued

Year	Estimated Total Cost (million $) [5]	Production (million $) [b]	November Year-End Capacity (mill. lbs.) [b]	Average Annual Capacity (mill. lbs.)	Capacity Utilization Rate (CUR) (percent) [6]
1976	4735.7	6626.6	9132.0	8784.0	75.4%
1977	5447.7	7327.9	9368.0	9250.0	79.2%
1978	5693.4	7783.0	9571.0	9469.5	82.2%
1979	6900.3	8436.6	9804.0	9687.5	87.1%
1980	7329.5	7892.5	9647.0	9725.5	81.2%
1981	8053.5	8005.9	9716.0	9681.5	82.7%
1982	6964.7	6459.9	9364.0	9540.0	67.7%

Sources: As per Table A6-1.

Notes: As per Table A6-1.

Table A7-1

U.S. Cellulosic Fibers Industry's Estimated Pretax Earnings Statistics

Year	Current Value of Shipments (mill. $) [a]	Estimated Current Total Cost (mill. $) [1]	Deflated Estimated Earnings before Taxes (DEEBT) (million 1972 $) [2]	Capacity Utilization Rate (CUR) (percent) [1]	GNP DEFLATOR (1972 = 100) [b]	Normalized [3] Indices DEEBT	Normalized [3] Indices Capacity Utilization Rate (CUR)
1958	722.8	644.3	117.0	73.8	67.1	18.7	10.6
1959	781.9	663.1	174.2	75.4	68.2	76.8	13.0
1960	709.1	648.4	87.6	71.0	69.3	-11.1	6.4
1961	643.8	534.0	156.4	70.0	70.2	58.8	4.9
1962	724.3	594.9	182.3	88.5	71.0	85.0	32.7
1963	731.8	572.9	221.0	91.6	71.9	124.3	37.3
1964	838.8	631.2	284.4	91.5	73.0	188.6	37.1
1965	903.2	694.5	280.5	91.3	74.4	184.7	36.8
1966	924.1	714.2	273.3	88.6	76.8	177.4	32.8
1967	902.8	695.1	262.6	105.0	79.1	166.5	57.4
1968	1017.4	799.0	264.7	93.8	82.5	168.7	40.6
1969	872.2	674.7	227.5	91.5	86.8	130.9	37.1
1970	620.5	515.6	114.6	79.8	91.5	16.4	19.6
1971	662.4	556.3	110.5	83.6	96.0	12.2	25.3
1972	589.5	531.4	58.1	89.1	100.0	-41.0	33.6
1973	641.4	543.4	93.3	90.3	105.0	-5.3	35.3
1974	926.4	916.3	8.8	86.7	115.1	-91.1	30.0
1975	836.3	812.6	18.8	59.6	125.8	-80.9	-10.7

Table A7-1 Continued

	Current Value of Shipments	Estimated Current Total Cost	Deflated Estimated Earnings before Taxes (DEEBT)	Capacity Utilization Rate (CUR)	GNP DEFLATOR	Normalized [3] Indices	
						DEEBT	Capacity Utilization Rate (CUR)
Year	(mill. $) [a]	(mill. $) [1]	(million 1972 $) [2]	(percent) [1]	(1972 = 100) [b]		
1976	944.1	917.6	20.0	69.2	132.3	-79.0	3.7
1977	1002.8	1010.2	-5.3	78.7	140.1	-105.5	18.0
1978	1105.0	1093.9	7.4	84.2	150.4	-92.3	26.2
1979	1244.9	1184.8	36.8	84.7	163.4	-61.5	27.0
1980	1357.3	1293.1	36.0	79.9	178.4	-62.3	19.8
1981	1424.0	1378.4	23.3	85.2	195.6	-75.6	27.7
1982	1262.8	1262.1	0.3	65.2	207.4	-99.6	-2.3
Mean:			95.4	66.7			
t Ratio:			0.9621	7.9329			

Sources: a. Census of Manufactures, U.S. Department of Commerce.
b. Statistical Abstracts of the United States.

Notes: 1. Extracted from Table A6-1.
2. DEEBT = (Current value of shipments - estimated current total cost)/(GNP deflator/100).
3. The original series to the left were converted into indices by taking 100 times their individual values as a numerator, dividing it by the mean value of that series and subtracting 100 from the result.

250

Table A7-2

U.S. Noncellulosic [1] Fibers Industry's Estimated Pretax Earnings Statistics

Year	Current Value of Shipments (mill. $) [a]	Estimated Current Total Cost (mill. $) [2]	Deflated Estimated Earnings before Taxes (DEEBT) (million 1972 $) [3]	Capacity Utilization Rate (CUR) (percent) [2]	GNP DEFLATOR (1972 = 100) [b]	Normalized [4] Indices DEEBT	Normalized [4] Indices Capacity Utilization Rate (CUR)
1958	668.4	437.9	343.5	54.2	67.1	-49.5	-33.9
1959	815.1	562.3	370.7	82.4	68.2	-45.5	0.5
1960	868.3	568.3	432.9	78.8	69.3	-36.4	-3.9
1961	1039.5	684.0	506.4	76.1	70.2	-25.6	-7.2
1962	1192.1	776.7	585.1	85.5	71.0	-14.0	4.2
1963	1403.2	948.8	632.0	88.6	71.9	-7.1	8.0
1964	1580.6	1046.0	732.3	91.9	73.0	7.7	12.0
1965	1842.9	1284.5	750.5	94.5	74.4	10.3	15.2
1966	1991.8	1451.7	703.3	86.3	76.8	3.4	5.2
1967	2033.2	1489.8	687.0	79.3	79.1	1.0	-3.3
1968	2584.7	1706.6	1064.4	91.3	82.5	56.5	11.3
1969	2713.3	2049.2	765.1	84.7	86.8	12.5	3.3
1970	2869.8	2303.1	619.3	76.9	91.5	-9.0	-6.3
1971	3241.4	2517.2	754.4	83.5	96.0	10.9	1.8
1972	3638.9	2862.0	776.9	90.7	100.0	14.2	10.6
1973	4751.2	3044.5	1625.4	93.9	105.0	138.9	14.5
1974	4716.1	4170.3	474.2	84.0	115.1	-30.3	2.4
1975	4933.8	4298.7	504.8	72.6	125.8	-25.8	-11.5

Table A7-2 Continued

Normalized [4] Indices

Year	Current Value of Shipments (mill. $) [a]	Estimated Current Total Cost (mill. $) [2]	Deflated Estimated Earnings before Taxes (DEEBT) (million 1972 $) [3]	Capacity Utilization Rate (CUR) (percent) [2]	GNP DEFLATOR (1972 = 100) [b]	DEEBT	Capacity Utilization Rate (CUR)
1976	5307.3	4735.7	432.0	75.4	132.3	-36.5	-8.1
1977	6379.7	5447.7	665.2	79.2	140.1	-2.2	-3.4
1978	6921.0	5693.4	816.2	82.2	150.4	20.0	0.2
1979	8227.2	6900.3	812.1	87.1	163.4	19.4	6.2
1980	8529.9	7329.5	672.9	81.2	178.4	-1.1	-1.0
1981	9602.2	8053.5	791.8	82.7	195.6	16.4	0.8
1982	7976.7	6964.7	487.9	67.7	207.4	-28.3	-17.5
Mean:			680.3	82.0			
t Ratio:			2.6285	9.3214			

Sources: As per Table A7-1.

Notes: 1. Excludes fiberglass.
2. Extracted from Table A6-2.
3. DEEBT = (Current value of shipments - estimated current total cost)/(GNP deflator/100).
4. The original series to the left were converted into indices by taking 100 times their individual values as a numerator, dividing it by the mean value of that series and subtracting 100 from the result.

Table A7-3

Pretax Returns on Gross Value of Fixed Assets

U.S. Cellulosic Fibers Industry

Year	Current Value of Shipments (mill. $) [a]	Estimated Current Total Cost (mill. $) [2]	Pretax Profit (mill. $) [3]	Gross Value of Fixed Assets (mill. $) [2]	Pretax Return on Gross Value of Fixed Assets (percent) [4]
1958	722.8	644.3	78.5	583.9	13.4%
1959	781.9	663.1	118.8	603.9	19.7%
1960	709.1	648.4	60.7	624.4	9.7%
1961	643.8	534.0	109.8	623.0	17.6%
1962	724.3	594.9	129.4	618.4	20.9%
1963	731.8	572.9	158.9	625.6	25.4%
1964	838.8	631.2	207.6	710.7	29.2%
1965	903.2	694.5	208.7	749.1	27.9%
1966	924.1	714.2	209.9	800.8	26.2%
1967	902.8	695.1	207.7	912.1	22.8%
1968	1017.4	799.0	218.4	963.4	22.7%
1969	872.2	674.7	197.5	871.1	22.7%
1970	620.5	515.6	104.9	614.3	17.1%
1971	662.4	556.3	106.1	623.7	17.0%
1972	589.5	531.4	58.1	611.1	9.5%
1973	641.4	543.1	98.3	612.6	16.0%
1974	926.4	916.3	10.1	877.5	1.2%
1975	836.3	812.6	23.7	917.6	2.6%
1976	944.1	917.6	26.5	818.5	3.2%

Table A7-3 Continued

	U. S. Noncellulosic [1] Fibers Industry					All U.S. Manufacturing		
Year	Current Value of Shipments (mill. $) [a]	Estimated Current Total Cost (mill. $) [5]	Pretax Profit (mill. $) [3]	Gross Value of Fixed Assets (mill. $) [5]	Pretax Return on Gross Value of Fixed Assets (percent) [4]	Pretax Profit (bill. $) [b, 6]	Gross Value of Fixed Assets (bill. $) [c, 6, 7]	Pretax Return on Gross Value of Fixed Assets (percent) [4]
1958	668.4	437.9	230.5	915.9	25.2%	23	118	19.5%
1959	815.1	562.3	252.8	893.6	28.3%	30	128	23.4%
1960	868.3	568.3	300.0	894.6	33.5%	28	135	20.7%
1961	1039.5	684.0	355.5	961.5	37.0%	28	141	19.9%
1962	1192.1	776.7	415.4	1025.9	40.5%	32	149	21.5%
1963	1403.2	948.8	454.4	1160.9	39.1%	35	158	22.2%
1964	1580.6	1046.0	534.6	1288.7	41.5%	40	168	23.8%
1965	1842.9	1284.5	558.4	1587.3	35.2%	47	130	36.2%
1966	1991.8	1451.7	540.1	1892.6	28.5%	52	200	26.0%
1967	2033.2	1489.8	543.4	2428.7	22.4%	48	218	22.0%
1968	2584.7	1706.6	878.1	2670.4	32.9%	55	232	23.7%
1969	2713.3	2049.2	664.1	2977.9	22.3%	58	249	23.3%
1970	2869.8	2303.1	566.7	3598.3	15.7%	48	267	18.0%
1971	3241.4	2517.2	724.2	3839.1	18.9%	53	279	19.0%
1972	3638.9	2862.0	776.9	4159.3	18.7%	63	301	20.9%
1973	4751.2	3044.5	1706.7	4603.7	37.1%	81	316	25.6%
1974	4716.1	4170.3	545.8	4924.3	11.1%	92	340	27.1%
1975	4933.8	4298.7	635.1	5491.8	11.6%	80	369	21.7%
1976	5307.3	4735.7	571.6	5875.9	9.7%	105	395	26.6%

U.S. Cellulosic Fibers Industry

Year	Current Value of Shipments (mill. $) [a]	Estimated Current Total Cost (mill. $) [2]	Pretax Profit (mill. $) [3]	Gross Value of Fixed Assets (mill. $) [2]	Pretax Return on Gross Value of Fixed Assets (percent) [4]
1977	1002.8	1010.2	-7.4	806.9	-0.9%
1978	1105.0	1093.9	11.1	799.2	1.4%
1979	1244.9	1184.8	60.1	843.0	7.1%
1980	1357.3	1293.1	64.2	884.0	7.3%
1981	1424.0	1378.4	45.6	951.6	4.8%
1982	1262.8	1262.1	0.7	992.7	0.1%
				Mean:	13.8%
				t Ratio:	1.4240

Table A7-3 Continued

| | U. S. Noncellulosic [1] Fibers Industry | | | | | All U.S. Manufacturing | | |
Year	Current Value of Shipments (mill. $) [a]	Estimated Current Total Cost (mill. $) [5]	Pretax Profit (mill. $) [3]	Gross Value of Fixed Assets (mill. $) [5]	Pretax Return on Gross Value of Fixed Assets (percent) [4]	Pretax Profit (bill. $) [b, 6]	Gross Value of Fixed Assets (bill. $) [c, 6, 7]	Pretax Return on Gross Value of Fixed Assets (percent) [4]
1977	6379.7	5447.7	932.0	5920.6	15.7%	115	439	26.2%
1978	6921.0	5693.4	1227.6	6112.1	20.1%	133	479	27.8%
1979	8227.2	6900.3	1326.9	6255.2	21.2%	154	523	29.4%
1980	8529.9	7329.5	1200.4	6445.2	18.6%	145	574	25.3%
1981	9602.2	8053.5	1548.7	6567.8	23.6%	159	630	25.2%
1982	7696.7	6964.7	732.0	6662.5	11.0%	108	692	15.6%
				Mean:	18.8%			18.5%
				t Ratio:	2.5419			5.5843

Sources: a. Censuses of Manufactures, U.S. Department of Commerce, Bureau of the Census.
         b. Statistical Abstract of the U.S.
         c. Annual Surveys of Manufactures and Historical Statistics of the U.S. Colonial Times to 1970,
           U.S. Department of Commerce, Bureau of the Census.

Notes: 1. Excludes fiberglass.
      2. Extracted from Table A6-1.
      3. Equals current value of shipments less estimated total cost.
      4. Equals pretax profit times 100 divided by gross value of fixed assets.
      5. Extracted from Table A6-2.
      6. "Data not necessarily comparable from year to year due to changes in accounting procedures,
         industry classification, sampling procedures, and so forth."
      7. Equals total assets less total current assets; total current assets equals cash plus notes and
         accounts receivable less allowances plus inventories.

Bibliography

Boulnois, L. The Silk Road. Translated by Dennis Chamberlain. New York: E. P. Dutton & Co., 1966.

Carroll, S. "The Market for Commercial Airliners." In Regulating the Product, edited by R. E. Caves and M. J. Roberts. Cambridge, MA: Ballinger, 1975.

Chandler, A. D., Jr. Strategy and Structure. Garden City, NY: Anchor Books, 1966.

Coleman, D. C. Courtaulds: An Economic and Social History, vol. 2. Oxford, England: Clarendon Press, 1969.

Commodity Research Bureau, Commodity Year Book. New York: 1954-1987.

Competitive Economic Factors in Man-Made Fiber Production Costs. Cambridge, MA: Arthur D. Little, 1975.

Corbman, B. P. Textiles: Fiber To Fabric. 5th edition. New York: McGraw-Hill, 1975.

Cotton Counts Its Customers. Market Research Service, Memphis, TN: National Cotton Council, 1950-82.

Dean, J., Managerial Economics, Englewood Cliffs, NJ: Prentice-Hall, 1951.

Donald, J. R., F. Lowenstein and M. S. Simon, The Demand for Textile Fibers in the United States. Technical Bulletin no. 1301, Washington, DC: U.S. Department of Agriculture, Economic Research Service, 1962.

Dudley, G. E. U.S. Textile Fiber Demand: Price Elasticities in Major End-Use Markets. Technical Bulletin no. 1500, Washington, DC: U.S. Department of Agriculture, Economic Research Service, 1973.

Evsyukov, V. S., N. V. Leontev, A. S. Chegolya, V. M. Malykh, E. M. Aizenshtein and L. Z. Novikov, "Some Economic Determinants in the Growth of Polyester Fiber Production in the U.S.S.R." Translated from Kimcheskic Volokna, no. 3, (May-June 1975), Ministry of the Chemical Industry of the U.S.S.R.; All-Union Scientific Research Institute.

Familiarity and Favorability with Synthetic Fibers and Brand Names and Their End Uses. Princeton, NJ: Opinion Research Corporation, 1969.

Forrestal, D. J. Faith, Hope & $5,000. New York: Simon and Schuster, 1977.

Freeston, D. W., Jr. The Competitive Status of the U.S. Fibers, Textiles, and Apparel Complex. Washington, DC: National Academy Press, 1983.

Goldenberg, D. I. "Economics' Contribution to Competitor Intelligence in Business." In Business Competitor Intelligence edited by W. L. Sammon, M. A. Kurland, and R. Spitalnic. New York: John Wiley and Sons, 1984.

Green, P. E. "Probability Models in Pricing Decisions." In Planning and Problem Solving in Marketing by W. Alderson and P. E. Green. New York: Richard D. Irwin, 1964.

Harrigan, K. R. Strategies for Declining Industries. Unpublished Harvard University Doctor of Business Administration dissertation, Ann Arbor, MI: University Microfilms, 1979.

Hollander, S. The Sources of Increased Efficiency: A Study of duPont Rayon Plants. Cambridge, MA: The M.I.T. Press, 1965.

Inderfurth, K. H. Nylon Technology. New York: McGraw-Hill, 1953.

Jewkes, J., D. Sawers and R. Stillerman, The Sources of Invention. London: Macmillan & Co., 1958.

Johnson, E. F. The Johnson Redbook. New York: Prescott, Ball and Turben, Inc.

Ketterling, V. Industrial Energy Study of the Plastics and Rubber Industries, SICs 282 and 30. Federal Energy Office/U.S. Department of Commerce (Contract no. 14-01-0001-1655 of the Bureau of Mines), Florham Park, NJ: Foster D. Snell, 1974.

Kornai, J. Rush Versus Harmonic Growth. Amsterdam: North-Holland, 1972.

_____, Anti-Equilibrium. New York: Elsevier, 1971.

Leibenstein, H. Beyond Economic Man. Cambridge, MA: Harvard University Press, 1976.

Liang, L. S. "Structural Profile of the U.S. Man-Made Fiber Industry." Reprint from Textile Industry, New York, Billian Publishing, 1971.

Lockhart, A. H., Jr. "Man-Made Fiber Outlook to 1980." In Chemical Market Research Meeting Papers, no. 938, November 1975.

Lowenstein, F. "Factors Affecting the Domestic Mill Consumption of Cotton." Washington, DC: U.S. Department of Agriculture, Economic Research Service, 1952.

Man-Made Fiber and Textile Dictionary. 3rd edition. New York: Celanese, 1975.

Man-Made Fiber Producers' Base Book 1951-1960. New York: Textile Economics Bureau, 1961.

Man-Made Fiber Producers' Base Book 1961-1965. New York: Textile Economics Bureau, 1966.

Man-Made Fiber Producers' Base Book 1966-1970. New York: Textile Economics Bureau, 1971.

Man-Made Fiber Producers' Base Book 1971-1975. New York: Textile Economics Bureau, 1977.

Man-Made Fiber Producers' Handbook. New York: Textile Economics Bureau, 1976-85.

Markham, J. W. Competition in the Rayon Industry. Cambridge, MA: Harvard University Press, 1952.

Modern Textiles. M. E. Denham, editor, Atlanta, GA: Billian Publishing, 1948-73.

Modigliani, F. "New Developments on the Oligopoly Front." Journal of Political Economy, 66 (1958).

Moncrieff, R. W. Man-Made Fibers. 6th edition. New York: John Wiley and Sons, 1975.

Press, J. J., ed. Man-Made Textile Encyclopedia. New York: Textile Book Publishers, 1959.

Reith, J. E. "Generalized Distribution Rule." Unpublished revised draft of an article. Wilmington, DE: April 27, 1967.

Saaty, T. L. The Analytic Hierarchy Process. New York: McGraw-Hill, 1980.

Sawyer, G. C. Designing Strategy. New York: John Wiley and Sons, 1988.

Scherer, Frederic M. Industrial Market Structure and Economic Performance, 2nd edition. Boston, MA: Houghton Mifflin, 1980.

Sosnick, Stephen, "A Critique of Concepts of Workable Competition," Quarterly Journal of Economics, vol. 72(3) (August 1958): 380-423.

Spandex Technology. Applications Research and Service Department, Decatur, AL: Chemstrand, 1964.

Stigler, G. J. "Report on Antitrust Policy - Discussion," American Economic Review, 46(2) (May 1956): 506.

Stigler, G. J., and J. K. Kindahl, The Behavior of Industrial Prices. New York: National Bureau of Economic Research, 1970.

TEDES Report. Fair Lawn, NJ: Systematic Forecasting, 1980.

Textile Economics Bureau, Rayon Organon, New York, vol. 5 (1934)--vol. 22 (1951).

Textile Economics Bureau, Textile Organon, New York, vol. 1 (1930)--vol. 4 (1933) and vol. 23 (1952)--vol. 57 (1986).

Tisdell, C. A., and P. W. McDonald, Economics of Fibre Markets. New South Wales, Australia: University of Newcastle, 1977.

"The U.S. Fiber Industry Running Out of Customers" Chemical Week, vol. 137(4) (July 24, 1985): 20-24. New York: McGraw-Hill.

U.S. Department of Commerce, Bureau of the Census, Historical Statistics of the United States Colonial Times to 1970, bicentennial edition, Washington, DC: 1975.

Veblen, T. The Theory of the Leisure Class, New York: The Modern Library, 1961.

Vietorisz, T. Programming Data Summary for the Chemical Industry, revised edition, New York: United Nation's Expert Working Group on Industrial Development Programming Data, May 1961.

Von Neumann, J., and O. Morgenstern, Theory of Games and Economic Behavior, 3rd edition. New York: John Wiley and Sons, 1967.

Ward, L., and G. King, Interfiber Competition with Emphasis on Cotton: Trends and Projections to 1980, Technical Bulletin no. 1487 Washington, DC: U.S. Department of Agriculture, Economic Research Service, 1962.

Williams, R., Jr. "Standardizing Cost Data on Process Equipment." Chemical Engineering, vol. 54(6) (June 1947a) 102-103.

_____ "Six-Tenths Factor Aids in Approximating Costs." Chemical Engineering, vol. 54(12) (December 1947b): 124-25.

Yale, J. P. Innovation: The Controlling Factor in the Life Cycle of the Synthetic Fiber Industry. Unpublished New York University doctoral dissertation, Ann Arbor, MI: University Microfilms, 1965.

Index

About the Author

DAVID I. GOLDENBERG is the chairman of Systematic Forecasting, Inc., a management advisory firm, and Adjunct Professor of Business Economics at Fairleigh Dickinson University. He has written numerous articles on the textile industry for a variety of business journals.

DATE DUE